Uniting Struggles

Critical Social Research in Critical Times

Alternate Routes 2012

A Journal of Critical Social Research

www.redquillbooks.com

ISBN 978-1-926958-15-6

Printed on acid-free paper. The paper used in this book incorporates post-consumer waste and has not been sourced from endangered old growth forests, forests of exceptional conservation value or the Amazon Basin. Red Quill Books subscribes to a one-book-at-a-time manufacturing process that substantially lessens supply chain waste, reduces greenhouse emissions, and conserves valuable natural resources.

Includes bibliographical references.
ISBN 978-1-926958-15-6

Also published as a serial:

"Alternate Routes"
ISSN 1923-7081 (online)
ISSN 0702-8865 (print)

Red Quill Books is an alternative publishing house. Proceeds from the sale of this book will support future critical scholarship.

Alternate Routes: A Journal of Critical Social Research 2012

JOURNAL MANDATE

Established in 1977 at the Department of Sociology and Anthropology, Carleton University, Alternate Routes' central mandate has been to create outlets for critical social research and interdisciplinary inquiry. A scholarly peer-reviewed annual, AR works closely with labour and social justice activists to promote the publication of non-traditional, provocative and radical analyses that may not find a forum in conventional academic venues. AR seeks to be a public academic journal and encourages submissions that advance or challenge theoretical, historical and contemporary socio-political, economic and cultural subjects and issues. In addition to full-length articles, we welcome review essays sparked by previously published material, interviews, short commentaries, as well as poetry, drawings and photographic essays. AR publishes primarily special-themed issues and therefore requests that submissions be related to the current call for papers. Submissions should be free of racist or sexist language, have limited technical or specialized terms and be written in a style that is accessible to our diverse readership.

Table of Contents

Articles

Interventions

Book Reviews

Editorial Notes

Uniting Struggles: Critical Social Research In Critical Times

With the reverberations of the Great Recession still wreaking havoc throughout much of the world, this issue of *Alternate Routes* unites articles based on their dedication to critical social research in critical times. Beginning with Anjali Pandey who surveys filmic evidence from over forty post-9/11 Hollywood pictures, she examines how the U.S.'s military presence in Iraq and Afghanistan continues not only on the ground but on the silver screen. Pandey's analysis investigates how the context of two ongoing wars finds linguistic coding and audience approval or disapproval in and through filmic content. She asks, how is public sentiment shaped by and affected through film? What are the verbal and visual strategies employed to stereotype the 'enemy' and 'other' them? How do these linguistic and visual renditions affect ideological perceptions? And, what function does such 'othering' in and through film serve culturally and politically? In "A Rough Climate for Migration", Elaine Kelly examines how climate change and environmental degradation is affecting mass migration today. Her contention is that if work is not done to assert an ethical foundation for responding to climate-induced migration, law and public policy will be dominated by a national security paradigm. Rather, drawing on Jacques Derrida's concept of hospitality, Kelly points toward the importance of ethical models that may help reorient the public policy choices of privileged states as a result of environmentally-induced displacement and migration.

The following article by Martijn Konings develops an alternative conceptualization of the state-market relationship and then discusses how such a framework allows us to make sense of key aspects of the neoliberal era. Its central claim is that neoliberalism was a return to classical liberalism only on an *ideological* level; neoliberal *practices* were never about institutional retreat or the subordination of public and private actors to the discipline of disembedded markets, but precisely involved the creation, legitimation and consolidation of new institutional capacities and mechanisms of control. As such, while the idea that neoliberalism has enhanced political control may seem a counter-intuitive conceptualization, Konings' article suggests that this is precisely the case because neoliberal ideology has such a hold of our common sense and intuitions. Engaging indirectly with many of the theoretical and empirical arguments put forth by Konings, Randall Germain articulates an alternative view exploring how the consequences of the global financial crisis are now making themselves felt on all aspects of global politics and the world political economy. Drawing on the work of Susan Strange, Germain investigates the changing global articulation of power. He suggests that the trajectory of the financial crisis, and the political responses to it, is indicative of a new architecture of power shaped by the intersection of dynamics associated with the rise of emerging market economies together with the re-assertion of the authority of the nation-state. This is an important task, Germain suggests, since some of the key elements of American power are being hollowed out, even as other elements remain intact without new ones yet forming. He concludes that the result will be a period of uncertainty as some key foundations of the global political order are recast along new lines of power.

The fifth article in this issue by Carlo Fanelli and Priscillia Lefebvre seeks to add to the growing body of literature examining the changing nature and content of government political economic intervention, social welfare provision, growing attacks against labour unionism and general restructuring of the federal public service in Canada. Fanelli and Lefebvre overview the transition from Keynesian to neoliberal public policy prescriptions, with a focus on precarious work and shifting labour market conditions. Their research is empirically grounded in an analysis of striking museum workers in the Ottawa and Gatineau region. They suggest that the Public Service Alliance of Canada (PSAC) Local 70396's efforts in achieving job security and fair wages for its members offer valuable insights from which to learn in the continued struggles against precarious work and neoliberal public policy. The PSAC strike illustrates how increasing trends in non-standard, temporary, and contract work are making inroads into the public sphere. Fanelli and Lefebvre conclude with some cursory projections as to the hardening relationship between employers and employees, particularly those unionized and in the federal public service, followed by some general observations on the in/adequacy of union responses. The succeeding analysis by Richard Fidler explores a new left political party, Quebec Solidaire, which was created during the last decade and is attracting considerable interest and support as an anti-neoliberal alternative to Quebec's three capitalist parties. While not explicitly anti-capitalist or socialist, it defines itself as a party "resolutely of the left, feminist, ecologist, altermondialiste, pacifist, democratic and sovereignist." In his important essay, Fidler outlines how this party originated, how it functions, and explores how it is coming to terms with some of the major challenges it now confronts.

Complementing many of the critical insights derived from Fidler's article, Aziz Choudry's essay begins by suggesting that the contributions, dynamics and politics of knowledge production in social movements and other activist contexts are often overlooked. Yet social movements, he argues, actively produce knowledge and provide crucial conceptual resources in social and ecological justice and liberation struggles. Choudry's article discusses informal and non-formal learning in social action contexts, tensions and power dynamics around the politics of these forms of knowledge production, activist research and the actual and potential contributions and challenges to theory arising out of the intellectual work of social activism. To conclude, he argues that critical scholarship should strive to engage concretely with today's social struggles and the knowledge produced in these contexts for both political and intellectual reasons. The final article by Jeff Noonen, "Socialism as Life-Coherent Society", suggests that notwithstanding the real achievements of capitalism, an alternative is ultimately necessary because the social processes through which capitalism reproduces and develops itself are ecologically unsustainable and socially, politically, and culturally contradictory. Noonen argues that beneath the apparent freedom of interest and activity enabled by capitalism lies a structure of social dependence upon possession of money-value for the satisfaction of life's requirements. Peering into this structure of dependence discloses the secret of capitalist unsustainability and contradiction: it systematically confuses life-value with money-value. He contends that a socialist alternative to capitalism is necessary because capitalism generates life-crises in the natural and socio-cultural dimensions of life-support and life-development. Nevertheless, however, conceiving socialism as a life-coherent society requires important revisions to prevailing interpretations of its traditional justificatory values.

Moving forward, new to *AR* for 2012 is an *Interventions* section. The current issue includes short analytical pieces, editorials and interviews with Michael Parenti (Profit Pathology and Disposable Planet), Pat Armstrong (Canadian Health Care: Privatization and Gendered Labour), Sut Jhally (Articulation, Cultural Studies, and Education), Michael Perelman (The Invisible Handcuffs of Capitalism), Noam Chomsky (Democracy and the Public University) and Garry Potter (Imaginaries and Realities, Utopia and Dystopia). As in previous issues, a number of contemporary book reviews are included as well. Needless to say, this issue could not have come together without the professionalism and courteousness of our many contributors. We would like to extend a great deal of gratitude to all of them for making our twenty-third issue and thirty-fifth anniversary edition an important and memorable one. An immense amount of appreciation is also due to our editorial board and many others informally affiliated with *AR* who lent their time, energy and expertise to see this issue through. Your leadership by example and passion is what keeps us motivated. *AR* is also very pleased to announce that all twenty-two of our previous issues are now fully available free of charge online (www.alternateroutes.ca). At *AR* we strongly believe in the liberation of knowledge–that is, knowledge produced through our shared experiences and efforts intent on not only interpreting the world, but changing it. We hope that readers will continue to support *AR* in various ways; whether by participating in our annual conference (see subsequent pages), submitting an article for inclusion, spreading the word through social media and in-person, visiting us online or purchasing a copy of our annual. We thank you most of all for giving us a reason to continue producing and disseminating radical analyses that may not find a forum in conventional venues. We dedicate this issue to you and all others who have supported us over the last thirty-five years!

"War on Terror" via a "War of Words": Fear, Loathing and Name-calling in Hollywood's Wars in Afghanistan and Iraq

Anjali Pandey[1]

9-11 AND THE WAR ON TERROR

The causal connection between the September 11, 2001 attacks and the war in Afghanistan and Iraq was strategically and carefully construed on the part of the Bush Administration—providing a perfect political alibi for the subsequent U. S. military invasion and occupation of these two sovereign nations. Former President Bush is famously remembered for declaring: "We wage a war to save civilization itself. We did not seek it. But we will fight it" (Excerpts, 2001, p. 6). Across the Atlantic, Tony Blair's matching war cry was: "To safeguard peace, we have to fight" (Cowell, 2001, p. 6) Also chronicled is the Anglo-American alliance formed to combat the global "war on terror" (Hoge, 2001) with Britain vowing to stand "shoulder to shoulder with the US" (Ford, 2001, p. 7) defending itself against what President Bush called "acts of unimaginable horror" (Excerpts, 2001, p. 6), and his British ally called "the worst terrorist outrage" (Cowell, 2001, p. 6). A decade later, the wars still rage both on the ground and on the silver screens of Hollywood. The overt attacks on the people and places in these two war-zones have had a noticeable ripple affect domestically in terms of 'reported' public sentiments and reactions. Most are aware for example of the firestorm of fear-driving attempts in the recent, highly publicized church-sponsored Koran-burning event. Equally prominent is the inflammatory reaction from some New Yorkers to the building of a mosque near Ground zero. Adams (2010, p.5) reports on these events:

---

1 Anjali Pandey is Professor of Applied Linguistics at Salisbury University (Maryland, U.S.A) with a doctorate from the University of Illinois. Her research encompasses issues of linguistic disempowerment in film with a forthcoming book entitled: Manufacturing Linguistic Insecurity. She can be reached at: axpandey@salisbury.edu

> The Florida Pastor [Terry Jones] who inflamed the debate over construction of an Islamic center near Ground Zero in Manhattan faded from public view, but anger simmered during a weekend marked by a memorial for 9/11 victims and dueling protests near the site of the proposed project.

How has such a fear of the 'other' occurred? Can films produced in the decade since 9/11 be implicated in such reactions?

OUTLINING THE RESEARCH FOCUS

While in any analysis of film, the context of filmmaking is as pertinent to the analysis as the content of the film *per se*, the scope of the current paper impels a particular focus on filmic content—in particular, linguistic choices. The analysis aims to spotlight *how* the context of two real wars finds linguistic encoding, and ultimately, mimetic (audience) approval or disapproval in and through filmic content. Downing (1980) compellingly argues that the power of film lies in its seeming capacity "to shape public feeling while appearing only to express it." It is this duality of rendition and representation that the current paper aims to understand. After all, the exploitation of media content in the service of state-driven agenda is not new (Moritz, 2005). Strategies of euphemism and mystification in the media marketing of the Vietnam War for example have been well chronicled particularly from a linguistic point of view (Bolinger, 1980, p. 132; Hughes, 1988, p. 220-220). Similar research has looked at World War II language. Of particular interest has been the manner in which the Nazi propaganda of *Gleichschatung*—"putting everyone in the same gear"—(Ehlich, 1989) was prominently and successfully accomplished via meticulous linguistic manipulations—in particular, via strategies of "lexical hardening" (Ehlich,1989); micro linguistic manipulations of emotion-inducing language steeped in cultural connotation and stereotype in a bid to both co-opt and mobilize German working-classes in the Nazi propaganda-machine's attempt at conflating anti-Semitism with nationalistic ideology (Ehlich, 1989).

Consequently, while filmic analysis can benefit from a macro-analysis of the context of filmic production (Miller *et al.*, 2005), a micro-analysis of textual renditions in particular films (Bleichenbacher, 2008) provides yet another manner to investigate the ideological role of film in the 21st century. The current paper is focused on *how* consent is manufactured in and through film. Linguistic data collected and coded from a randomly viewed list of over 40 film titles—all produced in the decade after September 11, 2001 (henceforth, 9/11)— underscores a number of key research questions. Firstly, *how* do these post-9/11 filmic productions represent the peoples, places, styles, rituals and names—in short, the culture of Arab and Muslim peoples in Afghanistan and Iraq—two countries experiencing U.S. military presence. Secondly, what are the specific verbal (linguistic) and visual (semiotic) strategies employed by such post 9/11 films to stereotype the 'enemy' and in effect "other" them? Thirdly, what might the ideological affects of these linguistic renditions have on audiences domestically as well as abroad, who are currently part of the so-called 'Global War on Terror'. Finally, what function could the 'othering' of the enemy in and through film serve both rhetorically and politically?

Filmic evidence from over 40 titles coded in the decade after the events of 9/11 reveal the workings of verbal and visual name-calling strategies which resonate with and reproduce Anglo-American phobias about Arab and Muslim people. Furthermore, these linguistic devices occur in the form of two consistent linguistic strategies. Firstly, via seemingly peripheral linguistic comments conflated against powerful visual reminders, numerous films in the data set reveal the workings of the device of *cinematic reminiscing*—defined in this paper as linguistic reminders of 9/11 which subversively as they historically "sign-post" audience-awareness about a nation's trajectory towards and engagement in war. Additionally, via a strategy of *cinematic acquiescing*, another device employed in several films, we see overt encodings of disparagement—systematic dysphemia, and name-calling of the peoples and places encapsulated in the war-zones in a bid to gain public consent for these militaristic invasions. Ultimately, it is argued, the complementary workings of *cinematic reminiscing* and *acquiescing* in 21st century films released in a post-9/11 decade reflect at the very same time as they reinforce a classic "orientalist" (Said, 1980) othering of the constructed enemy. Why this treatment of the enemy? Could it be that this *othering*—evoked in and through "a series of crude, essentialized caricatures of the Islamic world is presented in such a way as to make that world vulnerable to military aggression" (Said, 1980)? Could it also be possible that in instigating a 'fear' of Arab and Muslim peoples domestically, public policy regarding this geopolitical space goes unquestioned?

WAR IN FILMS VS. FILMS IN WAR

The explicit propagandist role of film in the recent 'war on terror' has been chronicled by numerous scholars (Kellner, 2010; Prince, 2009; Boggs and Pollard, 2005; Valantin, 2005; Suid, 2002; Shaheen, 2001). Film scholars such as Moritz (2005) recount how a mere two months after the September 11th attacks "Bush's advisor Karl Rove invited a crew of hand-picked directors and producers to exchange ideas. The topic: possible Hollywood contributions to the war against terrorists" (p. 120) – a move which ushered in a new era in filmmaking—what Moritz (2005) aptly labels, "militainment" (120). Such facts underscore commonly held perceptions—namely, that "movies are undoubtedly a powerful means of direct influence" (p. 124) particularly for "the target groups of 14-29 year old males" (Thomsen, 2005, p. 12)—a target audience who we are apprised are "conditioned to permanent aggressive militarism" in lieu of diplomacy (Thomsen, 2005, p. 12), and coincidentally also the age group which signs up for soldiering.

For most theorists, this marriage of media, ideology and profit-making trends both prior to and post 9/11 continues—particularly in a culture industry premised on "business as usual" (Thomsen 2005, p. 27). Valantin (2005) chronicles at length the seeming synergy between filmmaking and governmental directive, or rather, imagery in the service of acceptability in and through what he describes as "national security cinema" (p. ix)—an explicit manufacturing of mimetic consent for the American War machine. This 'reading' of film's recent role has also been reiterated by Boggs and Pollard (2007) who examine at length the manner in which the culture industry legitimizes war in and through filmic content which skillfully as it subversively skews audience orientations towards a predominantly nativistic, hyperpatriotic "spectacularization" or "chauvinistic patriotism" (Thomsen, 2005, p.160) of war imagery in a post-9/11 America. The continued use of film imagery for the glorification and legitimation of US corporate interests lends credence to the claim that "In Hollywood, profit and patriotism seem to be marching forward harmoniously in step." (Moritz, 2005, p. 125). Reiterating this analysis, Suid (2002) examines the glamorization of war in film as serving more of a psychoanalytic function—what he labels to be "an escapist entertainment that appeals to viewers' most basic, most primal instincts." (p. 3-4). While for most, it is the analysis of images or the political orientation of filmic content which is the subject of analysis, this paper examines the linguistic manner in which either consent or dissent for war is construed. The constructivist function of film—using "language and images... and other media creating fragments of reality consciousness in our mind" (Thomsen, 2005, p. 9) has been reiterated by a number of scholars (McDonald and Wasko, 2008). After all, "in the age of moving images" writes Thomsen (2005) "the film industry is deeply involved in the creation of a set of collective mind patterns from the very beginning" (9)—a concern to which we now turn.

THE FILM CORPUS IN THE CURRENT STUDY

Analysis of linguistic data in the current film corpus reveals two strategies of microlinguistic action at work. Firstly, we see numerous examples of the manner in which seemingly innocuous 'dialoging' in films function in an intertextual capacity—an appropriation and incorporation of post-9/11 sentiment. In such instances, "war-on-terror" parlance forms part of the linguistic *mis-en-scene* of dialog exchanges in films—even in films thematically removed or unrelated to these wars. Such commonsensical contextualizations of film as post-9/11 creations abound in and through a strategy of *cinematic reminiscences,* a clever filmic strategy which works in a contextual capacity—setting the film in a historical period—as a post 9/11 film, while also serving as a subliminal reminder of America under attack, with a concomitant need for 'self-preservation'. Several films in the data corpus fall in this category.

The second strategy of *cinematic acquiescence* examines films whose thematic focus is primarily the 'war on terror' and its aftermath. In such cases, linguistic evidence goes beyond reminiscing about 9/11, to functioning in an overt ideological role—one of manipulating audience opinion towards mostly consent towards these wars—rarely do we see dissent against these wars in films. In such cases, we see an overt 'othering' of reel enemies in filmic wars in a bid to effectuate and legitimize mimetic (audience) approval for 'real' enemies in actual ground wars. In the interests of space, narrative details surrounding films are kept to a minimum. An exhaustive filmography is provided at the end of the paper for readers interested in the titles covered.

The current study spans linguistic data culled from films spanning approximately a decade (2001-2010). This period encompasses the historically relevant decade after the events of 9/11— a type of "terrorism which changed the nature of war" (Thomsen, 2005, p. 19). Why such a corpus? To borrow the astute wording of one of the reviewers of the current paper,[2] the filmic corpus spanning this decade while united in terms of temporal space and thematic focus, differs in filmic genre and semiotic treatment of the wars. So, while all the films from which data is utilized are in fact, post 9/11 filmic productions featuring references to 9/11 and its aftermath—the so-called "war on terror"— they are also artistic creations which attempt to render geopolitical representations of Muslim/Arab peoples and places via different filmic genres. As the excerpts below demonstrate, films in this period range in a continua of different genre-types ranging from fictionalized film genres at the one end of the continuum such as: *Superbad* (Teenage Comedy); *Eagle Eye* (Science Fiction); *A Mighty Heart* (Thriller Drama); *Stoploss* (Realist War Drama); *This Is England* (Historical Drama) to on the other end of the continuum— realist docu-dramas such as *Where in the World is Osama Bin Laden?* –even including a blended genre of realist fiction such as *The Hurtlocker*. These are a few titles from the litany of examples under scrutiny in the current paper.

Furthermore, while seemingly randomized, examples in the current study exemplify two broad filmic strategies at work: films which utilize the events of 9/11 to situate and explicate upon the unfolding action in the form of implied backgrounding or context-building strategies; and secondly, films which engage in an overt foregrounding of the 'war on terror' as spotlighted thematic content. In the former instance, seemingly tangential linguistic allusions are evoked and invoked in the unfolding action in the form of *cinematic reminiscences* —reminders of September 11 and its aftermath. In such examples, manifold linguistic comments abound in the filmic scripts in reference to 9/11 and the 'war on terror'. A complementary strategy used in a plethora of films involves using the events and aftermath of 9/11 as spotlighted content in a bid to induce *cinematic acquiescence*—name-calling strategies meant to 'other' the enemy. Such filmic detailing of cinematic wars is rendered across a number of filmic genres via dialogic strategies which implicitly as they explicitly manufacture consent and acquiescence for the current ground wars raging outside the theater experience. Film scholar Lacy (2003) argues that "Cinema is a space involved in the process of actively forgetting and actively producing history" (p. 1). Data analyses in this paper point to post-9/11 filmic productions as doing much more. This decade of filmic produc-

2 The author would sincerely like to thank all three reviewers: Drs. T. Mirrlees, G. Rigakos and P. Lefebvre respectively for their meticulous and useful suggestions in refining the original argument of this paper.

tion simultaneously engages in a re-remembering and a re-producing of history—the outcomes of which are explored in the conclusion.

Film as both a reflector and shaper of public opinion emerges not from viewing a few samples of representations from a number of isolated films per se, but rather is most potent when we examine the corpus as a whole—in tandem—as a sample of production over a decade. After all, most moviephiles see not one, not two, but several films (Epstein, 2009). In line with such a context, filmic evidence is worthy of examination for "every linguistic interaction however personal and insignificant it may appear, bears the social structure that it both expresses and helps to reproduce." (Mesthrie et al., 2009, p. 335). Since the focus in the current paper is on the *how* of consent manufacturing, filmic clips are organized around the taxonomy of linguistic strategy adopted rather than chronologically presented—thus traversing a multiplicity of genre types. To rephrase, the discussion of films in this analysis is presented not chronologically but in terms of taxonomy—in particular, via the type of dysphemistic strategy being employed.

LOCATING HOLLYWOOD

A distinction between "Hollywood" as a place versus Hollywood as a culture industry is made in this paper. The analysis utilizes the word 'Hollywood' in the economic sense in which current parlance employs the term— a metonymic location of a culture industry. This media conglomeration— situated within a 'borderless' and globally expansive world (Miller et al 20005; Macdonald and Wasko 2008; Pandey 2013) lacks a geographical location *per se*. Hollywood in this sense, both serves at the very same time as it culls global talent via the strategy of what Cowen (2002) defines as "cinematic clustering" (p. 87) which at its best entails "the strategic use of cinematic talent from around the world" in a bid to "strengthen the market position" (p. 87) of Hollywood-produced films. With the fluid and seemingly "flat world" (Friedman, 2005) dissolution of national boundaries emerging in the 21st century we are increasingly witnessing what Wasser (2005) calls the "transcendent power of Hollywood". In a sense then, it is becoming much harder to 'locate' where Hollywood really is. In a poignant sentence opening his essay on the "Transnationalization of Hollywood," Wasser (2005) goes as far as claiming that "Hollywood is booming while the American film industry weakens" (p. 63). Recent film scholars (MacDonald and Wasko, 2008; Pandey 2010; Pandey 2013), have increasingly chronicled how globalization forces in the 21st century have created globally-spanning blockbusters with directorial and aesthetic talent garnered from multiple continents both in a bid to expand the "dream factory's" reach (Tyrell, 1999) while at the same time quell competition from national cinema endeavors (Miller et al. 2005).

So, while some of the data in the current paper is elicited from films which have obvious roots in British filmmaking, the transnational nature of Hollywood in terms of both production and distributions channels (Epstein, 2009) prompts the use of the term, "Hollywood" as a generic, metonymic term for films produced in English for broad mass appeal, and maximum market-output both domestically and abroad (Epstein 2009). Important to emphasize is that the films produced in the decade after 9/11 are not homogenous in their representations of the wars. However, there is no doubt that in the market-oriented nature of the film industry, it is ticket-sales which constitute a common denominator (Epstein, 2009). Thus, most of the films in the corpus are big budget films with mass audience exposure.

LOOKING AT EXAMPLES: CINEMATIC REMINISCING

For many, the consistent allusions to the 2001 attacks in a plethora of movies comes as no surprise. Linguistic comments about the 9/11 attacks, and the subsequent London bombings, form a consistent verbal detail in Hollywood movies of the past decade—even movies with themes unrelated to the war such as *Sugar*—a film whose primary focus is: the transnational capitalist baseball industry. *Sugar* uses a filmic strategy of "staged authenticity" (Thomsen, 2005, p. 18) to underscore its docu-drama filmic style. The film is quick to tell audiences of a son 'in Iraq'—a fact unsurprising considering Moritz's (2005) report that since the attacks, the government has sought ways of deploying the entertainment industry in the war against terrorism. The consequence: a consistent presence of the aftermath of 9/11 in the Visio-verbal syntax of post-9/11 films. As films are a conflation of imagery and language, Visio-syntax refers to the orchestrated manner in which post 9/11 filmic productions index allusions and remembrances to 9/11 in and through both visual imagery (montage) and verbal detail (dialoging).

Often, the verbalizations of the attacks are overt as in the film, *Reign Over Me*, a movie which overtly explores the theme of loss as a consequence of 9/11. In the film, a grieving widow tells audiences: "Then those monsters flew over here from across the world". The use of the term "monster" for the hijackers is both a reminder of what happened as well as a commentary on the need for 'self-preservation'. The use of the events of 9/11 to introduce both character and plot is another comment strategy seen at work in the science fiction film *Knowing*, which examines a child's supernatural powers in predicting an impending natural disaster. In *Knowing*, the toll of terrorism is stated in numeric terms. Details of lives lost is presented as a cipher which only the child can decode. Consequently, via dialog inclusions sporadically included in the film, audiences are constantly reminded of the "2,996' lives lost".

A myriad of such verbal reminders abound in the post 9/11 decade—often in the form of seemingly incidental details. Consider the film *Vantage Point* which tracks the assassination plot of a world leader in a bid to proffer a commentary about global terrorism. In *Vantage Point* via a powerful strategy of cinematic 'replay,' audiences are voyeuristically and verbally reminded of the death toll as a consequence of terrorism not just domestically, but internationally. On numerous occasions in the viewing of the film, we are told that "Since 9/11, more than 4,500 people have been killed in the rising tide of global terror." Terror we can argue through such a strategy is no longer local, but global.

A similar strategy of *cinematic reminiscing* takes center-stage in the film *Remember Me*—a 2010 drama which explores the psychological trauma of loss on those left behind. The film culminates with the events of 9/11 metaphorically filmed through the windows of the now defunct World Trade Center. In an attempt to foreshadow the impending action, a professor is shown in the opening scenes of the film, *Remember Me*, launching a lecture delivered to a group of attentive students seated in an amphitheater with the following opening: "In the wake of recent terrorist attacks, do you think there's a place for a discussion about ethics when we are talking about the root causes of terrorism?"

Cinematic reminiscing is not always verbal. It is sometimes visually plotted as in the opening and culminating scene bookmarking *The Stone Merchant*, a film which uses the events of 9/11 to examine *how* terrorists plan and execute their destruction. In this 2006 film starring Harvey Keitel, there is a careful spotlighting of a historicity of Islamic domination with its parallel in modern times—what Said (1980) so poignantly describes to be an Islamic threat of a: "resurgent atavism, which suggests not only the menace of a return to the Middle Ages but the destruction of the democratic order in the Western world." This 'fear' is carefully rendered for audiences to see in the form of the following still (see, below). Here, we see the chalk etchings of a university professor, himself an amputee, and victim of an Islamist terrorist bomb attack in Nairobi. The teacher draws a graph on the board for all students in his class after he testily responds to a student's objection that "Not all Muslims are terrorists" with the curt response: "But, almost all Terrorists are Muslims." The following still forms the last lingering close-up scene in the film. As an aside, both *The Stone Merchant,* and *Remember Me* use the powerful trope of 'teaching' to evoke their speech acts of *cinematic reminiscing*.

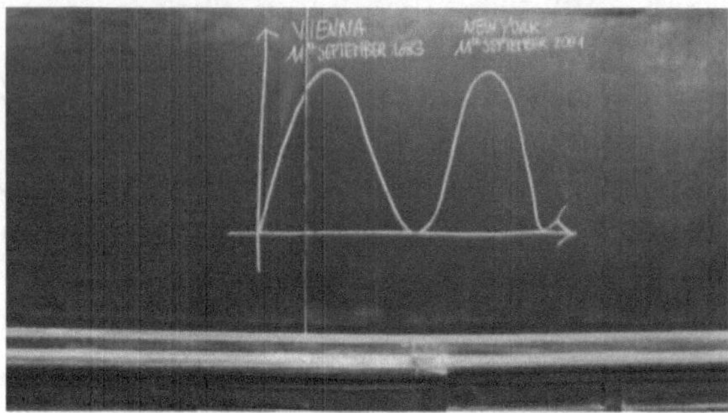

Still excerpted from: Djaoui, A. et al (producers); Martinelli R. (director). March 2006. *The Stone Merchant*. USA: Monarch Home Video.

While one may quibble with the politics underpinning filmic representations, and posit the convincing argument that not all of Hollywood's 9/11 portrayals are homogenous, what is crucial is that this strategy of *cinematic reminiscing* is used with consistency. Consequently, even in left-leaning films such as *Rendition*—a film which explored the 'hyper-control' exerted by the CIA in the Bush administration particularly in its treatment of foreign captured insurgents jailed in the infamous Guantanamo Bay prison, we see overt inclusions to 9/11. In *Rendition,* the allusions are semiotically rendered in the form of cinematic re-simulation as in the chilling reminder which opens the film.

Still excerpted from: Golin, S. *et al.* (producers); Hood G. (director). October 2007. *Rendition*. USA: New Line Cinema.

There is no doubt that the attacks have left "people resentful, hurting and looking for someone to blame" (Allan and Burridge, 2006, p. 10) with no easier target than the people and places encapsulated in the two war zones seen as the source of the attack by the Bush Administration. This mimetic angst (audience fear) is voyeuristically captured and commented upon in several movies. In the film, *Reign over Me,* a movie focused on the trauma of loss suffered as a consequence of 9/11, audience members watch as the actors themselves watch a television screen posting new threats:

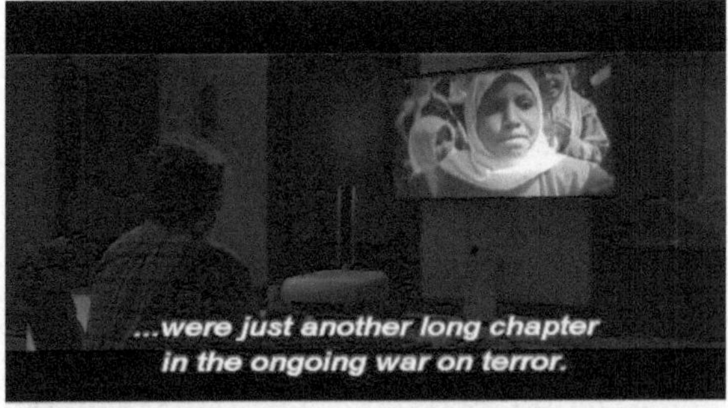

Still excerpted from: Binder, J and M. Rotenger (producers); Bender, M. (director). March 2007. *Reign Over Me*. USA: Columbia Pictures.

Still excerpted from: Binder, J and M. Rotenger (producers); Bender, M. (director). March 2007. Reign Over Me. USA: Columbia Pictures.

The above visuals show the dual workings of *cinematic reminiscing* both as a contextual and filmic strategy. So, while the film does draw audience attention to "the United States heading towards a *Big-Brother-is-Watching-You* society of continuous and networked surveillance" (Thomsen, 2005, p. 16), this cinematic spotlighting also manages to reflect fear at the very same time as it sustains it.

This device is used with generous abundance in the film *Incendiary*—a film exploring a similar theme of grief and guilt which the London mass-transit bombings have had on the families of both victim and assailant. Thus, across the Atlantic, the London bombings see visual and verbal memorialization in the film, *Incendiary*—accomplished via a lingering shot on the following filmic still which both condones the utility of mass surveillance at the very same time as it insidiously assures audiences of a 'free press' doing its job.

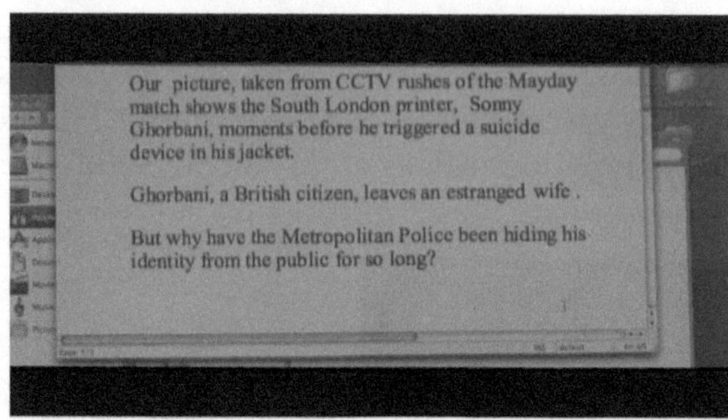

Still excerpted from: Paterson, A et al. (producers); Maguire, M. (director). October 2009. *Incendiary*. UK: Image Entertainment.

LOCATING REASONS AND LOCATING THE WARS

For audiences subjected to films in the decade after 9/11, it is filmic causation for the ground wars which see overt verbalization. Consider the film *The Kingdom,* a cinematic foray into the FBI's role in investigating a bombing attack in a Riyadh-based foreign workers compound. In, *The Kingdom,* Jennifer Garner's character is quick to warn a child (of all people) about "all the bad people out there who plan, organize, train, brainwash, and preach extreme violence," concluding: "These are the men we are fighting"—a message which locates the reason for war in overt terms for both child and viewing audience alike. Again, even in pacifist-focused films, the causation of war sees center-stage. In the film, *Lions for Lambs,* we see an intellectual analysis of the politics of war-mongering. This cinematic feat is accomplished via a juxtapositioning of the consequences of elite orders meted out by politicians, and their effects on ground soldiers—another polemic analysis of the cause of war in Afghanistan. In *Lions for Lambs,* a commanding officer tells soldiers: "Al Qaeda and the Taliban have been whittled down to small wolf-packs," adding, "we've successfully pounded the enemy into something much smaller." Several films choose to utilize filmic close-up shots of the war-zones made especially visually prominent in *Lions for Lambs*. Here, both wars are fore fronted via a camera pan of the map location of the wars. Consequently, war-parlance works in an intertextual capacity—there seems to be both an appropriation and incorporation of war parlance stated in "commonsensical" terms (Fairclough, 1989)—in the role of *mise-en-scene* construction.

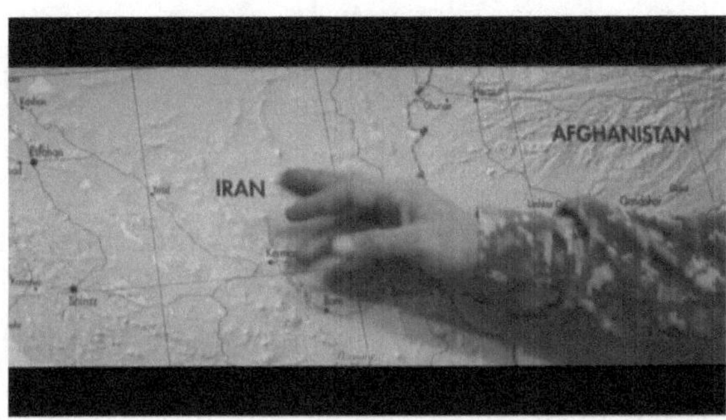

Still excerpted from: Redford, R. et al. (producers); Redford R. (director). November 2007. *Lions for Lambs.* USA: MGM.

What then follows is clever strategy to connect the two wars in the mind of audiences evoked via a deictic declarative: "They're allowing Wahhabi insurgents to hike from Iraq to Afghanistan"—said with a careful pontification of location for viewing audiences. For many viewers, the two wars seem indelibly connected. While it is matter of debate as to whether the film sought to spotlight this connection in a bid to garner dissent, it seems clear that for many—a decade after the invasions—that the lack of any real weapons of mass destruction—not terrorism, the 'supposed' cause of war in Iraq, has been relegated to the dustbin of historical amnesia.

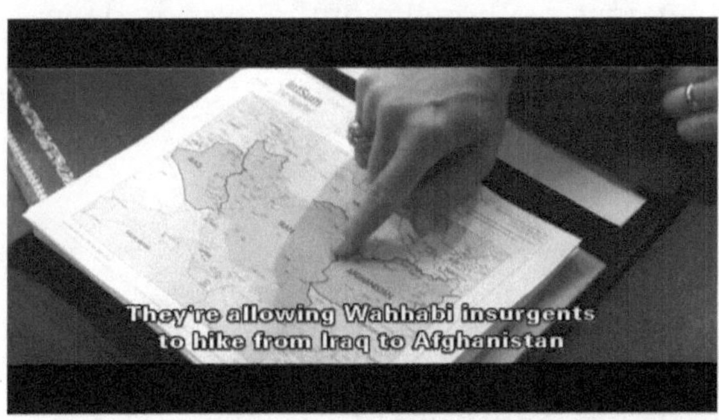

Still excerpted from: Redford, R. et al. (producers); Redford R. (director). November 2007. *Lions for Lambs.* USA: MGM.

A "dramaturgical and aesthetic shift" (Thomsen, 2005, p. 18) identified in post 9/11 film-making has been the use of "the cross-referentiality and intertwinement of different media" (Thomsen, 2005, p. 18) in film-making in a bid to instigate a sense of authenticity in films replicating our media-obsessed world. We witness the use of this strategy for example, in the science fiction thriller, *The Invasion,* a suspense film which uses the context of terrorism to locate an epidemic of somnambulance triggered by extraterrestrial fungi. In a bid to highlight the tactics used by what are labeled 'the insurgents' the film uses interruptive voice-overs. Consequently, in *The Invasion,* a radio reports the following grim details as Nicole Kidman's character eats breakfast: "Hundreds were killed in the bloodiest attack in Iraq since the start of the occupation." The voice-over proffers minute details in the form of: "A mixture of toxic chemicals was strapped to suicide bombers." We see a similar verbal focus on suicide bombers in *Lions for Lambs* where Tom Cruise's character argues for a need for the wars saying: "They butcher the people who helped us, who voted."

Cinematic reminiscing also occurs in visual terms. Consider a powerful scene taken from the widely successful film *Charlie Wilson's War*, a grand, Hollywood production of selective history, and "post-cold war triumphalism" (Chalmers, 2010, p. 1) which subversively as it overtly condones the 'arming' of nations—in this case—Afghanistan—in the cold-war period. Entertaining as *Charlie Wilson's War* was to watch, the film failed to make any overt links to the mujahedeen of yore and their causal links to the Taliban to today. It is also rumored that "The film's happy ending came about because Tom Hanks, "just can't deal with this 9/11 thing," according to Melissa Roddy, a Los Angeles filmmaker with inside information on the production of the film" (Chalmers, 2010, p. 90). Sometimes, the prod is visual as in the still from *Charlie Wilson's War* where the semiotically significant crescent moon is juxtaposed against a silhouette of the mujjahadeen.

Still excerpted from: Hanks, T. et al. (producers); Nichols, M. (director). December 2007. *Charlie Wilson's War*. USA: Universal Pictures.

THEORETICAL MODEL: DYSPHEMIA AND CRITICAL DISCOURSE ANALYSIS

The current paper presents a taxonomy of name-calling strategies directed at the people and places, in both wars. Evidence demonstrates the consistent use of dysphemic language—name-calling—uttered on the silver screens of Hollywood at the people, places and practices—linguistic and cultural—construed as Iraq and Afghanistan. The paper lends credence to the claim that "language is used as a weapon against enemies, and as a release valve when we are angry, frustrated or hurt" (Allan and Burridge, 2006, p. 2)—both strategies currently at work in the silver-screen wars raging also for a decade. The theoretical framework utilizes taxonomies of dysphemia as outlined by Allan and Burridge (2006) who define dysphemia as "speaking offensively"; a verbal practice which entails use of "taboo language" (p. 31) such as "curses, name-calling, and any sort of derogatory comments directed towards others in order to insult or wound them." Nuessel (2008) has used the term "ethnophaulism" (p. 29) to describe words used to "deprecate and disparage a group of people."

In the extensive taxonomy proffered by Allan and Burridge (2006), the following seven classifications of epithets are identified all of which are heard in the verbal and visual syntax of films pertaining to the wars in the post 9/11 decade examined in this paper. The insults and maledictions (Allan and Burridge, 2006, p. 79-85) include: comparisons of people with animals; slurs derived from tabooed bodily organs/ effluvia; dysphemistic epithets picking on physical characteristics treated as abnormalities (i.e., clothing practices); imprecations involving mental subnormality/derangement, and stereotyping (Karim, 1997); and finally, insults which Allan and Burridge (2006) label "-IST-dysphemisms (racist, sexist and ethnic slurs) on the target's character" (p. 85).

These linguistic strategies encode word-manufacturing strategies—labeled as morpho-semantic strategies since they involve unique morphological and semantic processes (O'Grady *et al.*, 2010). Evident in the analysis of such name-calling is the use of innovative morpho-semantic strategies including but not limited to: blended morphemes; the use of innovative compounding strategies as well as the use of borrowed pro-clitic forms (O' Grady *et al.*, 2010). The analysis is framed within current approaches to critical discourse analysis (Fairclough, 1992) in which "the intricate relationships between text, talk, social cognition, power, society and culture" (van Dijk, 1993, p. 253) are examined, and some recent societal effects examined. While critics of critical discourse analysis are quick to point out its potentially reductionist methodology—in particular, its "too strong a focus on the grammatical effects of texts" (Blommaert, 2005, p. 35), and a concomitant lack of historicity, the current paper argues that the microanalysis of text in and thorough a focus on the now—a synchronous analysis of textuality in current media such as film— permits for an alternate means to comprehend *how* the diachronicity of context—history— sees interpellation and intertextualization in and through popular media such as film. After all, language is "a reality-creating social practice" (Fowler, 1985, p. 62). In film, as we shall see, linguistic inclusions strategically as they systematically "constrain content in a bid to favor certain interpretations" (Fairclough, 1989, p.52).

NAME–CALLING THROUGH MORPHEMIC STRATEGIES: SEEKING CINEMATIC ACQUIESCENCE

One highly negative appellation apparent in the film corpus involves the innovative use of compounding of a historically charged racial slur (Essed, 1997) matched with a geographic marker in the form of the endocentric compound "Sand Nigger", whose use in the movie *Crossing Over* occurs as an incorporated form (O'Grady *et. al.*, 2010, p. 142). In the film *Crossing Over,* we are exposed to the bureaucracy surrounding illegal immigration into the United States, and presented with parallel stories of illegal immigrants trying to work in the United States under the real threat of deportation. The threat of terrorist illegals also forms a backdrop of the unfolding action. In the film, a group of teenagers jeer at a fellow Muslim student dropped off at school by her cab-driving father with the imprecation: "It's the sand-nigger express". That this malediction is hurled out by African-Americans successfully deletes the historical accretion of insult encoded in this taboo term (Asim, 2007).

Still excerpted from: Kramer, W and Marshall,W. (producers); Kramer, W. (director). February 2009. *Crossing Over.* USA: The Weinstein Company

"Pronouns, names and address forms are particularly clear and well defined sub-systems of language that reveal asymmetries of power" (Mesthrie *et al.,* 2009, p. 312). This same power which accrues from naming the 'other' sees reoccurrence in several films in the post 9/11 decade. Consider for example, the political drama *The Walker*—a film which examines Capitol politics in the form of a high suspense thriller involving murder. *The Walker* manages to hurl out similar insults. This same appellation—matched with visual violence is witnessed by audiences in a scene in which the epithet is hurled out at knife-point to a by-standing Arab extra. Here, as in several examples in the data corpus, verbal violence is synchronized with visual violence making the insult doubly-intimidating.

Still excerpted from: Nayar, D. (producer); Schrader, P. (director). November 2007. *The Walker*. USA: Kintop Pictures.

The use of the eponym 'Haji' as a form of insult is another fashionable epithet in current Hollywood—confirming Allan and Burridge's (2006) claim that insults function in an "us vs. them situation" (p. 49). The original semantic meaning of the term "haji" refers to "the holiness of one who has made a pilgrimage to Mecca" (Mesthrie *et al.*, 2009, p. 326). In current Hollywood productions however, the term has gone through a process of relexification (Halliday, 1978, p. 175)—a pejorization of the term to the point of encoding an entirely irreverent meaning which even audiences unfamiliar with the term soon internalize through repeated exposures to this word. We see multiple tokens in the data corpus of this strategy. Consider for example, the visualization and verbalization of the term even in a left-leaning film such as *War Inc.*—a movie which attempts a political satirization of the war in Iraq (a box office flop). In the film, John Cusack in the role of a contractor, with the clever eponym, Brand Hauser, attempts to unravel the economic underbelly of the war in Iraq in a fictionalized country called Turaqistan. No other imprecation seems more used than 'Haji' whose variable spelling is consistently conflated with other dysphemistic terms of high semantic import. In *War Inc.*, the imprecation is foregrounded against a tapestry of tolerance. While this powerful image conflates the two conflicting positions on the war, the camera's angle—a foregrounding of the insult, against an imperative for tolerance, lends enough conviction to the argument that the image functions subversively—as an overt attack against an "oppressive" climate of political correctness (Lakoff, 2000). The image further confirms Essed's (1997) claim of "the contradiction between the normative rejection of racial slurs and the lived reality in which tolerance of racism prevails" (143-144). It is a matter of debate whether the film merely attempts to spotlight the 'militaristic racism' in a bid to condone dissent. What is fascinating however is that in the construction of the image –the dysphemia is foregrounded rather than backgrounded. Could this image be one of those dual semiotic creations which shape public opinion while only merely appearing to express it, and already referred to at the outset of the paper?

Still excerpted from: Cusack, J. et al (producers); Seftel, J. (director). May 2008. *War Inc.*, USA: First Look Studios.

The theme of the war in Iraq and its after-effects on soldiers suffering the consequences of trauma forms the subject matter of *Stop-Loss,* a film which uses this invective with generous abandon. In this gritty movie, the 'realism' of the war in Iraq is captured on screen via the incessant use of 'Haji' as in: "I got two hajis right across the street"; or when a soldier confesses: "I'm tired of going and killing a haji in his kitchen and his bedroom."

Still excerpted from: Goodman, G. and S. Rudin (producers); Pierce, K. (director). March 2008. *Stop-Loss* USA: MTV Films/ Paramount.

One could argue it is perhaps easier to kill a haji (a thing) than an Afghani or Iraqi (a person) for actor and audience-members alike. While some may argue that the mere use of the term 'Haji' as a decontextualized term is not sufficient evidence of its use as a dysphemic inventive particularly since in realism-oriented films such as *Stop-Loss,* language is not 'cleaned-up' or sanitized to match audience sensibilities, but rather, reflects the reality of 'real war' where soldiers are not exactly nice to each other (which would be a mystification of war), there is sufficient evidence in *Stop-Loss* to point to the term being used in a dual capacity—to reflect as well as sustain an 'othering'. Consider for example, the manner in which visual evidence is carefully conflated in this film. We see a careful match of a badly disfigured face of an American soldier as a consequence of an IED which we are told is exploded by a 'haji'. This cost of war in *Stop-Loss* is viscerally showcased in the close-up of a badly burned soldier who refers to the cause of his injuries—the infamous IEDs as: "The hajis new bombs" (see still below). The shock of his disfigured face mitigates the semantic import of his own name-calling. No complementary images of burned Iraqi victims of war for example, are spotlighted in the film.

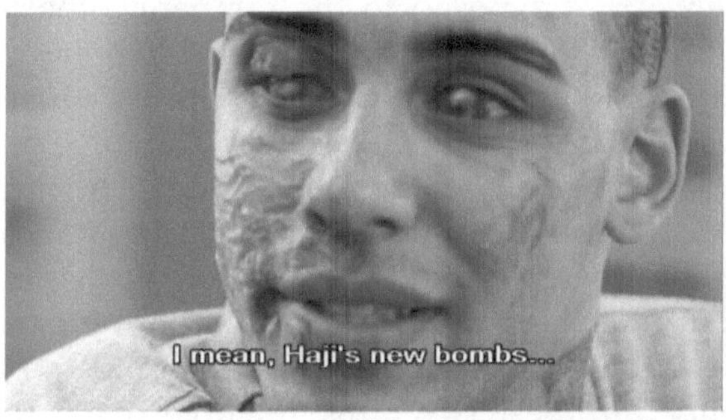

Still excerpted from: Goodman, G. and S. Rudin (producers); Pierce, K. (director). March 2008. *Stop-Loss* USA: MTV Films/ Paramount.

So, in reflecting current war-parlance, the silver-screen also provides viewing audiences with an inventory of invectives for the wars. In the Oscar-nominated movie, In the *Valley of Elah*, a film which confronts the lies, racism, hate and animalistic output of militarism—albeit in the most subtle of terms, we also encounter the use of this invective. We are witness to a returning war veteran, and criminal, coldly remarking to a baffled investigator played by Charlize Theron: "We arrested some hajji who was wounded" continuing with "and the haji screamed. . ." The specific conflation of the term 'haji' with the murdering veteran has to be read differently here than in the film *Stop-Loss*. Here, the invective functions in the capacity of exposure—a cinematic attempt at highlighting troop bigotry towards the 'enemy'. There is an overt depersonalization of the enemy confirming that "flippancy toward what is feared is a means of coming to terms with fear by downgrading it" (Allan and Burridge, 2006, p. 40)—in this case a semantic move on the part of the soldier from animism to animalism.

Still excerpted from: Haggis, P. and Hayward, B. (producers); Haggis, P. (director). September 2007. In *The Valley of Elah*. USA: Warner Independent Pictures.

In, *The Green Zone*, another film which attempts a questioning of the 'weapons of mass destruction' alibi used by the Bush Administration in its invasion of Iraq, we see the use of the invective in a similar vein. In the film, audiences are exposed to the rampant 'othering' given free rein in the military. Thus, in *Green Zone*, a soldier is filmed using this term of disparagement for all Iraqi nationals, as when he informs his commanding officer—played by Matt Damon—with: "This Hajji says he needs to talk to you about something" A similar venting of anger sees reoccurrence in the same film, when a bystanding guard superciliously asks of Matt Damon's translator, "What's up with the Hajji?"—a careful inclusion of the label used on the part of the directors in both these films to encode the attitude of most of the troops towards the 'enemy'. In these two films, the invective is used sparingly and critically—with none of the lead characters using the terms, and instead, watching in astonishment its use. See for example, the facial expression on Charlize Theron's character in the still below excerpted from *The Valley of Elah.*

Still excerpted from: Haggis, P. and Hayward, B. (producers); Haggis, P. (director). September 2007. In *The Valley of Elah*. USA: Warner Independent Pictures.

The invective *Haji* is conflated not just with verbal attack, but with visual violence as in the following scene from *Stop-Loss* where a marine who has lost a platoon member hurls out the invective—confirming that slurs can be both "directly and indirectly intimidating" (Essed, 1997, p. 142). The camera seems sympathetic to the plight of the soldier—who only seems to be interested in 'rescuing' his platoon-mates—using whatever means necessary to gather intelligence as to their whereabouts in a carefully construed 'an all-is-fair in-love-and-war' type of scene.

Still excerpted from: Goodman, G. and S. Rudin (producers); Pierce, K. (director). March 2008. *Stop-Loss* USA: MTV Films/ Paramount.

The seemingly 'innate' propensity for violence of the constructed 'enemy' is filmic fodder in many an acclaimed film. Consider for example the macabre content contained in the 2010 Academy Winner, *The Hurtlocker*—a film which meticulously chronicles the bravery of bomb dismantlers in the Iraq war. In one scene, we are given the grisly details of dismantling a bomb stuffed in a cadaver packed with explosives—'a body bomb'. The question is does this cinematic concoction successfully utilize fetishization, and the dismemberment of Iraqi society in the service of triumphalism and militarism? One has to watch the DVD commentary to find out that the contraption of the 'body bomb' was a creative concoction devised on the part of Kathryn Bigelow's filmic team. In the DVD commentary Bigelow claims that "this prosthetic is a heavily loaded symbolic moment…the idea of a bomb put inside the body of the Iraqi people." Most audiences will unlikely get this fictional symbolism 'seeing' instead the gruesome 'reality' of a cadaver strapped with real bombs—a macabre indictment against a people who will stop at nothing—who this film seems to insinuate –seem maliciously keen on using their dead to create more dead. After all, *The Hurtlocker* was touted as a film based on true soldier accounts. The lingering still on a "butcher shop" which opens the action of *The Hurtlocker*— a film which swept the stage at the Academy Awards— is proof enough of the point-of view being proffered in the film. We have three occurrences of this dysphemic term used to describe civilian Iraqis. Consider the still below with its verbalization:

Still excerpted from: Bigelow K. et al. (producers); Bigelow, K. (director) June 2009, *The Hurt Locker.* USA: Universal Studios.

In other examples, a soldier remarks: "The nine is now pressing into the haji's forehead" with a much more disparaging comment uttered by another soldier who proclaims in exasperation: "You've got two infantry platoons behind you whose job it is to go haji hunting." The conflation of hunting 'hajis' and militaristic fighting is not lost on viewers. Afterall, for most, it is the hunter's prowess that is spotlighted—and not his/her kill.

Haji with other dysphemic terms occurs in *Harsh Times*—a film which examines the psychosis of a veteran suffering from post-traumatic stress disorder. In the film, an unstable war veteran unleashes anger and guilt in a cathartic tirade and metonymic claim: "You know what they were—they were fuckin' hajjis, terrorists, the bad guys."

Still excerpted from: Ayer, D. and Sperling A. (producers); Ayer, D. (director). November 2006. *Harsh Times.* USA: MGM.

A similar semantic juxtapositioning occurs in *Stop-loss* where a bereaving father is given license to vent via a compounded invective: "I'd go back tomorrow to get that Haji bastard that killed Preacher."

Still excerpted from: Goodman, G. and S. Rudin (producers); Pierce, K. (director). March 2008. *Stop-Loss* USA: MTV Films/ Paramount.

PLACE NAMES: A CLINE OF NEGATIVITY

The most obvious output of war depictions on the silver screen involve novel morphophonemic blending and clipping strategies involving the suffix "istan" used to insult the geographic space encapsulated in the war zones. In *Harsh Times,* an Afghan war veteran smugly calls the country: "Trashcanistan."

Still excerpted from: Ayer, D. and Sperling A. (producers); Ayer, D. (director). November 2006. *Harsh Times*. USA: MGM.

In an article written soon after the 9-11 attacks titled: "Clan of Stans" Shen (2001) defined "*Istan*" of Persian etymology as 'place of' (p. 12), and then proceeded to examine the semantic roots of seven place names/ countries utilizing this morphemic suffix.

This insult of place also sees occurrence in films attempting a more serious investigation of the wars in the form of docu-dramas such as *Where in the World is Osama Bin Laden?* This film attempts a critique of the state-run machinery set up in the service of 'the hunt for Osama Bin Laden.' Surprisingly we find this multimorphemic blend being used for 'comedic' effect as in the following nonsensical agglutinative form which opens the film. Narrated in his voice, Morgan Spurlock speculates on his plan of action with: "Was I supposed to go look for him in *Afghanibaluchapakiwaziristan*?" he asks? The inevitable effect is one of 'othering' the entire region—a 'foreignization' that many a mainstream viewer perceives this geographic space to be. After all, in a close-up shot as seen below, audiences are subjected to the word photographed against a backdrop of the entire map of the region.

Still excerpted from: Spurlock, M (producer); Spurlock, M (director). April 2008. *Where in the World is Osama bin Laden*? USA: Weinstein Company.

The use of '–istan' as a means to denigrate is consistent—there is even a 2009 release called *Absurdistan*. Sometimes the insult is extreme as in *War Stories*—a film which attempts to explore the global spread of terrorism in this geopolitical space as it tracks the lives of two reporters. In the film, Uzbekistan is conflated with 'whore'. Eager to underscore the chaos of the region, the same blending strategy occurs in, *Lions for Lambs* as "Trash-gani."

Still excerpted from: Redford, R. et al. (producers); Redford R. (director). November 2007. *Lions for Lambs*. USA: MGM.

The cline of insult while more subtle, but perhaps as derogatory, progresses to metonymy—where "the part stands for the whole" (Sebeok, 1994) in the film, *Charlie Wilson's War* where Tom Hanks' character eagerly solicits support for a plan to arm the mujahedeen in a 'faraway' place in the form of: "It's in a pile of rocks called Afghanistan."

Still excerpted from: Hanks, T. et al. (producers); Nichols, M. (director). December 2007. *Charlie Wilson's War.* USA: Universal Pictures.

The choice of label in *In the Valley of Elah,* slides further down the cline of negativity when an irate father calls Afghanistan "a shithole"—a term used with generous abundance in the film, *Brothers*. This latter film attempts to explore the psychological toll of trauma on returning soldiers and their families.

The effect of place on the psyche of both viewer and soldier alike is most vividly vocalized in the 2010 Academy Award winner, *The Hurtlocker* where audience members hear soldier comments in the form of: "Let's get out of this fucking desert"; "I fucking hate this place"; followed by a sarcastic rejoinder in the form of "You don't like waiting around in this beautiful neighborhood?" –uttered at the very same time as the camera carefully pans across a garbage-strewn street. As an aside, one has to hear the director commentary by Kathyrn Bigelow fourteen minutes into the film [in the DVD] to find out that this scene was cinematically created—*a mis-en-scene* whose workings she explains at length as: "It was a pretty clean street—yeah we brought in quite a lot of garbage. I remember personally picking up the garbage and scattering it around as I remember it…" Why such a detailing of place one wonders especially for a film shot in Jordon instead of the real Iraq? Why such a careful attempt at rendering a sense of place? This cline of labeling confirms Allan and Burridge's (2006) finding that: "terms of pejorization" (p. 54) often range in "scale with fear, abhorrence, loathing, and contempt at the one end, and nothing worse than low social esteem at the other" (p. 54). With such consistent and predictable verbal and visual bombardment in current film, it becomes easy to see just what little effort it takes to rile citizens over Koran-burning or mosque building in the 'homeland'. Could the cognitive effects of such filmic labeling be having their desired social effect on viewing audiences?

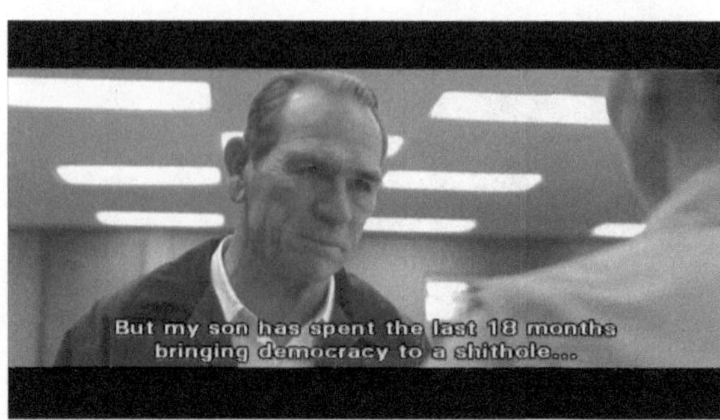

Still excerpted from: Haggis, P. and Hayward, B. (producers); Haggis, P. (director). September 2007. In *The Valley of Elah*. USA: Warner Independent Pictures.

The use of the suffix "istan" as a 'trendy' form of insult finds reoccurrence in *Lakeview Terrace*—a psychological thriller of a cop-turned-rogue. In the film, a deranged police officer played by Samuel Jackson hurls out the morphemic backformation: "You a Euro-Mexi-Japa-Chine-stani or what?" Again, while such wordage functions to reflect current war parlance, its effect on sustaining such prejudices cannot be discounted. For most audiences, the label is cathartic—a reflection of the frustration of many.

Still excerpted from: Lassiter, J and W. Smith (producers); LaBute, N. (director). September 2008. *Lakeview Terrace*. USA: Screen Gems.

It is not just Afghanistan that bears the brunt of insult but also Iraq. In, *Stop loss* an officer takes great care to describe the country for audiences saying: "Sand, Fleas, Flies, Heat, Boredom or you get shot at or blown up," he sardonically tells the camera—ending with "That's pretty much it." Iraq as a term for insult finds allusion even in films unrelated to the theme of war. Consider the film *The Departed,* another Academy-Award winner focused on the Irish mob workings post-civil rights, but whose 9-11 contextual adaptation sees overt spotlighting. Denigration of Iraq occurs in the form of a similie in the Oscar-winner *The Departed* where Inspector Dignam, played by Mark Walberg, calls the Boston Police Unit a "shithole" with "more leaks that the Iraqi navy."

It is perhaps this 'disgust' of place that Brad Pitt's character in the film *Babel*—a movie focused on the interconnectivity of violence on three continents seems keen on exposing. In *Babel,* an irate tourist in an unnamed middle-eastern country vents his geographical frustration with the following dysphemic diatribe: "This is your fucked-up country!" For viewing audiences, could such insult terms serve cathartic as well as subversive roles. The question is could these consistent insults possibly shape and re-shape fear, attitudes and feelings about people in faraway places?

NAME-CALLING OF PEOPLE AND CULTURAL PRACTICES:

Name-calling is rampant in the imprecations used to describe the clothing of individuals in the war zones evoked via novel compounding strategies. Consider for example the film, *Body of Lies,* a high-octane spy thriller which attempts to examine the global tentacles of terrorism presented from the point-of view of a CIA officer played by Leonardo DiCaprio. In, *Body of Lies,* a middle-eastern contact appropriates a co-opted invective to describe the government as: a "towel-head monarchy." The use of "towel head" as an invective is spotlighted in films which seek to question the fallout from 9/11 on Arab American citizens. Thus, in the film *American East* whose focus is just this, a restaurant proprietor confesses: "The rednecks yell: *towel-head* at me also."

It is not just customs but clothing preferences which are the subject of overt attack in several post-9/11 filmic productions. The deprecation of clothing sees overt attack in the film *Crossing Over*—a movie explicitly focused on border security in a post-9/11 America. In the film, an insult is levied out at a young Muslim girl when two schoolmates use the epithet to dually jeer and taunt her appearance and religion with: "Rag-head chick can hide her face and nobody even know she butt-ugly." This confirms Nuessel's (2008) finding: "Ethnopaulisms are pejorative names or designations for people who belong to an ethnic group and they are usually based on several observable phenomena including skin color, clothing customs, culturally determined eating and drinking practices and other aspects commonly associated with a particular group" (p. 29-30).

Still excerpted from: Kramer, W and Marshall, W. (producers); Kramer, W. (director). February 2009. *Crossing Over.* USA: The Weinstein Company

For critics who argue that such cinematic insulting exists merely to reflect current temperaments of a nation at war—a reflection of Islamophobia for instance—consider the manner in which anti-Islamic sentiment is deftly woven into the filmic content of this film. In the same movie, audiences are privy to the grisly details of an 'honor killing' of an Iranian girl murdered by her brother. How can audiences not leave the theater wondering about the mores of these screen-constructed 'enemies'.

Across the Atlantic, we see the use of historical dramas with 'timely' showcasings of a post-globalization Britain unwilling to accept its multicultural diversity. In the acclaimed film, *This is England,* history is anachronistically rendered via a focus on present-day concerns—the attitude of some Britishers to Muslim immigrants. So, while the film is not about terrorism per se, its thematic treatment of anti-Muslim sentiment makes its release anything but coincidental particularly in a culture making industry such as filmmaking in which it is ticket sales which drive production content (Epstein, 2009). Thus, *This is England,* a film about a gang of 1980's pre-teen and teen skinheads becomes historically relevant to a 21st century English society still 'reeling' from its own bout of domestic terrorism. How else can one explain the consistent focus on Muslim discrimination in the film—a discrimination which overtly reflects at the very same time as it subversively asserts its bigotry. Islamophobic invectives see reoccurrence in the form of diminutive eponyms for a pair of young Muslim boys wearing traditional skull-caps—seen in the film *This is England,* where they are pejoratively called "Fucking Tweedledum and Tweedledee" by an angry British Gang.

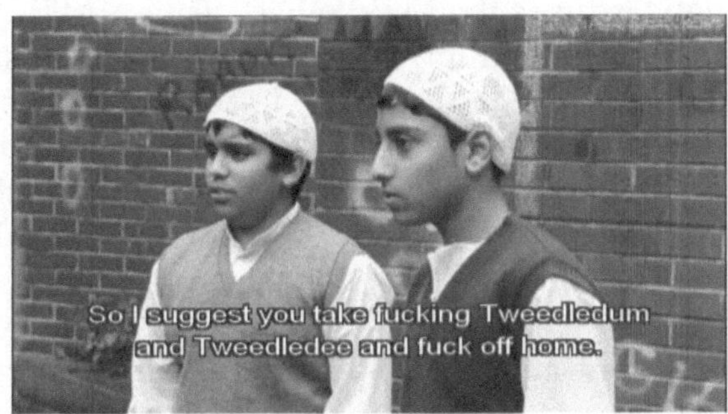

Still excerpted from: Herbert, M (producer); Meadows, S. (director). April 2007. *This is England*. UK: Film4

NAMES: SPOTLIGHTING PEJORIZATION

It is not just the cultural routines of clothing, but naming practices which see attack in a plethora of films produces in this decade. Screen-time is often used to 'comment' on names from these war zones. Consider the vigilante film *Domino* which uses the unlikely plot of a trio of bounty hunters to offer commentary on a post 9/11 America. The film opens with a voice-over by Keira Knightley's character who introduces audiences to their driver— shown ravenously devouring meat. "That's our driver Alf. He's from Afghanistan" she tells audiences, and then hastens to add: "He once ate a cat. We can't understand how to pronounce his fuckin' name, so we just call him the cat-eating alien." Allan and Burridge (2006) claim "An assault on one's name is treated as comparable with, or even worse than, an assault on one's body" (p. 125).

Perhaps the most 'innocuous' of insult-levying occurs in the genre of comedy where all seems to be fair in the art of making audiences laugh. Consider the following insult in the teenage-comedy, *Superbad*, where the pejorization of Muslim names forms the subject of protracted debate and ridicule. This direct assault on names occurs in, *Superbad* alongside other morphemes of dysphemia:

Fogell:	They let you pick any name when you get down there
Seth:	And you landed on McLovin?
Fogell:	Yeah, it was between that or Mohammed.
Seth:	Why the fuck would it be between that or Mohammed? Why not just pick a common name of a normal person?

The dyad demonstrates the power of film in establishing 'normative' versus unmarked naming trends. Few will miss the correlation of 'non-normalcy' with Muslim names. What better way to 'other' than to de-normalize? This spotlighting of non-normativeness is commented upon even in films whose thematic focus is the Middle East. Thus, Middle-eastern names are presented as marked forms on both a sociolinguistic and semantic level in the film, *Body of Lies,* where via a strategy of pretend misunderstanding, the movie reiterates the seeming complexity and 'otherness' of these 'Arab-sounding' names which 'inherently' warrant confusion. This theme of 'foreignization' is played out in the following dyad:

Ed: Thank you. You have done an incredible job developing this guy Karoobi—Katoomi
Hani: Karami.
Ed: Karami [irritated].

How does one remember these 'similar' sounding names audiences are likely to ponder? The dual reality of both reflecting as well as sustaining insult comes in *Syrianna*—a left-leaning film which attempts to demonstrate the bigotry of state officials keen on pillaging the Middle-East at any cost. In the film, the titular forms of address of the Middle East are the butt of insult. We see a pejorative dimunitization and insult of a titular address form — a dyad in which 'Emir' is substituted for an insult.

Board-head: So, I want to talk about the gulf and how a goddamn Emir.... What is an Emir anyway?
Member: King. It's a King.
Board head: A king. Well, how some Podunk king tossed you out on your ass.

The lack of any real need for this dialog leaves one wondering whether in reflecting prejudice, films successfully manage to sustain such attitudes.

It is not just clothing, but also the culinary traditions of the Arab world which form food for insult in a plethora of post 9/11 films. Consider the off-handed remark in the bizarre comedy: *You Don't Mess with the Zohan*—a film which attempts to examine post 9/11 ethnic tensions among multicultural residents in New York City. In the film, an imprecation is levied out in the form of an innocuous comment on hummus as: "it's a very tasty, diarrhea like substance." This same pseudo qualification occurs in *War Inc.,* when John Cussack's character invites a fellow journalist out for tea with: "Would you like to go out for a cup of tea? I hear they make it great here, cardamom mace—the good kind?" With a people 'prone' to violence, this qualification of edible mace in its contrast with explosive mace is anything but coincidental. After all, in film where every milli-second of action is a product of careful orchestration (Epstein, 2009) nothing is accidental.

Still excerpted from: Cusack, J. et al (producers); Seftel, J. (director). May 2008. *War. Inc.*, USA: First Look Studios.

Sometimes the denigration is matched with harsher semantic pejoratives. Consider for example, the overt denigration of the cuisine of Pakistanis as the subject of insult in the coprolalia-rich dialogue of the award-winning film, *This is England* where bigoted, skin-head gangsters harass a group of Pakistani boys with: "Now run home 'cause mommy's cooking curry. Go on." Later in the film, there is an all-out affront on a Pakistani proprietor with a machete matched with the following verbal assault: "I will slay you now where you fucking stand, you fucking Paki cunt. And clean the place up. It fucking stinks of curry. Fucking stinks! Reeks of the fucking shit!"

NAME-CALLING OF LANGUAGE: LINGUICISM

It is not just the physicality of place that bears the burden of cinematic name-calling, but also the linguistic practices contained in the war zones. The role of Hollywood in sustaining attitudes towards people (Bogle, 1991) and languages is well chronicled (Lippi-Green, 1997; Pandey 2001; Bleichenbacher 2008). Note for example the 'ancillary' comments made about Arabic in the film *Traitor*, which examines the counter-intelligence enterprise in a post 9-11 world keen on dismantling global terrorist cells. In *Traitor*, linguicism (Phillipson, 1992) against Arabic emerges in the following dialog between two FBI agents in which there is a clever conflation of Arabic with Jihad.

Officer 2: Claims he's been selected to become *shahid*.
Officer 1: You picking up a little Arabic?
Officer 2: Ah! Just your basic "Jihady"

The synchronization of Arabic with Jihad (war) is again anything but innocuous. Similar 'peripheral' comments occur in several post 9/11 films. Take note for example of the following utterance in the film *Lions for Lambs* where a young recruit asks of his superior: "So, Jihadi and Wahhabi terrorists are moving through Shiite Territory sir?" Most audiences may not catch the conflation of terrorist activity: 'Jihadi' (warring) with an entire sect of the Muslim faith 'Wahhabi' (religion) in the uncontested interrogative.

Even 'independent' (Thomsen and Krewani, 2005) movies with seemingly liberal political agendas seem eager to define the personality type of middle–easterners. Consider the following extraneous filmic detail introduced as an 'innocuous' toast in the Oscar-nominated film, *Rachel Getting Married*. Once again, a family drama centered on the difficulty of homecoming as experienced by a recovering addict forms the thematic focus of the film while still manages to insert its own 'liberal' dose of denigration of middle Easterners. Here, via the use of an interruptive, overlapping conversational turn (Coates, 1994) highlighting the name: 'Mahmood' in the dialog, audiences are subjected to a semantic stereotype framed as a conversational claim which denies at the very same time that it asserts the stereotype:

> Toaster: So, anyway, when the cab-driver finally caught up with us, she talked him down from his middle-eastern fury and like... []
> Rachel: [] Mahmood! Such a nice man! [sarcastically]
> Toaster: In like, um pretend Arabic, Farsi, Urdu, I don't know...

Rachel's inability—her non desire to distinguish between these languages goes uncontested—another example of foreignization at work. The reassertion of the stereotype of "Muslim rage" (Lewis, 1990, p. 47) coded as "middle-eastern fury" confirms that "these stereotypes and semantic scripts function as part of a collective cultural memory" (Karim, 1997, p. 153) and sees a sourcing in films.

Overt statements about Arabic abound in several movies. The conflation of Arabic with terrorism forms the opening sequence of the blockbuster, *Eagle Eye* for example. In this action-packed film which zooms in on a fantastical U.S governmental take-over by rouge agents, the threat of terrorism is ever present. In the opening of the film, audiences are carefully apprised of the following details: "Four males, one of them is speaking in a Rashkani dialect consistent with our Intel on Al-Khoei." The use of the suffix "-ani" as well as the proclitic marker "Al" make the allusion to 'afghani' and Al Qaeda sufficiently clear. A similar conflation of Arabic as a language of terrorist activity emerges in *The Kingdom*, where Arabic is simultaneously heard as a visual of a man with mutilated fingers shakes the hero's hand, confirming Karim's (1997) observation of "thematic clusters" (p. 157) with "entrenched images of Muslims as innately prone to violence" (p. 165).

Still excerpted from: Mann, M and S. Stuber (producers); Berg. P. (director). October 2007. *The Kingdom*. USA: Universal Pictures.

It is this seeming attention to ancillary content, but gruesome content nonetheless, presented within the context of biographically inspired truth-based film which is perhaps most powerful in its effect on audiences. One such film, is the Academy-Award nominated film, *A Mighty Heart*. The film chronicles the disappearance of journalist Daniel Pearle in Pakistan. Here, actress Angelina Jolie, playing the wife of the slain journalist takes great care to identify the language of the perpetrators of the heinous crime. She tells mortified audiences in monotonic detail the following: "They found Danny's body cut into 10 pieces. [...] Then one day, probably February first, three men who spoke Arabic were brought to the compound."

It is this very palpable 'fear' of the other which is the subject of cinematic comment in the film *Babel*, where a 'frightened' tourist informs fellow travelers with the following warning: "In Egypt, in a town like this they slit 30 German tourists' throats. They might do the same to us." Such verbal and visual indexing of violence confirms Karim's (1997) assertion of the persistence of "core images that can be efficiently manipulated to influence public opinion, especially when strong action is to be taken against nations whose populations are primarily Muslim" (p. 155). Arabic as a language of jihad is reinforced in *Body of Lies*, via a carefully construed but concocted suicide mission which is orchestrated entirely in Arabic and carefully translated on screen in real time for audiences to see —indeed confirming the stereotype that Muslims "revel in acts of terrorism" (Karim, 1997, p. 157). With such overt spotlighting of language, why would audience members want to learn Arabic?

ANIMAL IMPRECATIONS

The term 'camel' as a cultural marker and denigrator of the Middle East is another common insult form. In the highly acclaimed film, *Happy Go Lucky*, a psychological drama which cinematically juxtapositions normalcy against rage in a post-London bombings England, we are privy to the pent-up frustrations of a xenophobe who is given free license to utter the following racialized rant. In his role as a driving instructor, he testily yells out:

> Come on! Drive the car. You're not driving a camel. Okay? This is not a bazaar. We have rules in this country. We have regulations and you keep to them!

The conflation of camels with lawlessness is not lost on audiences able to pick up on other semantic links to the Middle East in the form of "bazaar". So, while the victim of the insult is never within the view of the camera, this covert yet potent insult's intent remains overtly obvious to viewers. A similar allusion to camels for insult occurs in *The Departed*, where Inspector Dignam reports on the danger of missing computer processors to a laughing audience with: "These are the kind they put into computers that could put a cruise missile up the ass of a camel." Once again, the allusion to a medieval technology-culture geopolitically sign-posted by the give-away "camel" makes it clear to audiences who the target of the insult really is. Animalistic denigration occurs in *Superbad* in angry overtones. An angry adolescent yells: "These fucking terrorists multiply like bunnies." Why is film so keen on spotlighting this anger? While most audiences may explain this seemingly peripheral comment, as a joke, it confirms Said's (1980) prediction of a generation ago, namely: "So far as the United States seems to be concerned, it is only a slight overstatement to say that Muslims and Arabs are essentially seen as either oil suppliers or potential terrorists."

Still excerpted from: Apatow, J. et al. (producers); Mottola, G. (director) August 2007. *Superbad.* USA: Columbia Pictures.

In *This is England,* animal imprecations occur in the form of diminutives matched to a series of stringed invectives in the form of: "Look at these little, fucking sewer rats"—an insult yelled by an irate skin-head (another spotlighted angry person!) at the very same time that the camera positions the Muslim boys at the feet of the gangsters in the form of a deep-scope shot.

Still excerpted from: Herbert, M (producer); Meadows, S. (director). April 2007. *This is England.* UK: Film4

The eye of the camera semiotically as it hierarchically positions westerners vs. Arabs in this concocted world of hate. This trope of asymmetry encapsulated in a majority of films produced in this post 9/11 decade is worth spotlighting. Again, we see film functioning in the dual capacity of reflecting while it sustains the very asymmetry it attempts to spotlight.

Such duality of filmic imprecation sees occurrence in comedic films such as *Soulmen*—a film which explores the reuniting of two estranged friends. Again in and through peripheral comments Arabs become the victim of angry insult (anger again). On-screen verbalizations of dysphemia occur in this film as a tirade from an irate employee by the name of Hinds played by Samuel Jackson who provoked to anger by a bigoted middle-eastern boss yells out the following outburst:

> You know there was a time, I would have knocked your teeth down your throat for saying shit like that to me. But I'm a changed man. Now I could'a called you a unibrow-shaving, pilaf-eating, greasy-ass, goat fucker, but I didn't, did I? Because I didn't want to hurt your feelings, and I didn't want to piss you off.

Again, verbal and visual violence are conflated. Also semantically significant is the manner in which the dysphemism is framed—as a possibility rather than an actuality—in a sense, it is an insult which is denied at the very same time that it is asserted—a brilliant strategy of Hollywood's doublespeak.

Still excerpted from: Friendly, D. T et al. (producers); Lee, M.D. (director). November 2008. *Soul Men*. USA: MGM.

POST-LONDON BOMBINGS: THE CINEMATIC AFTERMATH

Cinematic acquiescence for group insult is often framed in films attempting to spotlight the theme of ethnic 'warfare' in a post globalization multicultural metropolis—the subject of scrutiny of the film *Rocknrolla*. In this film, the sociological analysis unfolds in the form of multicultural gang warfare in 21st century London. This same screen-anger as seen in countless other excerpts sees verbalization in the dysphemic rich film called RocknRolla where a bigoted crook is given free cinematic license to bully and insult. In one scene, he manages to match verbal threats with violence by threatening a banker of Pakistani origins with: "Don't you ever swear at me, you yellow puddle of immigrant piss. . ." (see, still below).

Still excerpted from: Clark-Hall, S. et al. (producers); Ritchie, G. (director). September 2008. *Rocknrolla*. USA: Warner Bros.

We have already examined several examples of such xenophobic hate encoded in the film aptly titled: *This is England*, where a temporally adapted (post-London terrorist sentiment) finds angry verbalization. In one scene in *This is England* a bigoted gang-member openly vents his frustration against Pakistani immigrants. It might be noted as an aside that the film uses 20 tokens of the dysphemic outburst "Fuckin Paki"—often hurled out by a child, and in the company of other explosive invectives such as: "filthy Paki bastard" (see, still below)

Still excerpted from: Herbert, M (producer); Meadows, S. (director). April 2007. *This is England*. UK: Film4

In the visual below, anger is conflated with a weapon of violence, when a machete-wielding, gang-leader threatens a Pakistani shopkeeper with: "I will slay you now where you fucking stand, you fucking Paki cunt." In their thoroughly comprehensive taxonomy of strategies of name-calling, Allan and Burridge (2006) state "It is generally accepted that 'cunt' is the most tabooed word in English" (p. 52). Again, the release of a film focused on a 1980s, neo-Nazi gangster group sees 'timely' applicability in present-day Britain—a timing of filmic production which is anything but coincidental in an industry where profit margins remain wedded to audience tastes in very real terms (Epstein, 2009).

Still excerpted from: Herbert, M (producer); Meadows, S. (director). April 2007. *This is England.* UK: Film4

SEMANTIC STEREOTYPING: TERRORISTS

Ultimately, it is the conflation of Arab peoples with Terrorists that sees dizzying occurrence either as an implied act (seen in previous examples), or used as a direct linguistic insult. Since the wars are causally linked to the 9/11 attacks in the mind of most, the predominant form of name-calling 'on-screen' pertains to the revival of the word: 'terrorist' consistently used as a metonym/semantic stereotype (Karim, 1997). The conflation of 'Terrorist' with the people encapsulated in the two wars occurs even in moves unrelated to the thematic issue of war. Consider the following offhanded comment made in *Rush Hour 3*—a martial arts comedy which manages to conflate Iranians with terrorism—confirming Nuessel's (2008) claim that "ethnophaulisms are metonyms, i.e., a particular physical trait or a behavior pattern stand for an entire ethnic group." (p. 30), and often form "the basis of stereotyping" (30). In *Rush Hour 3*, the following uncontested claim occurs:

> Captain: Last week you put 6 Iranians in jail for a week.
> Carter: You and I both know them Iranians was terrorists.
> Captain: They were scientists at UCLA!
> Carter: Big deal! 'cause they cure cancer in rats that doesn't mean they won't blow shit up!

Still excerpted from: Birnbaum, R. et al. (producers); Ratner, B. (director). August 2007. *Rush Hour 3.* USA: New Line Cinema.

While most audiences 'laugh off' this ridiculous assertion, the 'terrorist' fear remains uncontested. A similar phobia forms the opening claim uttered by a CIA officer in *Body of Lies*. He is heard saying: 'Listen to me! I am not getting my head cut off on the internet? If something happens, shoot me!' while in the film, *Brothers*, a whimpering hostage-soldier, vocalizes his fear with: "Are they going to cut our heads off?"

This same obsession with terrorism occurs in the Oscar-nominated film, *Frozen River,* a film which uses the post 9/11 world of American immigration to concoct a story of human trafficking across a Canadian border evoked in the form of an unlikely partnership forged between a Mohawk and Caucasian single-mother team trying to eek out an existence. In one scene in the film, Ray, the Caucasian-American heroine cautions her Mohawk partner as they get ready to smuggle a Pakistani couple with: "I just hope these aren't the ones who blow themselves and everyone else up." Having second thoughts, she tosses what she deems to be a suspicions bag out her car window saying: "Nuclear power, Poison gas! Who knows what they might have in there. I'm not gonna be responsible for that."

We see several of such overt ethnopaulisms in current movies. Consider for example, the abundance of insult levied out in the film, *From Paris with Love*—a big-budget blockbuster starring John Travolta in the role of a CIA operative on the hunt for global terrorist cells. In the film, the conflation of crime with ethnic group is overt. In one scene, a CIA operative inquires of John Travolta's character, "What am I looking for?" as he peers out a pair of binoculars. He is given the following shocking description: "You're looking for a Pakistani with a big bag of coke or a raghead pushing a wheel cart filled with cash." A few minutes later, at the sound of a knock on the door, Travolta's character announces to audiences: "It's probably that Pakistani pimp. Kill the fucker!" A few scenes later at a dinner party, in the same film— *From Paris with Love*— the following conversation transpires:

> Girlfriend: And what type of people did you kill today, James?
> James: The usual. Bad guys.
> Charlie: Bad guys? Baddest-ass, suicide vested, cold-hearted Pakistani motherfuckers this side of Karachi. No… well seriously I mean we took down a whole terrorist cell today.

The use of five invectives concatenatively structured in the dyad above serves as a final example of the working of *cinematic acquiescence*. After all, why wouldn't one want to exterminate a terrorist cell with suicide vested terrorists—a scene carefully rendered as an act of self – defense. Perhaps the same kind of self-defense argument underpinning the two ground wars in the mind of most?

CONCLUDING REMARKS:

The analysis above raises some final questions. Firstly, how exactly do we analyze the consistent name-calling levied out on the silver screen against the people and places in the current wars in Afghanistan and Iraq. What are the implications of these "labels of primary potency that act like shrieking sirens, deafening us to all finer discriminations that we might otherwise perceive" (Karim, 1997, p. 155). Thomsen (2005) alludes to the powerful role of film in shaping perceptions saying: "In the age of moving images, the film industry is deeply involved in the creation of a set of collective mind patterns from the very beginning" (p. 9). Do such invectives have an effect on audiences? What is the implication of this asymmetrical portrayal of the 'other', and finally, How is power in the hegemonic sense evoked via "the internalization of the norms and values implied by the prevailing discourses within a social order" (Mesthrie, et al 2009, p. 316).

We cursorily examine these effects on three journalistic outputs. Why journalists? Perhaps because they are often supposed to stand in diametric contrast to state-sanctioned hegemony. Said (1980) is quoted for claiming that: "Very little of the detail, the human density, the passion of Arab-Moslem life has entered the awareness of even those people whose profession it is to report the Arab world." One recent case may serve as appropriate evidence. Consider the esteemed journalist Juan

Williams' infamous commentary on the famed Fox TV channel:

> When I get on the plane, I got to tell you, if I see people who are in Muslim Garb and I think, you know, they are identifying themselves first and foremost as Muslims, I get worried. I get nervous. (Stelter, 2010, p. 1)

This comment cost Williams his job at *National Public Radio* at the very same time that it landed him a "three-year contract worth nearly $2 million in total" (Stelter, 2010, p. 10) with the right-wing news channel, *Fox News*. So while, the press debates whether Juan Williams had the right to voice his internal fears in a public sphere, the real question worth asking is: How did the erudite Juan Williams internalize such fears? Thomsen and Krewani (2005) allude to film's role in the internalization of attitudes claiming: "We owe much of our interior landscapes to the visions, the characters, and the stories of that most characteristic ingredient of American culture" (p. 8).

There is sufficient evidence in the data-analysis presented of the subversive role played by the film industry which reflects at the very same time as it sustains consenting attitudes about the people and places encapsulated in the wars—in some cases reflecting as well as endorsing the continued necessity for the two wars. The juxtaposition of the verbal violence of name-calling presented against a cinematic backdrop of visual violence it is argued serves a key mimetic function—one of filmic catharsis. After all, Allan and Burridge (2006) claim "There is no doubt, we are living in times of high anxiety" (p. 105). Name-calling in Hollywood serves a key socio-semiotic function: it provides an inventory of invectives in current war parlance while at the same time permits a viewing citizenry with free license to define and describe a faraway enemy—perhaps in the entertainment industry's bid to gain continued public approval for the wars.

This paper has demonstrated the *how* of othering—in particular, how innovative, word- manufacturing processes in cinematic wars serve to manufacture consent for real ground wars. In effect, perjorization precedes dehumanization in its trajectory towards exploitation. So, while the strategies of cinematic *reminiscing* and *acquiescing* seem to reflect at the very same time as they sustain the othering of the people, places and cultures encapsulated in the war-zones of Iraq and Afghanistan, audiences subjected to a decade of such linguistic bombardment are less likely to ask for clarification on the real question namely, the cause of these wars.

In the machinery of war, film serves as a powerful conduit in the manufacture of consent. The construction of 'suitable enemies' on reel screens subconsciously if not consciously we could argue sanctions real killings of real 'enemies' on the ground. After all, the lack of any sustained public or institutional outcry—particularly journalistic, against a war founded on concocted causation—'weapons of mass destruction'—in the invasion and subsequent occupation of Iraq for example, lends support to the claim that filmic 'othering' can indeed inoculate viewers into asking for accountability in the decisions to war—i.e. why stage fake reasons for a war? Instead, the causation of war continues to be shrouded behind current cinema's fog of reel enemies, and in its incessant focus on the effects of war on U.S. troops—not Iraqi or Afghani citizens for instance.

Perhaps the most potent output of cinematic creations rests on the effects that such portrayals have on a broad sociological level. Consider for instance the largely unopposed acquiescence of the state's expanded military incursions both domestically and abroad. Such a 'spotlighting' of the 'war on terror' either via the indirect strategies of *linguistic reminiscing* or via direct thematic focus in the form of *cinematic acquiescing,* guarantees unqualified institutionalized license for militaristic expansion at the very same time as it grants permission for an equally expanded machinery of national security operation. Consider for example, the fear-mongering which Hayworth (2006) appeals to in a bid to conflate a rightward shift in immigration policies in the post 9/11 decade. In the preface to his book, journalist Sean Hannity, is quick to inform readers of the impending 'doom' of illegal immigration cautioning readers with the following 'frightening' scenario:

> ...unless we act soon, we could be facing another catastrophe on the order of September 11. By allowing people to cross our borders unchecked, we invite a security risk into our homeland. There is no way of knowing if any—or how many terrorists have already slipped across our border. (p. ix-x)

Others seem eager to market the fear of 9/11 for expanded global control. In his uniquely titled publication, *Schmoozing with Terrorists,* journalist Klein (2007), utilizes a chronoscope of edited interviews with what he calls "jihad-urging sheiks" (p. xv) to call for an expansion of the war on terror, or what he calls "the war against America" on a global scale (p. xvi). For him "global jihad" is on the rise because,

> We have failed to carry out a coherent policy against terror. We have failed to understand global terror and how to annihilate it. As a result, the terrorists are much stronger today than before September 11, when our war on terror began. (p. xviii).

For journalists, such as Klein (2006) the war on terror is not just political, but rhetorical namely: a "war for our existence" (p. 191).

A final point concerns the one missing piece: the financial burden of these wars. Rarely do films focus on the financial cost of these two wars—a financial drain described most aptly by Chalmers (2010) as "running up the imperial tab" (p. 2) at the generous rate of "an estimated trillion dollars a year spent on the defense establishment" (p. 8). In 2009, the cost was at "30 billion per annum to maintain the war in Afghanistan alone" (Chalmers, 2010, p. 8). So, while the wars rage on the ground, Hollywood seems to be doing its part of selling public policy by waging its own verbal battle on the silver screen, and in viewers' minds—in and through its war of words. It is against such a backdrop of rhetorical contest that post-9/11 films I the last decade engage in their own trademark procedures of systemic 'forgetting' in a bid to spotlight a strategic 're-remembering' of 9/11 and the continued need for war.

REFERENCES

Adams, Russell, (2010). "Tensions Still on Boil in Mosque Fight." *The Wall Street Journal,* eptember 13, p. A.5.

Allan, Keith and Kate Burridge, 2006. *Forbidden Words: Taboo and the Censoring of Language,* Cambridge: Cambridge University Press.

Asim, Jabari, 2007. *The N word: Who can say it, who shouldn't and why,* New York: Houghton Mifflin and Company.

Bleichenbacher, Lukas, 2008. *Multilingualism in the Movies: Hollywood Characters and their Language Choices,* Tübingen: Franke Verlag Publishing Company.

Blommaert, J. 2005. *Discourse.* Cambridge: Cambridge University Press.

Bolinger, D. 1980. *Language: The Loaded Weapon.* New York: Longman.

Bogle, Donald, 1991. *Toms, Coons, Mulattoes, Mammies, and Bucks: An Interpretive History of Blacks in American Films,* New York: Continuum.

Chalmers, J. 2010. *Dismantling the Empire: America's Last Hope.* New York: Metropolitan Books/ Henry Holt.

Coates, J. "No gap, lots of overlap: turn taking patters in the talk of women friends," in D. Graddol, J. Maybin and B. Stierer (eds), *Researching Language and Literacy in Social Context.* Clevedon: Multilingual Matters, pp. 177-192.

Cowell, Alan, 2001. "A Nation Challenged," *New York Times*, October 8, p. B1: 6.

Cowen, Tyler. 2002. *Creative Destruction*. Princeton: Princeton University Press.

Downing, J. 1980. *The Media Machine*. London: Pluto Press.

Ehlich, K. (ed.) 1989. *Sprache im Faschismus*. Frankfurt am Main: Suhrkamp.

Epstein, Edward, J., 2009. *The Hollywood Economist: The Hidden Financial Reality Behind the Movies.* New York, Melville House Publishing.

Essed, Philomena, 1997. "Racial Intimidation: Sociopolitical Implications of the Usage of Racist Slurs," *The Language and Politics of Exclusion: Others in Discourse,* by Stephen Harold Riggins, pp. 131-152.

Excerpts from President's Speech: "We will prevail in War on Terrorism," *New York Times*, November 9, p. B.6.

Fairclough, Norman, 1992. *Discourse and Social Change,* Cambridge: Polity Press.

Fairclough, N. 1989. *Language and Power*. London: Longman.

Ford, Peter, 2001 "Britain's Blair Leads Roundup of support for US," Christian Science Monitor, October 9, 93(220): 7.

Fowler, R. 1985. "Power" in T. van Dijk (ed.). *The Handbook of Discourse Analysis, Vol. 4: Discourse Analysis in Society*. (pp.61-82). London: Academic Press.

Friedman, T. 2005. *The World is Flat: A Brief History of the Twenty-First century*. New York: Farrar, Straus and Giroux.

Halliday, M.A. K. 1978. *Language as Social Semiotic: The Social Interpretation of Language and Meaning.* London: Edward Arnold.

Hayworth, J.D. 2006. *Whatever it Takes: Illegal Immigration, Border Security, and The War on Terror*. Washington, DC: Regnery Publishing Inc.

Hoge, Warren, 2001. "A Nation Challenged; Afghan Peacekeeping; Britain to send up to 1,500 for Security force," *New York Times*, December 18, p.5.

Hughes, G. 1988. *Words in Time.* Oxford: Blackwell.

Karim, H. Karim, 1997. "The Historical Resilience of Primary Stereotypes: Core Images of the Muslim Other," *The Language and Politics of Exclusion: Others in Discourse*, Stephen Harold Riggins (ed.), pp. 153-182.

Klein, A. 2007. *Schmoozing with Terrorists: from Hollywood to the Holyland, Jihadists Reveal their Global Plans—To a Jew!* Los Angeles: World Ahead Media.

Lacy, Mark, J. 2003. "War Cinema and Moral Anxiety." *Alternatives: Global, Local Political*. November 1, 2003. www.highbeam.com

Lakoff, Robin Tolmach, 2000. *The Language War*, Berkeley: University of California Press.

Lewis, B. 1990. "The Roots of Muslim Rage" *Atlantic Monthly*, September Issue, pp. 47-60.

Lippi-Green, Rosina, 1997. *English with an Accent: Language, Ideology, and Discrimination in the United States*, New York: Routledge.

McDonald, P. & Wasko, J. 2008. (Eds.), *The Contemporary Hollywood Film Industry*. Oxford: Blackwell Publishing.

Miller, T, Govil, N., McMurria, J., Maxwell, R., & Wang, T., 2005. *Global Hollywood 2*, London: British Film Institute.

Mesthrie, R., J. Swann, A. Deumert and W. L. Leap. 2009. *Introducing Socio-Linguistics*. Philadelphia: John Benjamins.

Moritz, G. S. 2005. "Pentagon Pictures: How Hollywood has its Scripts censored by Washington" *Hollywood: Recent Developments*. Thomsen, C. W. and A. Krewani (eds.), pp. 120-125.

Neussel, Frank, 2008. "A Note on Ethnophaulisms and Hate Speech," *Names: A Journal of Onomastics*, 56(1): 29-31.

O' Grady William, John Archibald, Mark Aronoff and Janie-Rees-Miller, 2010. *Contemporary Linguistics.* New York: Bedford St. Martin's Press.

Pandey, Anjali. 2013. "World Englishes and Media." In *The Encyclopedia of Applied Linguistics* Chapelle, C.A. (Ed.), Vol. *Lingua Francas and World Englishes*. Oxford: Wiley-Blackwell, forthcoming.

Pandey, Anjali, 2010. "The Million Dollar Question: How do you Sell English on the Silver Screen?—A Visio-Linguistic Analysis of *Slumdog Millionaire,"Americana: The Journal of American Popular Culture*. n. 9:2, pp.1-33.

Pandey, Anjali, 2001. "Scatterbrained Apes' and 'Mangy Fools': Lexicalizations of Ideology in Children's Animated Movies." *Studies in Media and Information Literacy Education*. 1(3): 1-11.

Phillipson, Robert, 1992. *Linguistic Imperialism*, Oxford: Oxford University Press.

Riggins, Stephen Harold, 1997. *The Language and Politics of Exclusion: Others in Discourse*, Thousand Oaks, California: Sage Publications.

Said, E. W. 1980. "Islam Through Western Eyes," *The Nation* April 26, first posted online January 1, 1998, accessed September 27, 2011. http://www.thenation.com/article/islam-through-western-eyes

Sebeok, Thomas, 1994. *Signs: An Introduction to Semiotics*, Toronto, Toronto University Press.

Shen Fern, 2001. "A Clan of 'Stans," *The Washington Post*, October 19, 2001, C. 12

Stelter, Brian 2010. "One Comment, Two takes at NPR and Fox." *The New York Times*, October 22, P. B. 1

Suid, L. H. 2002. *Guts and Glory: The Making of the American Military Image in Film*. Lexington: University Press of Kentucky.

Thomsen, C. W and A. Krewani (eds.) 2005. *Hollywood: Recent Developments*. London: Edition Axel Menges.

Thomsen, C. W. 2005. "9/11. Before and After." In C. W. Thomsen and A. Krewani (Eds.), *Hollywood: Recent Developments*. (pp. 9-27). Stuttgart: Edition Axel Menges/University of Siegen.

Tyrrell, H. 1999. "Bollywood versus Hollywood: Battle of the Dream Factories." Eds. Tracey Skelton and Tim Allen. (pp. 260-273). *Cultural and Global Change*. New York: Routledge.

Van Dijk, T.A. 1993. *Elite Discourse and Racism*, Newbury Park, California: Sage Publications.

Wasser, F. (2005). The Transnationalization of Hollywood. In C. W. Thomsen and A. Krewani (Eds.), *Hollywood: Recent Developments*. (pp. 63-70). Stuttgart: Edition Axel Menges/University of Siegen.

FILMOGRAPHY

Apatow, J. *et al.* (producers); Mottola, G. (director) August 2007. *Superbad.* USA: Columbia Pictures.

Ayer, D. and Sperling A. (producers); Ayer, D. (director). November 2006. *Harsh Times*. USA: MGM.

Besson, L and Osborne, I. (producers); Morel, P. (director). February 2010. *From Paris with Love.* USA: Lionsgate.

Bevan *et al.* (producers); Greengrass, P. (director). March 2010. *The Green Zone*. USA: Universal Pictures.

Bigelow K. *et al.* (producers); Bigelow, K. (director) June 2009, *The Hurt Locker*. USA: Universal Studios.

Binder, J and M. Rotenger (producers); Bender, M. (director). March 2007. *Reign Over Me*. USA: Columbia Pictures.

Birnbaum, R. *et al.* (producers); Ratner, B. (director). August 2007. *Rush Hour 3.* USA: New Line Cinema.

Black, T. *et al.* (producers); Proyas, A. (director). March 2009. *Knowing.* USA: Summit Entertainment.

Boden, A *et al.* (producers); A. Bowden and R. Fleck (directors). April 2009. *Sugar*. USA: Sony Picture Classics.

Channing-Williams, S. (producer); Leigh, M. (director). April 2008. *Happy-Go-Lucky*. UK: Momentum Pictures.

Cheadle, D. *et al.* (producers); Nachmanoff, J. (director). August 2008. *Traitor.* USA: Overture Films.

Clark-Hall, S. et al. (producers); Ritchie, G. (director). September 2008. *Rocknrolla.* USA: Warner Bros.

Cusack, J. et al (producers); Seftel, J. (director). May 2008. *War. Inc.*, USA: First Look Studios.

Deluca, M. et al. (producers); Sheridan, J. (director). December 2009. *Brothers*. USA: Lionsgate.

Demme, J. et al (producers); Demme, J. (director). October 2008. *Rachel Getting Married*. USA: Sony Pictures.

Djaoui, A. et al (producers); Martinelli R. (director). March 2006. *The Stone Merchant*. USA: Monarch Home Video.

Fishcher, P. (producer); Singer R. (director). March 2003. *War Stories*. USA: NBC Films.

Friendly, D. T et al. (producers); Lee, M.D. (director). November 2008. *Soul Men*. USA: MGM.

Golin, S. et al. (producers); Hood G. (director). October 2007. *Rendition*. USA: Newline Cinema.

Golin, S. et al (producers); Iñárritu, G.A (director). October 2006. *Babel*. USA: Paramount Pictures.

Goodman, G. and S. Rudin (producers); Pierce, K. (director). March 2008. *Stop-Loss* USA: MTV Films/ Paramount.

Hadida, S. and Scott, T. (producers); Scott T. (director). October 2005. *Domino*. USA: Newline Cinema.

Haggis, P. and Hayward, B. (producers); Haggis, P. (director). September 2007. *In The Valley of Elah*. USA: Warner Independent Pictures.

Hanks, T. et al (producers); Nichols, M. (director). December 2007. *Charlie Wilson's War*. USA: Universal Pictures.

Herbert, M (producer); Meadows, S. (director). April 2007. *This is England*. UK: Film4

Kramer, W and Marshall, W. (producers); Kramer, W. (director). February 2009. *Crossing Over*. USA: The Weinstein Company

Lassiter, J and W. Smith (producers); LaBute, N. (director). September 2008. *Lakeview Terrace*. USA: Screen Gems.

Mann, M and S. Stuber (producers); Berg. P. (director). October 2007. *The Kingdom*. USA: Universal Pictures.

Moritz, N. H (producer); Travis, P. (director).February 2008. *Vantage Point*. USA: Columbia Pictures.

Nayar, D. (producer); Schrader, P. (director). November 2007. *The Walker*. USA: Kintop Pictures.

Nozik, M. et al. (producers); Gaghan, P (director). November 2005. *Syriana*. USA: Warner Bros.

Osborne, N. et al (producers); Coulter, A. (director). March 2010. *Remember Me*? USA: Summit Entertainment.

Paterson, A et al. (producers); Maguire, M. (director). October 2009. *Incendiary*. UK: Image Entertainment.

Pitt, B. et al (producers) Winterbottom, M. (director) June 2007. *A Mighty Heart*. USA: Paramount Vantage.

Pitt, B. et al. (producers); Scorsese, M. (director). September 2006. *The Departed*. USA: Warner Bros.

Rae, H. and Hourihan, C. (producers); Hunt, C. (director). August 2008. *Frozen River*. USA: Sony Pictures Classics.

Redford, R. et al. (producers); Redford R. (director). November 2007. *Lions for Lambs*. USA: MGM.

Sandler, A et al. (producers); Dugan, D. (director). June 2006. *You Don't Mess with the Zohan*. USA: Columbia Pictures.

Scott, R. and De Line, D. (producers); Ridley, S. (director). October 2008. *Body of Lies*. USA: Warner Bros Pictures.

Silver, J. (producer); Hirschbiegel, O. et al (directors). August 2007. *The Invasion*. USA: Warner Bros Pictures.

Singh, A. et al (producers); Issawi H. (director). October 2007. *American East*. USA: Distant Horizons.

A Rough Climate for Migration

Elaine Kelly[1]

> *"Understanding climate change as a security issue risks making it a military rather than foreign policy problem and a sovereignty rather than global commons problem." (Barnett, 2003, p.14)*

> *"This is the double law of hospitality: to calculate the risks, yes, but without closing the door on the incalculable, that is, on the future and the foreigner. It defines the unstable site of strategy and decision." (Derrida, 2005, p. 6)*

INTRODUCTION

In 2010, writer and director Michael Nash released a film detailing the impact of climate change and environmental degradation in terms of mass migration. Nash's film, titled *Climate Refugees* has since gone around the world, gaining official selection into countless film festivals. According to information contained on the official website http://www.climaterefugees.com, the film has made its way across much of the United States, presumably in an effort to educate Americans about the global nature of climate change as well as possible impacts at a domestic level with regard to displacement and migration. A call for political action, the film places emphasis on the negative implications of neglecting climate issues, casting this in terms of threats to national security. Given its dominant market (so far), its cover imagery of the U.S. and South America across a face, and its inclusion of prominent American academics, scientists and politicians, such as Al Gore, Paul Ehlrich and Lester Brown, it is not unreasonable to assume that U.S. national security is an important theme of the film. In fact, approximately two minutes into 'Trailer Two' is the following quote from Navy Vice Admiral Lee F. Gunn:

---

1 Elaine Kelly is Chancellor's Postdoctoral Candidate at the University of Technology, Sydney, Australia. Her work examines the political, ethical and scientific issues associated with the climate-migration nexus. She is particularly interested in the works of Jacques Derrida and the concept of hospitality in the context of climate-migration. She can be reached at: Elaine.Kelly@uts.edu.au

> Addressing the changes in the Earth's climate is not simply about saving polar bears and preserving the beauty of the mountain glaciers. Climate Change is a threat to our national security.

"Climate Change is a threat to our national security". Such a statement reveals some potentially important implications for policy directions in relation to international or cross-border climate-induced migration. An issue that has no formal recognition or (inter)national structures[2], environmental migration remains in a policy vacuum. This leaves it open to be being absorbed by a security platform. Thus the contention of this paper is that if work is not done to assert an ethical foundation for responding to climate-induced migration, law and policy will be dominated (in and for the Global North) by a national security paradigm. This is already an emerging trend with countries such as Australia deploying the Navy in 'deter and deny' migration strategies, and the US drawing heavily upon the military following the devastating earthquake in Haiti in 2010, an example I will return to later in this paper.

While the nation-state is usually assumed in security studies to be the bedrock for stability, I argue that it can be viewed as an active agent in producing insecurity when we examine the North-South divide and the ways in which in the Global North disaster narratives promote apocalyptic visions of environmental migration which in turn perpetuate racialised discourses of invasion and fear. For instance, one article warns of the 50 million environmental refugees who are set to "flood the global north by 2020" (SMH, 2011) or another which reports that 'Mexican "climate migrants" predicted to flood US' (naturenews, 2011). This nightmarish narrative functions in the Global North to stall policy development, while in the Global South many states continue to deal with the reality of regional and internal mass migration. Against the logic that posits this as a regional problem, I agree with Warner *et al.*, who argue that solutions must be thought through at a global level (Warner et al, 2009).

From here, I consider the privileged nation-state as bound up with the production of insecurity in numerous ways. Firstly, in relation to the ongoing complicity of many privileged states in the emission of the

---

2 Legal scholarship on climate refugees and environmental migration is available, but has not been put into action by the international community at present. See: Bierman and Boas, 2008; Warner *et al.*, 2009. Moreover there is a debate amongst legal scholars as to what mechanism and definitional system would be most appropriate. This paper is concerned with the dominance of national securisation and the impact of having no protective framework rather than with outlining the positions within this debate.

very pollutants that contribute to environmental and climate displacement and migration. In 2007, Namibian's representative to the United Nations, Kaire Mbuende, reportedly referred to the continued levels of Greenhouse Gas Emissions by developed nations as equivalent to "low intensity biological and chemical warfare" (cited in Brown *et al.*, 2007, p. 1142). Secondly, in relation to the policing of borders and the militaristic management of 'mass migration' and, thirdly, in reference to the ways in which these more dominant states may override another state's sovereignty or decision-making capacity in the event of natural disaster (or in the future, climate change disaster). This shifts the discourse away from positioning the privileged nation-state as a potential victim, in the position of impeding insecurity from *waves* and *floods* of migration, and toward an understanding of its active role in sustaining the conditions of instability and indeed insecurity for vulnerable states and populations. Throughout, I shift between examples of more broadly understood environmental disaster such as the 2010 earthquake in Haiti, and more specific climate change issues. This shifting is not to be understood as a conflation of environmental disasters with climate-related events. Rather, Haiti is drawn upon because it exemplifies the manner in which existing policy patterns toward specific forms of migration will contribute to, if not determine, potential responses to climate-related disasters in the future. Moreover, because the effects of climate change on migration are difficult to determine in advance, it is useful to "use past and current experiences as analogous" (Tacoli, 2009, p. 517).

By calling into question the logic of security at play, this paper attempts to disrupt the dominant political vocabulary of national security and securitisation more generally in relation to matters of migration and climate. Securitisation refers to the Copenhagen School's paradigm which regards security as the "social practice" of constructing an issue as a threat (Trombetta, 2008, p. 588). This in turn permits the suspension of the normal order of things and the deployment of a "'decisionist' attitude which emphasizes the importance of reactive emergency measures" (Trombetta, 2008, p. 588). Heeding Mark Neocleous' call for an "alternative political language" to contend with the dominance of securitisation (Neocleous, 2008, p. 186), I present the concept of hospitality as one way that we may be able to ethically engage with and prepare for climate-induced migration; to engage at the "unstable site of strategy and decision" (Derrida, 2005, p. 6) without shutting out the foreigner or reducing politics to the identification of enemies, as in Schmitt's logic.[3] Derrida's

3 See Huysman, 2006.

double law of hospitality refers to the notion that a fundamental unconditional openness must negotiate with the imperative to condition gestures of hospitality via programmes, rights discourse, and other policies, and vice versa, that the latter cannot be closed off. Using Derrida I argue that the concept of hospitality provides us with greater scope for ethical engagement with the issue. In so doing, I compare the mobilisation of the military by the US following the earthquake in Haiti to the gesture of radical hospitality put forth by Senegal President Abdoulaye Wade. Rather than bracketing 'hospitality' off as a utopian or unrealistic ideal, I argue that it must contest the political vocabularies that constitute the climate-security discourse.

SECURITISING CLIMATE-MIGRATION

Literature dealing with issues of security tends to be interdisciplinary in scope and thus encompasses a wide range of approaches. It is consequently impossible to generalise about the 'field'. A dominant area of research however concerns national security which is, according to Lester Brown, "as old as the nation-state" itself, but took on greater significance post-WWII when it was reduced, from this period until the end of the Cold War, to military might with a "policy of continual preparedness" (Brown, 1977, p. 4). Underpinning the operation of national security is a belief that the political and economic structures of the nation-state provide stability and protection, and that threats external may undermine this (traditionally this specified war/military threats). Before I get to an analysis of the potential response to climate migration to the Global North, it seems imperative to outline and analyse the ways in which security is tied to the nation-state and the development of this field to encompass the environment, migration and more recently, climate change.[4] This discussion is important in order to contextualise issues of migration and demonstrates the dominance of the security model when discussing the environment and climate change.

Lester Brown's foundational piece, *Redefining National Security* (1977), marks a discursive shift away from national security as a military issue and toward understanding the relationship between man and nature in terms of security. Brown outlines the environmental basis of much polit-

---

4 Anthropocentric climate change has and will continue to result in the increased frequency, duration and force of harsh weather events (storms, hurricanes and droughts for example), as well as rising sea levels. Such events occur in addition to more broadly understood environmental problems such as desertification, soil erosion, resource depletion, an expanding population and natural disasters such as earthquakes.

ical conflict, the importance of energy and resources, and the manner in which the economy is dependent upon the biosphere for its raw materials. It stands to reason then that if domestic political and economic stability is the objective of national security imperatives, the environment would need to be accommodated under such an umbrella. Brown concludes that "the purpose of national security deliberations should not be to maximize military strength but to maximize national security" (Brown, 1977, p. 37). Over fifteen years later, Joseph J. Romm likewise notes that the broadening of security outside of traditional military concerns and into areas like the environment witnesses the diminishing import of military security (Romm, 1993, p.1). In this sense, widening the concept acknowledges the diversity of issues that may impact the nation-state's sense of well-being as well as the variety of possible ways of responding to problems. Theoretically, 'human security' goes a step further, shifting the emphasis away from the state and toward the individual.[5]

However, even as the discourse of security is now recognisable in discussions outside of traditional military concerns, the alignment of the environment as a defence issue has become increasingly apparent. As Richard A. Matthew tells us, while many, especially environmentalists, saw the defence industry as inextricably bound up with the problems of ecological disaster, the environment soon emerged as an aspect of national security and, from the 1980s onward in the United States, continued to be included in its agenda (Matthew, 2000, p. 105). Despite some reservations on the left side of political activism, many fought for the inclusion of environmentalism in the national security policy domain (Matthews, 2000, p. 107). With this move, Matthew marks precisely what is at stake: while inclusion may have initially been desired as a result of a fear that without any recognition of the problem at a national level the response would be one of neglect and continued environmental degradation, the contemporary context reveals to us the costs of such inclusion. In the decision to include environmental security into its defence agenda, a large range of economic, social and political issues could now be interpreted utilising the rubric of defence and the apparatus of the military.

---

5 Roland Paris' much cited text "Human Security: Paradigm Shift or Hot Air" (2001), suggests that the umbrella term human security is too broad to assist policy makers or academic researchers alike. In a different manner, Migel De Larrinaga and Marc G. Doucet in "Sovereign Power and the biopolitics of human security" (2008), argue that the paradigm of human security extends the reach of sovereign and biopolitical modalities of power. In this sense, taking an approach popularised by Giorgio Agamben they contend that human security is simply another means via which sovereign power takes hold of life.

Drawing diverse issues under the same umbrella of securitisation has the effect of, as Jef Huysmans notes regarding migration, determining the operation of the political as the identification of an "existential" threat, in the tradition of politics handed down since Schmitt (Huysmans, 2006, p. 126). Across the Global North–for instance, in the EU[6], Australia, and the US–unexpected migration has witnessed the deployment of the military, something which United States Naval War College Associate Professor Paul Smith writes, "partially reflects a paradigm shift in how international migration is being considered. What was once a social or labor issue has now transformed often into a security matter" (Smith, 2007, p. 628). Following this, Smith argues that while this may present a workable short-term solution for the 'host' state, in the long-term, states must confront the "dilemma" of "how to accommodate the predicated surge in environmental migrants" (Smith, 2007, p. 633).

The dominance of the security paradigm can be seen in recent efforts to lock down a concept of climate security which can then be effectively mobilised by policymakers, extending its reach from environmental and migration discourse into climate change. Steen Nordstrom has suggested that even though climate change is an "odd security problem to address" (Nordstrom, 2010, p. 6), because it is a "threat multiplier" it needs to be more tightly tied to national security and multilateral discussion forums (Nordstrom, 2010, p. 9). Again the language of threat dominates. Because migration is a knock-on or one of the threats multiplied by unstable climatic conditions, one can only assume then that it should be subsumed under the umbrella of national security. Indeed, Joshua W. Busby has contended that the "spillover from neighbours" may in turn require "military mobilization to contain the population movement or provide essential services" (Busby, 2008, p. 477). In the following section, this blurring of humanitarian aid and military mission in the interests of national security will be discussed.

Marie Julia Trombetta recognises the difficulty of implementing climate security, arguing that its complexity arises in the paradoxical need to both transform and protect "the existing economic structure and way of life" (Trombetta, 2008, p. 591). While environmental security takes account of the entire biosphere, climate security concerns the "maintenance of stable climatic conditions as a prerequisite of all human enterprises" (Trombetta, 2008, p. 595). The ambition to secure stable climatic conditions is central to the issues of displacement and migration

---

6 Smith (2007, p.628) notes that the EU's border protection agency, Frontex, utilises the military regularly.

which arise when climatic conditions are destabilised and chaotic. And yet, the desire to tie political action to a notion of climate security reads ambiguously. How would this be achieved? Normative questions of responsibility arise: if a nation-state has benefited historically from high carbon emissions should it take on more migrants/refugees? How can we weigh this against the host nations own sustainability needs? How can we think through hospitality in this setting? It is at this juncture–of sustainability and social justice–that states need to do ethical work.

Even as the difficulties, paradoxes and oddities of merging climate and security are signposted by academics, the coupling of climate change with security, and thus the association to "potential or real threat" (Liotta, 2005, p. 49) can be seen in the establishment of major government and non-government bodies such as the CIA's Centre on Climate Change and National Security in late September 2009.[7] Indeed this development builds on what John Tirman has highlighted as the ways in which security discourse has taken a leading role in the administration and regulation of immigration post 9/11 in the US (Tirman, 2006). In addition to the formation of national bodies, the United States Department of Defence *Quadrennial Defence Review Report 2010,* which provides an overview of the strategic framework for its national defence force, includes the subsection "Creating a Strategic Approach to Climate and Energy". In this brief section we are told that that climate change, alongside energy, will play a key role "in shaping the future security environment" (p. 84). Taking a holistic approach, the document notes that "climate change, energy security and economic stability are inextricably linked" (p. 84). This echoes Brown, writing almost 40 years earlier, rhetorically tying national security to sustainability (even the defence force is involved in making its operations more ecologically sustainable!). The preservation or defence of the environment and climate is crucial for continued economic prosperity. The conclusion is drawn that the military as well as civil bodies will be required to deal with "instability or conflict" resulting from climate change (p. 85). Interestingly, *mass* migration is mentioned once - briefly and cautiously–pointing to the possibility that national responses will privilege national security over other possible modes of engagement.

The move toward heightened border protectionism[8] is crucial to scrutinise given the role of such privileged nation-states in the emergence of anthropocentric climate change as well as the uneven burden

7 See https://www.cia.gov/news-information/press-releases-statements/center-on-climate-change-and-national-security.html.

8 See Paul Smith (2007) for an overview of the various ways in which military security paradigms have been employed against migrants.

the Global South will be dealt in terms of migration (Tacoli, 2009, p. 515).[9] In the context of climate change and migration the apparatus of security extends in two directions: one, it simultaneously, and from afar, *contains* migratory movements by positing responsibility as a local or regional issue, rather than a global concern, a point reflected in the failure to generate an international definition of a climate and/or environmental migrant or refugee. As Simon Dalby has noted, "spatial strategies of containment" have always been part of security discourse (Dalby, 2002, p. 38). Even as pre-established migration routes suggest a local or regional trajectory, there needs to be a global focus to policy outlook and an appreciation of "mobility...as part of the solution rather than the problem" (Tacoli, 2009, p. 514). Part of this solution needs to be the reintroduction of hospitality into the debate. This would challenge the current practice of "warehousing" refugees, or what U.S Committee for Refugee's executive director, Levinia Limón, referred to as "coercing people who have fled persecution to live in crowded, destitute and dangerous encampments" (Limón cited in Fernandes, 2007, p. 142). Secondly, as outlined above, in the Global North, securitising migration promotes the deployment of the military in the event of mass migration, setting security against hospitality or ethics, and short-term reactionary politics against long term legislative and policy development.

While there seems to be an acknowledgement of the difficulty yet urgency of defining climate-induced migration, there is little argument over the fact that numbers are increasing (Kalin, 2010, p. 82). According to Norman Myers, a conservative estimate of environmental migrant numbers in the 1990s was 25 million, more than the figure of traditional refugees at the time (Myers, 2002, p. 609). Current figures put this between 50 million and as high as one billion by 2050 (Christian Aid, 2007), with 200 million often repeated (IOM). Many of these migrants come from "impoverished communities" (Myers, 2002, p. 612) where the environment has exceeded its carrying capacity and can no longer sustain life. Scholars indicate that when migration occurs it is usually regionally focused, leaving neighbouring countries in the position of having to negotiate large numbers of new arrivals (Matthews, 1989; Myers, 2002; Ramlogan, 1996; Swain, 1996; Fernandes, 2007; Tacoli, 2009). As Feldman and Hsu have pointed out, it is not simply a matter of chance that the effects of environmental damage, destruction and harm are unevenly

9 As Tacoli (2009) indicates, only a small proportion of movement is global in scope, with most migration occurring regionally or even within the same state (rural to rural, urban to urban or rural to urban).

distributed. They argue that the "distribution of environmental burdens and risks reflects the legacies of racialisation and colonialism" (Feldman & Hsu, 2009, p.199; also see Dalby, 2002).

When the political response by states such as the US, Australia and the European Union to the migration of peoples characterises their movement as illegal through, in the case of climate-induced migration, a failure of recognition, it could be argued that a model of security is reiterated in which racial privileging protects some at the expense of others (Feldman and Hsu 2009, p. 199). Ashok Swain reveals to us the fact that for years marginal peoples have called for an expansion of the concept of refugee beyond the post-WWII definition, which can be viewed as somewhat Eurocentric in nature. Swain informs us that the Organisation of African Unity as well as Central American bodies have lobbied for change and greater inclusion (Swain, 1996, p. 964). More recently, Bangladesh's finance minister, Abul Maal Abdul Muhith, noted that "The convention on refugees could be revised to protect people. It's been through other revisions, so this should be possible" (Grant, Randerson and Vidal, 2009). Stalled political action and legal implementation forces us to question the reasons for such reluctance to either re-define refugee or open up new categories of protection. P.H Liotta suggests that when threats are not deemed to be immediate and undeniable the political response is often one of refusal followed by reactive action:

> Given the uncertainty, the complexity, and the sheer non-linear unpredictability of creeping vulnerabilities, the frequent–and classic–mistake of the decision maker is to respond with the 'gut reaction': the intuitive response to situations of clear ambiguity is, classically, to *do nothing at all.* The more appropriate response is to take an adaptive posture. (Liotta, 2005, p. 52)

A reactive reaction can be juxtaposed to "an adaptive posture", which I suggest can be read as one open to the uncertainty inherent to hospitality (unconditional hospitality) while also preparing in advance–adapting–to changing circumstances (conditional hospitality). A security apparatus is mobilised in a reactive manner by Global North states and forecloses or dramatically restricts both a conditional economy of hospitality, and unconditionality. Moreover, in the movement from reaction to adaptation, a 'threat' can be re-signified. In this instance, while legal recognition has its limits, a more ethically informed conditional hospitality can be attained which responds to the needs outlined by vulnerable countries.

For the Global North then, the failure (or refusal?) to adapt protocols for protection or regulation leads then to the adoption of military tactics when confronting migration and reproduces a racialised apparatus of security in which privileged states must be protected from potential mass migration, while poorer states are left to deal with growing numbers of displaced peoples. Here I draw again on Feldman and Hsu who understand "racialisation as, in part, a function of differentially distributed vulnerabilities" (Feldman & Hsu, 2009, p. 204).[10] While there is an acknowledgment that some locales are more vulnerable to the impact of climate change, for instance the works of Myers and others brings to light the uneven effects of climate change; legacies of racialisation and colonialism are not fleshed out for their ongoing significance. In fact, the language deployed by Myers in his book *Ultimate Security* re-inscribes the sorts of racial fear invoked more casually in mainstream media. The rhetoric of flooding, spreading and waves, of poverty and destruction, has the effect of portraying such peoples in homogenising ways with the logic of 'us' and 'them' implicitly apparent. For example, take the following excerpt from Myers:

> We could eventually (or soon?) witness multitudes of despair-driven migrants heading from tropical Asia toward "empty" Australia, from China toward Siberia, from Latin America toward North America, and from Africa toward Europe…
>
> The repercussions would be profound. Refugees often arrive with what is perceived by host communities as "unwanted luggage" in the form of alien customs, religious practise, and dietary habits, plus new pathogens and susceptibility to local pathogens. Resettlement is generally difficult, full assimilation is rare. Economic and social dislocations would proliferate, cultural and ethnic problems would multiply, and the political fallout would be extensive if not explosive (Myers, 1993, p. 200-1).

---

10 At the time of writing this paper, a humanitarian catastrophe is occurring in the Horn of Africa, where at least 10 million people are affected by drought with many moving toward large refugee camps in the region. While I cannot do justice to this issue in this paper, the emergency presents us with an example of what Limón refers to as "warehousing". Near the borders of Ethiopia and Somalia, the Dadaab Camp usually holds 90,000 people at capacity, but currently has 400,000 people with more waiting to be processed. While not all of these people may be requesting resettlement in another country, all are moving because their homelands are at least temporarily unable to nourish them. In response, the British are leading the way with aid packages, pledging firstly £38 million and then another £52.25 million.

Although potentially well-intentioned (as a call for action to mitigate environmental destruction), Myers' disaster narrative positions the racialised 'other' as a bringer of disease, disorder, and incompatible cultural differences which may lead to conflict and political breakdown. The Global North faces invasion by "multitudes of despair-driven migrants". Dalby expresses this well when he writes that such representational strategies highlight "the modern impulse to control and the medical tropes of endangerment and disease, abnormality and threat" (Dalby, 2002, p. 154). Myers' scenario negatively overemphasises the risks and dangers of extending hospitality. Such framing is unhelpful to any constructive efforts to understand the necessary and inevitable role that migration and resettlement will play in the future.[11]

From this we can see that from the representational economies perpetuated in media, academic texts and so on, to the positions held by governments, security is privileged over hospitality; they are, in fact, placed in opposition to one another. In this section, I have traced the way in which environmental, migration and climate issues have been included in security debates. These debates have attempted to move beyond the national paradigm.

By introducing a discussion of climate-induced migration, I have suggested that despite this conceptual development, the nation-state continues to hold enormous power over the scope of policymaking with a policy vacuum at the international level in relation to climate and environmentally-induced migration. This in turn reiterates a racialised North-South divide, with the Global South carrying most of the impacts of environmental migration. Finally, I have started to highlight the potential for military models of security to become the norm in privileged states in response to the possibility of environmental and climate-induced disaster migration. In the next section, I will focus on the US response to the Haiti earthquake in 2010 in order to develop this line of argument.

---

11 That hospitality is not on the agenda for the Global North is evidenced in the unfolding Horn of Africa humanitarian crisis where emergency aid tops the international agenda (and rightly so), but the possibility of global gestures of hospitality in terms of resettlement is not addressed. While it is undeniably important to restore homelands, to provide funding for infrastructure and local resilience strategies, the plight of hundreds of thousands of peoples demands measures which extend beyond the maintenance of refugee camps.

A ROUGH CLIMATE FOR MIGRATION

"Border security–and the ability to decide who comes in and who is excluded–is an essential aspect of state sovereignty." (Smith, 2007, p. 621)

It has almost become a truism to say that humans have for thousands of years moved in response to climate, either opportunistically or as a result of circumstance (see Carto *et al.*, 2009; McLeman and Smit, 2006). With the system of nation-states firmly established since the Treaty of Westphalia in 1648, movement has been read through a paradigm of sovereign rights and responsibilities. The logic that Paul Smith expresses–that border security is central to state sovereignty–has been echoed in politics and law with, for instance, the former Australian Prime Minister stating that "[w]e will decide who comes to this country and the conditions in which they come" (Howard, 2001) following an influx of asylum seekers arriving by boat from Iraq, Afghanistan and Iran between 1999 and 2001.[12] This mode of politics, one which Barnett–in the quote which opens this paper–refers to as a security paradigm tying military efforts and sovereignty together (Barnett, 2003, p. 14), contains an extremely conditional version of hospitality reliant upon invitations. Barnett contends that a paradigm change is needed in which climate change should be put under the banner of foreign policy and regarded as a global commons concern. What this means is that it must look outward instead of inward; it must understand the nation-state as in-relation with other states and non-state actors. In our current political environment and imagination turning to foreign policy may only confirm the priority of the nation-state even as it demands global engagement and puts into question traditional understandings of responsibility, ownership and sovereignty. While this shift in perspective has potential, its relationship to security discourse needs to be carefully thought through. Part of this demands that we disentangle hospitality from discourses of insecurity and threat.

In 'The Case against Linking Environmental Degradation and National Security' (1990), Daniel Deudney carefully thinks through the ramifications of linking the environment with security. Writing in response to figures such as Jessica T. Matthews and Lester Brown, Deudney contests the relevance of national security–as concerned with interstate violence–with the environment. There are two other points Deudney highlights that have importance for this paper. Firstly, Deudney points out that national security has traditionally been understood as imposing a form of "*organised violence*" (Deudney, 1990, p. 462)

12 see Pugliese, 2002; Perera, 2002.

and secondly, nationalism is always coupled with national security. Indeed, Deudney argues that "[n]ational security thinking and action is all premised upon a relatively sharp distinction between 'us' and 'them', between friend and foe" (Deudney, 1990, p. 467). Thus, if we continue to promote a national security approach to climate change and environmental migration, the baggage of nationalism comes along too, with strong racialised distinctions between 'us' and 'them', between 'citizen' and 'foreigner', and 'friend' and 'enemy'. Before considering ways in which we can intervene ethically into this complex political issue, ways that break down the reliance on national security, the case of the 2010 Haiti earthquake will be discussed. Is there a form of organised violence functioning in the actions of the US government, despite its humanitarian guise? Is there a nationalistic sense of 'us' and 'them' evident in the response? What understanding of hospitality does this entail? Is hospitality even possible within security regimes, or do we need an entirely different language?

Haiti: 'Compassionate Invasion'?

A compelling example of the use of a national security paradigm by the US is the event of the Haitian earthquake of January 2010.[13] The response to this crisis provides insights into ways in which climate security across national borders or in the name of defending one's borders may in the future be militarised. The use of the US defence force for humanitarian aid following natural disaster is not something new. Indeed in 2005, following Hurricane Katrina in New Orleans, the US military was deployed to 'restore order' and assist with aid, with a 'public health emergency' declared, effectively placing New Orleans under martial law.[14] For the American critical theorist, Henry Giroux, Hurricane Katrina revealed a "politics of disposability" in which some US citizens were blatantly "abandoned" by the US government (Giroux, 2006, p. 180). This systematic neglect, according to Giroux, reflected larger racial and class divides in America, which came to determine a differential response in the event of disaster.

The case of Haiti takes on several additional troubling dimensions. Although I am not focusing on the biopolitical dimensions of national security, it is possible to adjust and apply Giroux's critical framework to the situation in Haiti and argue that a "politics of disposability" has been operational. Departing from Giroux, I am interested in the ways in

13 'Compassionate Invasion' was how one *Times* editor put it for Mark Thompson's piece "The U.S. Military in Haiti: A Compassionate Invasion', 12 January 2010. Available Online at: http://www.time.com/time/specials/packages/article/0,28804,1953379_1953494_1954326,00.html .

14 See Giroux 2006, for a critical analysis of Hurricane Katrina.

which US national security measures *contained* any possible migratory movements out of Haiti as well as the ways in which Haitian sovereignty has been completely undermined in the year following the tragedy. This, in and of itself, may be considered an exercise of biopower as distinct from biopolitics (Esposito, 2008, p. 15). According to Roberto Esposito, biopolitics, or "politics in the name of life" is sometimes conflated with "biopower" which refers to "life subjected to the command of politics" (Esposito, 2008, p. 15). This is not what Giroux does, preferring the term necropolitics derived from Achille Mbembe to discuss life negatively affected by politics–disposable life–and deploying the term biopower in relation to the operation of racialised and classed neoliberalism:

> Given the increasing perilous state of the those who are poor and dispossessed in America, it is crucial to re-examine how *biopower functions within global neoliberalism and the simultaneous rise of security states organised around cultural (and racial) homogeneity.* This task is made all the more urgent by the destruction, politics, and death that followed Hurricane Katrina (Giroux, 2006, p. 182, my emphasis).

Giroux's inclusion of security states defined here as enforcing a "cultural (and racial) homogeneity" is a useful way to frame the response of the US to the Haitian earthquake, and ties in with Deudney's argument concerning nationalism. The security apparatus around migration in the US-Caribbean region has been developing since the 1980s, increasingly reinforcing national sovereignty and the right to protect its borders, and culminating in Operation Vigilant Sentry introduced in 2007:

> this plan provides guidance for four, broad mass-migration activities: (1) at sea rescue and interdiction operations in response to a mass migration from Cuba, Haiti, or other Caribbean nations; (2) deterrence and dissuasion; 3) land-based-law enforcement operations; and (4) migrant processing, protection, and detention procedures (Homeland Security Fact Sheet, 2007).

Deepa Fernandes argues that Haitians in particular have been "disproportionately targeted" by US immigration and homeland security measures (Fernandes, 2007, p. 123). For instance, Fernandes brings our attention to the automatic denial and deportation of Haitians arriving by boat while historically refugees from neighbouring nations like Cuba are provided the opportunity to apply for asylum (Fernandes, 2007, p.

133), a point overturned with the passage of Vigilant Sentry. That Haitians occupy a particular place as a security threat in the US imaginary is highlighted by two things in particular. Firstly, it was in 1972 with the arrival of Haitians fleeing political violence that indefinite detention was introduced, and secondly, the US government's funding of the Haitian Coast Guard (Fernandes, 2007, p.135-138). It is against this background that the response to the 2010 earthquake must be read.

On 12 January 2010, an earthquake of 7.0 magnitude struck the small island state of Haiti leaving its major city, Port-au-Prince, in ruin and resulting in the death of 300, 000 locals.[15] The response of the US government was swift and significant, with a massive deployment of military personnel issued within hours; "one of the globe's biggest warships" in addition to 10,000 troops (Thompson, 2010). In the words of *Times* journalist Mark Thompson, "Haiti for all intents and purposes, became the 51st [American] State…[or] ward of the state" (Thompson, 2010). While this is certainly true in terms of the liberties the US government took with Haitian state sovereignty, the US government did not extend all of the benefits of US citizenship to Haitian victims of the earthquake.[16] Thompson's language is of import here: to become a ward of the state is to be placed under the state's care, to be regarded as unfit to govern oneself, a condition usually placed upon minors who are deemed to no longer have adequate parental supervision. This move has been discussed with reference to colonisation across a range of contexts, with designated populations being under the control of the coloniser's law while not offered citizenship. That the US sought to dominate aid and, later, reconstruction efforts, undermines the political independence of Haiti, the 'first black republic' in the world (overthrowing its French colonisers in the late 18th/early 19th century). Repeating the phrase "Only the U.S. Military" throughout the second half of the article, Thompson's nationalistic piece gives the impression that the US government has taken on the responsibility of a Big Brother, compassionately pouring resources into the vulnerable region, taking the lead–even outnumbering the international community efforts with only 9,000 UN peacekeepers initially sent out (Thompson, 2010).

The actions of the US government to this natural disaster were, from the outset, framed in terms of national security even as they sought to provide essential aid. The use of such a paradigm for an environmental

15 The Haitian population is approximately 10 million.

16 The US government did provide temporary rights to undocumented Haitians in the US at the time of the disaster, but this ended in February 2011 when the US started deporting 4,000 undocumented Haitian immigrants back to Haiti.

catastrophe makes it a relevant example for more speculative discussions of climate security and migration to the Global North. The US government did not make any secret of its security imperatives, immediately deploying its national security team led by Deputy National Security Adviser, Denis McDonough (Thompson, 2010). The US gained air traffic control at the major airport in Port-au-Prince, regulating the arrival of aid and international personnel and, perhaps equally importantly, who could *leave* Haiti (AFP, 2010). The impact of this was heavily scrutinised in the media when a group of critically ill patients scheduled to be flying out of Haiti to Florida for immediate care, were delayed treatment for four days (Padgett, 2010). It has been reported that the majority of US money was spent on military endeavours with only a small amount allocated to the Haitian government to spend on food for its displaced population (which exceeded one million in the capital city). Haitian President Rene Preval's comments were paraphrased by *Democracy Now!* journalist in the following manner: "his government is receiving less than a penny for each dollar the US spends on aid efforts in Haiti. Thirty-three cents of every dollar goes to US military aid, over three times the nine cents spent on food" (*Democracy Now!*, 2010). Aid and defence worked hand in hand with a large Navy hospital anchored off the coast of Haiti. Thus, in addition to securing the right to control the airport, the US government's deployment of a Navy hospital in conjunction with Coast Guard worked to prevent passages across the sea to Miami, only 681 miles away from the small island. The show of force was clear: US Coast Guard Commander Christopher O'Neal saying that "The goal is to interdict them at sea and repatriate them" conforming to the directives of Operation Vigilant Sentry outlined above (cited in Rezouni, 2010, p.12; Waterfield, 2010). Salaheddine Rezouni has noted that immediately following the earthquake, "US soldiers in Guantanamo Bay have already set up tents and beds as a prudent measure to prepare for possible refugees" (Rezouni, 2010, p. 12). Thus, Guantanamo Bay, a site of exception from US law whilst firmly under its jurisdiction, would function as an *ad hoc* emergency detention camp in the event of mass migration. This provision had been initiated in the early 1990s by George Bush Senior, who set up Guantanamo Bay for use "as a refugee camp exclusively for Haitians" (Fernandes, 2007, p. 136).

If we are to understand biopower as the subjugation of life to the demands of political power, in this instance a foreign sovereign force has effectively sought control over movement of bodies out of another sovereign territory, as well as blocking off the avenues for migration across the sea. The decision to intervene in Haiti and assume a degree of sovereign right perhaps signals a changing conception of sovereignty in the era of climate change and natural catastrophe. Such changes are not geared toward recognising interdependence and forming cooperative forms of responsible action or "shared identity", a movement toward globalism (Matthews, 1989, p.175); rather this example illustrates the vulnerability of another's state sovereignty in the interests of US national security and US biopower. This occurred under the seemingly more ethical umbrella of humanitarian aid, but it is useful to recall Deudney's warning that "taken to the absurd extreme–as national security threat sometimes are–seeing environmental degradation in a neighbouring country as a national security threat could trigger various types of interventions, a new imperialism of the strong against the weak" (Deudney, 1990, p. 468). Writing twenty years ago, Deudney's fear can be seen unfolding in Haiti at least, most explicitly, until the US military withdrew in late April 2010 and, implicitly, in the internationally organised reconstruction process which has followed. Haitian writer and activist Jean Saint-Vil argues that this reconstruction effort is "mobilizing resources to maintain the status quo" with all but two of the construction contracts given to US contractors (*Democracy Now!*, 2011).

Against this sort of response "[f]or those countries already dealing with large influxes of migrants, and for those likely to receive increasing numbers of migrants as a consequence of climate change, forward looking assessments and forward planning for climate immigrants should be a policy priority" (Barnett, 2003, p. 12).

MOVING BEYOND SECURITY: HOSPITALITY AND THE CLIMATE-MIGRANT/REFUGEE

Following the devastation in Haiti, a gesture of hospitality shone through the wreckage and systematic *organised violence* of US national security. Amidst the blurring of humanitarianism and militarism and the firm commitment to US power, the President of Senegal, Abdoulaye Wade, offered land to Haitian victims: "The repeated calamities that befall Haiti prompt me to propose a radical solution: to take measures to create somewhere in Africa, the conditions for Haitians to return". Such a gesture of goodwill recognised an historical context of colonialism and slavery: "They did not choose to go to that island. It is our duty to recognise their right to come back to the land of their ancestors" (ABC, 2010). More than this, on offer was fertile land, to ensure the sustainability of any potential community. While there was no mass permanent migration from Haiti to Senegal, by October 2010, 163 Haitian students had been granted full scholarships to study in Senegal. Even this gesture is exceptional given the economic backdrop in Senegal where half the population is unemployed and literacy rates remain low (39.3%).[17] In a speech to the students, President Wade invoked the language of hospitality: "Your ancestors left here by physical force...You have returned through moral force... You are neither strangers nor refugees. You are members of our family" (cited in Bojang, 2010). This message was reinforced by Iba Der Thaim, Vice-President of Senegal's national assembly, when he spoke of giving the world "a lesson in humanity": "Senegal has shown that it's in the hearts of the poor that you can find the gift of generosity...A country that is neither rich nor developed has agreed to share the little it has with its brothers" (cited in Bojang 2010). While both officials deploy the language of brotherhood and familial ties, thus "introducing the circles of conditionality" (Derrida, 2000a, p. 8), it was under the dominance of security discourse that this act of radical hospitality was put forward. I call this gesture radical because it goes beyond determined rights and responsibilities and speaks to the particularities of the situation. What are the solutions, radical or otherwise, that we in the Global North, are willing to put forward? In the Global North, it is necessary to re-think our conditional modes of hospitality (as well as our inhospitable responses) and learn to more ethically adapt to the unconditionality of hospitality.

While it may read strangely to say that we must prepare for what we cannot know in advance, for the unexpected, this is precisely what much action in the realm of climate change requires. In so doing, there is an ethical necessity to move beyond the notion of security. While some have pointed out that the constructed nature of the discourse gives it the capacity to work in the name of progressive outcomes (see Trombetta (2008) for instance, as well as the acceptance of the term 'human security'), others have argued that the term is irredeemable (Neocleous, 2008). Trombetta's claim that "[s]ecuritization is not about applying a fixed meaning of security as exceptionality that inscribes enemies in a context... it is 'an always (situated and iterative) process' [citing Stritzel, 2007, 366] of *generating* meaning" (Trombetta, 2008, p. 591), is correct. However, introducing hospitality as the lens through which we should plan for movements of people holds moral appeal and seeks to short-circuit dominant security discourse. While security is discursively maintained, the dominance of militarisation in the realm of migration is evident in the ways in which many privileged nation-states are deploying deterrence techniques.

---

17 See: https://www.cia.gov/library/publications/the-world-factbook/geos/sg.html

As we have seen, in the context of climate change Paul Smith acknowledges the need to move beyond the security paradigm and in the direction of morally defensible positions, while Jef Huysmans' analysis of migration demands that we rethink our understandings of the political, security and the relationship between the two. Dalby also argues that a shift away from "exceptional measures" and toward "routine political and economic" procedures is important in de-securitising a range of issues (Dalby, 2006, p. 10). Barnett and Tacoli both state the need to include mobility as part of any solution to climate-induced migration. However, such dispositions are not available from within the logic of militarisation which inherently requires the violent closure of the border and thus denies the question of ethics or a more pluralistic notion of politics (Huysmans, 2006, p. 127). Nor, I would argue, are they available within the discourse of security even if it does not automatically infer the use of the military. Because security produces "a practice of exclusion: a practice of identity and being through exclusion" (Burke, 2008, p. 5), the logic that motors policy and discourse around (national) security perpetuates a form of identity that is separate from the 'other' or, when pushed, views alterity as a threat to selfhood/statehood. A politics of (in)security assumes that a fully protected state can be realised through force, and the re-establishment of borders, something pursued under the rubric of national security. The need to root sovereignty in forms of national securitisation denies what Butler thinks of as a pre-existing interdependency and vulnerability, "an impressionability and violability that are ineradicable dimension of human dependency and sociality" (Butler, 2004, p. xiv).

As noted above, hospitality is a double law, requiring the movement between the unconditional and the conditional. This movement is deconstructive in the sense that rather than taking an either/or position, hospitality arises out of the negotiation of the two poles. This process is also bound up with the construction of subjectivity and statehood. Hospitality involves the negotiation rather than reconsolidation of identity. As Derrida writes it is "the foreigner...the one who, putting the first question, puts me in question" (Derrida, 2000b, p. 3). Why is this significant? Returning to Burke, we saw that security imposes a mode of identity premised upon exclusion. Deconstructive reasoning challenges the possibility of discrete identities by emphasising the interdependent relationship between self/other, host/guest and so on. For Derrida, the performance of hospitality is not merely the reiteration of the categories of host and guest, but demonstrates how they rely upon and challenge one another. In this way, notions of interdependency and sociality are compatible with deconstructive engagements with hospitality and provide a theoretical foundation for ethically informed practice.

I opened this paper with a quote from Derrida which suggests that hospitality contains an inherent riskiness and incalculability. This has two central implications for proposing a political vocabulary of hospitality in the context of climate-migration. Firstly, the acknowledgement of risk as something needing recognition could potentially be read as re-imposing the language of security, or justifying its presence (security is, after all, one strategy for eliminating or reducing potential risks). This raises the following questions: outside of security measures how can risk be responded to ethically? Does hospitality as a conceptual alternative provide a way to take account of risk without returning us to a political space of threat and danger, characteristic of securitisation? It is at this critical intersection that further work is needed, work which exceeds the scope of this paper. Secondly, in spite of every effort to calculate and prepare in advance, the incalculable remains. What this means is that even if we create protocols and legal frameworks of recognition, something will remain excessive to these measures and disrupt them. In this sense, Derrida's double law gives space for hospitality outside of legal imperatives. The implication for our concern is that the currently undefined nature of climate migration should not result in a default defensive reaction; rather, it is a chance for hospitality. This philosophical reorientation is where a new discussion of practices of hospitality can be generated, where perhaps we can "reorient the politics of the state" (Derrida, 2001, p. 4).

Jon Barnett's argument, captured in the other quote opening this paper, suggests that we shift away from a military-sovereignty response to a foreign policy-global commons framework. This may provide us with a starting point for such a reorientation and is certainly compatible with the concept of hospitality. However, in order to avoid the exclusionary logic of security, this would need to renegotiate the binary relations of 'us' and 'them' or 'inside' and 'outside' and 'host' and 'guest' which tend to underpin foreign policy considerations. It is precisely by privileging a deconstructive language of hospitality that this may be achieved. In the domain of migration, this would require co-operative action and equitable responsibility-sharing at the level of programs, as well as rethinking concepts of identity and belonging at a conceptual level. It is here that the theoretical approach of a global commons discourse may be useful in conjunction with discourses of hospitality. If global commons regards ownership, sovereignty and responsibility in ways that stretch the dominant western tradition, understandings of host and guest and of citizen and foreigner may be able to be rethought.

CONCLUSION

Despite efforts to expand the security discourse beyond the state and to mark it as constructed, the "national referent dominates discussions of security" (Barnett, 2003, p. 2). If national security inherently excludes the concerns of non-citizens by privileging national priorities, the protection of citizen rights and the "classic national security burden–ensuring its territorial inviolability" (Romm, 1993, p. 4), I have asked if it is the most appropriate paradigm to utilise in response to climate-induced migration. My critical intervention is not an attempt to argue for the dissolution of the state in the name of a world of open borders. Rather it seeks it highlight limitations and point toward the importance of *ethical* models that might help re-orient the response of privileged states to climate-induced displacement and migration. If our critical work has to take place within the context of nation-states, then it needs to imagine ethical solutions to major problems. Part of this will involve making more central the language of hospitality. As such, this paper has offered a review of the dominant security literature and its inclusion of the environment, climate change and migration. From here, I sought to unpack and scrutinise the implications of tying climate-migration to a security paradigm. In response to the limitations of this coupling, I introduced the concept of hospitality, drawing particularly on Jacques Derrida's interventions.

REFERENCES

ABC. (2010, January 18). Senegal offers Haitians a new home. *ABC News Online*. Retrieved from: http://www.abc.net.au/news/stories/2010/01/18/2794995.htm.

AFP. (2010, January 15). US takes over Port-au-Prince airport after Haiti earthquake. *news.com.au*. Retrieved from http://www.news.com.au/breaking-news/us-takes- over-port-au-prince-airport-after-haiti-earthquake/story-e6frfku0-1225819945319.

Barnett, J. (2003). Security and climate change. *Global Environmental Change* 13: 7-17.

Bierman, F and Boas I. (2008). Protecting climate refugees: The case for a global protocol. *Environment*. 50 (6): 8-16.

Bojang, S.(2010, October 14). Senegal takes in Haitian student refugees. *The Guardian*. Retrieved from: http://www.guardian.co.uk/world/2010/oct/14/senegal-haiti-earthquake-student-refugees.

Brown, L. (1977, October). Redefining national security. *Worldwatch Paper14.* Washington D.C. Worldwatch Institute.

Brown O., Hammill, A., McLeman, R. (2007). Climate change as the 'new' security threat: implications for Africa. *International Affairs*, 83:6, 1141-1154.

Busby, J.W. (2008). Who cares about the weather? Climate change and U.S. national security. *Security Studies*, 17:3, 468-504.

Burke, A. (2008). *In fear of security: Australia's invasion anxiety*. Port Melbourne. Cambridge University Press: 1-14 (introduction only).

Butler, J. (2004). *Precarious life: The powers of mourning and violence*. London and New York. Verso.

Butler, J. (2010). *Frames of War: When is life grievable?* London and New York. Verso.

Carto, S.L, Weaver, A. J, Hetherington, R, Lam, Y, Wiebe, E.C. (2009). Out of Africa and into an ice age: On the role of global climate change in the late Pleistocene migration of early modern humans out of Africa. *Journal of Human Evolution*. 56: 139-151. *Climate Refugees*. (2010). Retrieved from: http://www.climaterefugees.com/.

Dalby, S. (2002). *Environmental security*. Minneapolis. University of Minnesota Press.

De Larrinaga, M., and Doucet.M.G. (2008). Sovereign power and the biopolitics of human security. *Security Dialogue*. 39(5): 517-537.

Demoracy Now! (2010, January 28). US military spending in Haiti more than triples assistance to Haitian government. Retrieved from: http://www.democracynow.org/2010/01/28/headlines#3.

Democracy Now! (2011, January 12). Haitian writer Jean Saint-Vil: One year after earthquake, Haitian population treated as a threat, not an asset. Retrieved from: http://www.democracynow.org/2011/1/12/haitian_writer_jean_saint_vil_one.

Derrida, J. (2000a). Hostipitality. *Angelaki: Journal of Theoretical Humanities*, 5(3), 3-18.

Derrida, J., and Dufourmantelle, A. (2000b). *Of hospitality*. (Trans. Rachel Bowlby). California. Stanford University Press.

Derrida, J. (2001). *On Cosmopolitanism and Forgiveness*. London. Routledge.

Deudney, D. (1990). The case against linking environmental degradation and national security. *Millennium: Journal of International Studies,* 19: 461-479.

Esposito, R. (2008). *Bios: Biopolitics and philosophy*, (T. Campbell. Trans.). Minneapolis and London. University of Minnesota Press.

Feldman, M. B., and Hsu, H. L. (2009). Introduction: Race, environment, and representation', *Discourse*, 29(2&3): 199-214.

Fernandes, D. (2006). *Targeted: National security and the business of immigration*. New York. Seven Stories Press

Homeland Security Fact Sheet. (2007, March 2). Fact Sheet: Operation Vigilant Sentry. Retrieved from: http://www.hstfse.com/go/doc/1038/148670/FACT-SHEET- Operation-Vigilant-Sentry.

Howard, J. (2001, October 28). Transcript of the Prime Minister. (Speech delivered at the Federal Liberal Party Campaign Launch, Sydney). Available online at: http://www.australianpolitics.com/news/2001/01-10-28.shtml.

Huysmans, J. (2006). 'De-securitising migration: Security knowledge and concepts of the political', in *The politics of Insecurity: fear, migration, and asylum in the EU*. USA and Canada. Routledge.

Giroux, H.A. (2006). Reading Hurricane Katrina: Race, class, and the politics of disposability. *College Literature*. 33.3: 171-196.

Grant, H., Randerson, J., Vidal, J. (2009, December 4). UK should open its borders to climate refugees, says Bangladeshi minister. *The Guardian*. Retrieved from: http://www.guardian.co.uk/environment/2009/nov/30/rich-west-climate-change

International Organisation of Migration. Retrieved from: http://www.iom.int/jahia/Jahia/complex-nexus.

Kalin, W. (2010). Conceptualising climate-induced displacement. In *Climate change and displacement: multidisciplinary perspectives*. Ed. Jane McAdam. Oxford and Portland, Oregon. Hart Publishing.

Kelly, E. (2006). White hospitality: a critique of political responsibility in the context of Australia's anti-asylum seeker laws. *Continuum: Journal of Media and Cultural Studies*. 20:4, 457-469.

Liotta, P.H. (2005). Through the looking glass: Creeping vulnerabilities and the re- ordering of security. *Security Dialogue*. 36(1): 49-70.

McLeman, R, and Smit, B. (2006). Migration as adaptation to climate change. *Climatic Change*. 76, 31-53.

Matthew, R.A. (2000). The Environment as a national security issue. *Journal of Policy History*. 12(1), 101-122.

Matthews, J.T. (1989). Redefining security. *Foreign Affairs*. 68(2), 161-177.

Moon, B. K. (2007, September 24). 'Address to High-Level Event on Climate Change'. UN News Centre. Retrieved from: http://www.un.org/apps/news/infocus/sgspeeches/search_full.asp?statID=121.

Myers, N. (2002). Environmental refugees: a growing phenomenon of the twenty-first century. *Philosophical Transactions of the Royal Society of London B*. 357, 609- 613.

Myers, N. (1993). *Ultimate Security: The Environmental Basis of Political Instability*. New York and London. W. W. Norton & Company, Inc.

Nordstrom, S. (2010, March). Climate security: From agenda-setting to policy. Royal Danish Defence College.

Neocleous, M. (2008). *Critique of Security*. Edinburgh. Edinburgh University Press.

Padgett, T. (2010, January 31). Who's to blame for suspending Haitian medevac flights? *Time*. Retrieved from, http://www.time.com/time/specials/packages/article/0,28804,1953379_19534 94_1957926,00.html.

Paris, R. (2001). Human security: Paradigm shift or hot air. *International Security*. 2(Fall), 87-102.

Perera, S. (2002). A line in the sea: the Tampa, boat stories and the border. *Cultural Studies Review*. 8(1), 11-27.

Pugliese, J. (2002). Penal asylum. *borderlands e-journal*. 1(1). States of America. Retrieved from: http://www.defense.gov/qdr/images/QDR_as_of_12Feb10_1000.pdf.

Ramlogan, R. (1996). Environmental refugees: A review. *Environmental Conservation*. 23, 81-88.

Rezouni, S. (2010). Illegal immigration: Causes, consequences, and national security implications. Strategy Research Project. Carlisle Barracks, PA. Army War College. Retrieved from, http://www.stormingmedia.us/59/5902/A590225.html.

Romm, J. R. (1993). *Defining national security: the nonmilitary aspects*. New York. Council on Foreign Relations Press. *Sydney Morning Herald*. (2011, February 22). 50 million 'environmental refugees' by 2020, experts say.

Sydney Morning Herald. Retrieved from, http://www.smh.com.au/environment/climate-change/50-million-environmental- refugees-by-2020-experts-say-20110222-1b31i.html

Smith, P. (2000). Transnational security threats and state survival: A role for the military? *Parameters*. Army War College. US. 30(3).

Smith, P. (2007). Climate change, mass migration and the military response. *Orbis*, 51(4), 617-633.

Swain, A. (1996). Environmental migration and conflict dynamics. *Third World Quarterly*. 17(5), 959-973.

Tacoli, C. (2009). Crisis or adaptation? Migration and climate change in a context of high mobility. *Environment and Urbanisation*, 21, 513-525.

Thompson, M. (2010, January 16). The U.S. military in Haiti: A compassionate invasion. *Time*. Retrieved from, http://www.time.com/time/specials/packages/article/0,28804,1953379_1953494_1954326,00.html.

Tirman, J. (2006, July 28). Immigration and insecurity: Post 9/11 fear in the United States. *Border battles: The U.S immigration debates*. Retrieved from, http://borderbattles.ssrc.org/Tirman/

Trombetta, M, J. (2008). Environmental security and climate change: Analysing the discourse. *Cambridge Review of International Affairs*, 21:4, 585-602.

Warner, K & Ehrhart, C, de Sherbinin, A, Adamo, S. & Chai-Onn, T. (2009). *In search of shelter: Mapping the effects of climate change on human migration and displacement.* Cooperative for Assistance and Relief Everywhere.

Waterfield, B. (2010, January 19). Haiti earthquake: US ships blockade coast to thwart exodus to America *The Telegraph.* Retrieved from, http://www.telegraph.co.uk/news/worldnews/centralamericaandthecaribbean/haiti /7030237/Haiti-earthquake-US-ships-blockade-coast-to-thwart-exodus-to- America.html.

Westing, A. H. (1992). Environmental refugees: a growing category of displaced person. *Environmental Conservation.* 19, 201-207

Neoliberalism and the State

Martijn Konings[1]

INTRODUCTION

Many political economists have tended to view the Global Financial Crisis as a turning-point, leading us out of neoliberalism and into a more regulated form of capitalism (Gamble, 2009; Altvater, 2009; Wade, 2008).[2] The fact that even financial elites felt that insufficient regulatory constraints might have been a factor in the making of the crisis was taken as indicating the demise of free-market dogmas. Further confirmation of this diagnosis came in the form of the massive public interventions in the wake of the crisis, which ran counter to all the core tenets of neoliberalism. Such arguments often follow the logic of a Polanyian conceptual framework, according to which market expansion will generate contradictions that trigger a double movement whereby society organizes to re-impose its values on the market's commodification logic. In Polanyian metaphors, after several decades of market 'disembedding' we are potentially witnessing a new phase of regulatory're-embedding'.

By now, this optimism has been tempered somewhat: it has become clear that the public interventions in the wake of the crisis represent some of the most inegalitarian uses to which state power has ever been put–that is to say, that massive amounts of public funds have shielded financial elites from experiencing the consequences of bad bets while ordinary people are suffering the full effects of the crisis, including unprecedented rates of eviction and unemployment. Yet what persists is the notion that the crisis and the governmental responses it triggered

---

1 Martijn Konings is Lecturer in Political Economy at the University of Sydney (Sydney, Australia) and has published widely on American and global finance. His current research interests relate to the changing ways in which households are connected to financial institutions, shifts in pension funds' investment strategies since the onset of the subprime crisis, and the need for political economy to enrich its understanding of core economic categories by drawing on perspectives in social psychology and psychoanalysis. He recently edited The Great Credit Crash and American Empire and the Political Economy of Global Finance (with Leo Panitch). He can be reached at: martijn.konings@sydney.edu.au

2 This article incorporates material previously published in Neoliberalism and the American state, *Critical Sociology*, 36 (5), 741-765.

represent a progressive moment: according to this reasoning, some form of regulated capitalism is not just imperative from an ethical point of view, but it is a practical necessity, as the self-regulating market will sweep away the very conditions of social and political order.

This article argues that such assessments of the current situation are based on a misappraisal of the past three decades, and it will elaborate this argument with reference to the US case. Its central claim is that neoliberalism was a return to classical liberalism only on an *ideological* level; neoliberal *practices* were never about institutional retreat or the subordination of public and private actors to the discipline of disembedded markets, but precisely involved the creation, legitimation and consolidation of new institutional capacities and mechanisms of control. To view the neoliberal era through the lens of institutionalization is to say that it has been a process whereby financial forms penetrated more deeply into the everyday life of ordinary Americans, financial innovation assumed a certain systemic coherence and functionality, and regulators created new policy channels that gave them more grip on financial expansion. This had little to do with the generalized subordination of private and public actors to market imperatives but rather involved a contraction of the room to maneuver available to the bulk of the population that found its counterpart in the growth of the state's capacities and the increased leverage commanded by financial elites. In the construction of these new relations, the *idea* of a return to a pre-Keynesian free market has played a crucial role, but it is the task of the critical social scientist to show how practices diverge from (even if they are also profoundly shaped by) people's ideas about them.

The idea that neoliberalism has enhanced political control represents a counter-intuitive conceptualization, but this article suggests that that is the case precisely because neoliberal ideology has such a hold on our common sense and intuitions. In order to uncover the nature of neoliberal practices we need to shift to a conceptual register not shaped by neoliberal free-market discourse–to a framework that allows us to see what such practices affect and do rather than say and project. This means that, in order to uncover precisely those dimensions of power that neoliberal discourse obscures, we need to broaden our conception of political authority and learn to operate with more capacious concepts of statehood and state power. Attempts to counter the hegemony of neoliberalism often rely too much on a narrow conception of public authority that, by seeking to reassert the salience of the official state vis-à-vis the market, tend to remain within the conceptual parameters set up by neoliberal thought. This article first develops an alternative conceptualization of the state-market relationship and then discusses how this allows us to make sense of key aspects of the neoliberal era.

NEOLIBERALISM AND INFRASTRUCTURAL POWER

We may usefully draw here on Mann's (1984) conception of 'infrastructural' power: whereas 'despotic' power refers to fairly direct authority over a specific set of actors that is backed up by the threat of coercion, infrastructural power denotes a capacity to implement political projects through social life–that is, an ability to employ institutionalized networks of connections among social actors for the transmission of authority. Infrastructural power is more indirect and diffuse and confers more control over the systemic properties of social interaction. It is crucially dependent on the kind of hegemonic socialization that secures active cooperation from social actors. Such legitimacy is constructed through institutions that present us with formal, idealized accounts of the operation of our social relations.

That norms and institutions should not reveal everything about social life is essential to the emergence of stable mechanisms of social control: their full exposure would entail continuous questioning and so prevent them from becoming entrenched in the routines of everyday life. At the same time, however, the complexity and opacity at the heart of modern power means that its operation is often highly unclear to its participants, making it difficult to wield even for those who are positioned favourably in its networks. In other words, actors may exercise power without being aware of it or without knowing how to wield it most effectively. The capacities that modern power builds are contradictory and fragile, precisely because they require the navigation and manipulation of indirect social relations. Although dominant actors like financial elites and policymakers are likely to have more systemic oversight than subordinate actors, their actions are refracted by institutional mediations in ways that they cannot always control or fully foresee.

These considerations suggest a particular angle from which to view the dynamics of the neoliberal era. From this perspective, the fact that the modern American state's capacity to manage economic life and secure financial stability is regularly under threat should not be seen primarily as evidence for the idea (prevalent especially in (IPE) International Political Economy) that capitalism tends to destroy its institutional preconditions and that neoliberalism has given free rein to this tendency. The interpretation proposed here relies on the idea that, instead, the tensions faced by and running through the neoliberal state are the very process through which the state's modalities of control evolve, reflective of the difficulties involved in managing more intricately interwoven social relations. From a historical perspective the unprecedented infrastructural capacity of the modern American state's institutional complex to steer and regulate social processes is much more remarkable than the fact that, like all relationships of political control, it is characterized by myriad problems, contradictions and unintended consequences. The infrastructural power wielded by the modern American state is without historical precedent, and so is the intensity of the contradictions that it must negotiate.

Infrastructural power cannot be easily conceptualized using the categories of political economy. While IPE has not only tried to bring the state and regulatory institutions back in but also tried to distance itself from a 'state vs. markets' perspective, its emphasis on the fluidity of the distinction between these spheres has not yet generated the conceptual instruments to understand the role of the neoliberal state in a qualitatively different way. Despite the attention to the state and its institutions, financial globalization is still conceptualized as the 'disembedding' of financial markets from their erstwhile 'embedded liberal' institutional environment and the resulting imposition of market discipline on public and private actors (e.g. Helleiner, 1994; Best, 2003; Ruggie, 2007).

To suggest that the lingering influence of a 'state vs. markets' perspective is apparent in the continued reliance on Polanyian metaphors of 'embeddedness' and 'disembedding' might seem to be inconsistent with the fact that many scholars use the work of Polanyi precisely in order to conceptualize markets as institutional structures. Polanyi's (1957) central argument was that markets are institutional constructions and that the periodically recurring tendencies of markets to disembed themselves from their institutional context would give rise to a counter-movement through which social forces would emerge seeking to re-embed and re-regulate the market. But, as Gemici's (2008) analysis of Polanyi's writings demonstrates, the way the problematic is framed–i.e. the tendency of markets to escape their institutional environment and the possibilities for re-embedding–suggests that a pre- or extra-institutional logic is at work. That is, insofar as the role of institutions is primarily conceptualized in terms of their ability to regulate and embed markets, the expansionary logic of markets is not *itself* seen as an institutional construction. Rather, it features as a pre-social mechanism that will emerge and expand whenever it is not actively prevented from doing so. This point echoes recent critiques of the notion of embeddedness as a metaphor to theorize the locus of markets and exchange in social life, which argue that it allows for the persistence of an economistic understanding of the market as a sphere governed by actors' natural, pre-social propensities and not structured and produced through the norms, conventions and rules provided by institutions (Krippner 2002, Beckert 2003, Jones 2008).

We need to move beyond an account of neoliberalism that is consistent with its self-description, i.e., as the subordination of governmental authority and public purpose to the disciplinary pressures of disembedding markets. This argument needs to be differentiated from other perspectives that emphasize the continued salience of institutions in the era of financial globalization and neoliberalism. One of the central theoretical points of critical IPE has been the role of the state in fostering the globalization of financial markets. Moreover, it is widely recognized that neoliberal policies do not involve a literal retreat of the state from society and that deregulation is always re-regulation (i.e. that 'freer markets' mean 'more rules', in Vogel's (1996) terms). However, such interpretations tend to generate conceptual problems characteristic of a Polanyian understanding of markets, which stresses on the one hand their many institutional preconditions and on the other their periodically surfacing tendency to escape from that environment and to reverse the direction of causality as their own logic comes to prevail over the control that can be exercised through institutional structures. That is to say, even if it is acknowledged that markets are always dependent on institutional supports, neoliberalism still tends to be considered in terms of the declining capacities of states vis-à-vis disembedded financial markets, the diminished control of political authority over the financial system.

The argument made here is different–it is that neoliberalism has involved a process of institutional reconfiguration that adjusted some of the key parameters of the existing financial regime in a way that enhanced rather than diminished the infrastructural capacities of the American state, as well as multiplied the strategic leeway available to those who enjoy privileged access to the state's mechanisms of infrastructural control (Panitch and Gindin, 2005). Neoliberalism did not represent a return to a purer form of capitalism more in line with the prescriptions of classical liberalism, i.e., 'an attempt once again to disembed the market from society' and as such 'merely the latest iteration of Polanyi's double movement' (Blyth 2002: 4). Rather, it connected the state's formal institutions in more functional ways to the networks of governance and control that had evolved at the level of financial intermediation and everyday life, thereby improving the state's ability to manage those dynamics.

The understanding of market expansion implicit in the political economy literature contrasts in an interesting way with the way such processes have been conceptualized in other fields. In recent years, authors working in the field of 'cultural economy' have attempted to go beyond the residual economism of IPE to conceptualize financial expansion not as a dynamic of disembedding that destroys social bonds and cohesion, but precisely as a process through which new social forms and relations are created, whereby hitherto uncharted aspects of human life become incorporated into the webs of disciplinary social power and subsumed under the organizational forms of modernity (e.g. Aitken, 2005; Langley, 2008).

The argument in this article bears some similarities to these Foucauldian approaches. But it prefers the theoretical lens of 'infrastructural power' over concepts such as 'governmentality' or 'disciplinary power' because it permits us to foreground two key dimensions of contemporary capitalism that have generally not received sufficient attention in the cultural economy literature: the role of the state and the inequality embedded in the operation of power. Foucauldian perspectives have tended to assume that the proliferation of governance mechanisms in social life has meant an attenuation of the centrality of the formal state, but this tends to reproduce the image of neoliberal capitalism as a movement of 'disembedding'. Second, such approaches have tended to conceptualize the discursive structures of market governance as a somewhat anonymous *nebuleuse* that exerts its disciplinary effects evenly across the social field. The market may now be considered as a network of social relations, but these have become so web-like and anonymous that it still does not allow us to think of discipline as an asymmetrical relationship of control. The argument advanced in this article is built on the notion that discipline does not affect social actors in uniform ways, but consists of institutional mechanisms through which some actors build and leverage their agency and expand their strategic options at the expense of the room for manoeuvre and capacities available to others.

RE-INTERPRETING THE NEOLIBERAL ERA

In order to fully understand the configuration of social forces out of which the neoliberal era emerged, we need to begin with a schematic look at the nature of the preceding era (from the New Deal to the 1970s), which saw the emergence of modern mechanisms of infrastructural power. The development of this order during the post-WWII period was characterized by contradictions that motivated new strategies and policies that would consolidate and extend the mechanisms of infrastructural power during the neoliberal era. IPE usually understands the post-New Deal era as a Polanyian mix of markets and state intervention. However, the concept of 'embedded liberalism', which suggests a balance of governmental institutions and market forces, doesn't give us much conceptual grip on that period. Far from being contained or suppressed, the post-New Deal American financial system underwent a dynamic of vigorous expansion. The point of many New Deal reforms had been not to reduce, but precisely to promote, the integration of the American middle and working class into the financial system. This was evident above all in public sanction and support for the use of securitization techniques in order to increase the supply of popular (especially consumer and mortgage) credit. Finance was seen not as a force of social fragmentation but as a cluster of institutions that could be used as a means of social integration (Calder 1999).

The New Deal had thus created institutional foundations for the deeper penetration of financial forms into the fabric of American life. And such financial expansion was seen not as increasing but undermining public control: policymaking in the post-New Deal era reflected an emerging awareness of the mechanisms of infrastructural control, of the potentially symbiotic relationship between public authority and economic expansion. This was allied to growing awareness of the fact that the proliferation of economic connections produced network characteristics and systemic properties that allowed for more effective institutional steering and manipulation (Mitchell 2005)–expressed in the prominence of Keynesian economics.

For a range of complex (and mostly familiar) reasons, this order came under pressure during the 1960s and 1970s. In this context, the demand for consumer and mortgage credit accelerated in a way that the existing financial system was not designed to accommodate. In order to respond to this demand, banks initiated a huge wave of innovation, dramatically expanding their securitization options. This had contradictory effects: it promoted the state's institutional capacities in one respect but complicated them in another. On the one hand, the expansion of popular credit compensated for the growing gap between wages and economic aspirations, integrated Americans into the discipline of indebtedness and repayment and in this way was crucial in blunting the political edge of social discontent and fortifying the logic of capitalist socialization. On the other hand, innovative financial constructions created tremendous regulatory problems: policymakers did not have the instruments to stabilize this pattern of financial expansion (Degen 1987). While finance was increasingly important as a means of social integration, the fact that this function was insufficiently supported by the existing institutional regime was visible in high levels of inflation.

It is in this context that the emergence of a neoliberal regime should be situated. One of the key moments here was the Federal Reserve's turn to monetarism. Monetarism is often described as a return to more traditional, pre-Keynesian financial policies, but this is a misleading portrayal. Pre-New Deal financial authorities simply did not have the kind of policy levers that might have permitted them to manipulate financial markets in such a comprehensive way. It had taken the developments of the intervening decades to produce the financial connectivity that permitted such policy leverage. Monetarism was a policy to address problems that proceeded on the basis of institutional capacities built up over the previous decades. The standard view of neoliberalism in terms of the subordination of policy and politics to the discipline of the market fails to capture either its origins or effects: the turn to monetarism was initiated by policymakers within the state who sought not to abandon but precisely to increase regulatory control; and it had the effect of enhancing regulatory control over financial markets.

Monetarist policies involved putting strict limits on the amount of federal funds that banks could access, resulting in higher interest rates. This did not, however, suppress the creation of money and credit. Rather, it triggered a new wave of innovation and liquidity creation. Banks benefited from the increased price of credit without suffering the downside of restricted quantity (Greider, 1987, p. 139-40). Capital markets activity surged and financial markets began to function as a kind of vortex, sucking in economic activity. Monetarism therefore did not stamp out inflationary pressures but rather re-directed them: inflation was concentrated in the financial sector and so transformed from a generalized problem into a dynamic beneficial to financial capital.

The flipside of this development was the recession in the manufacturing sector, which, in combination with the social policies of the Reagan administration, had a devastating impact on the income of the lower strata of the American population, pushing these groups to borrow against unfavourable rates and often to borrow more in order to be able to repay their loans and interest charges. Everyday life and high finance, Main Street and Wall Street, became connected in a highly asymmetrical relationship. In other words, what neoliberalism meant was not across-the-board market discipline but a *redistribution* of discipline and constraints: it gave financial capital much more leeway, and the other side of this was the intensification of economic discipline on the lower strata of the American population.

This redistribution of financial discipline was highly functional from the systemic perspective with which policymakers were concerned: the inflation of asset prices was much more manageable than the consumer-price inflation of the 1970s. So the monetarist shock reconfigured the financial regime in such a way as to eliminate its most serious institutional contradictions and to bolster the infrastructural capacities of the US state. Debt-based socialization could now proceed without creating the kind of regulatory contradictions that had marked the 1970s.

This did not mean that active financial management had become unnecessary, but that the American state had created sufficient policy room for itself that it could deal with the contradictions of financial markets in more constructive ways. Increased public capacities were evident in the Treasury's ability to sell massive amounts of public debt in expanding financial markets, allowing it to finance large budget deficits with relative ease. These public financing capacities would become crucial in the American state's management of the crises of the 1980s (like the debt crisis and the Savings and Loan crisis (S&L)), as it permitted the Treasury to bail outs firms that were considered 'too big to fail'. And such interventions created expectations for the way in which financial authorities were likely to respond to the threat of large financial intermediaries failing in the future, i.e., it created a regime of implicit bailout guarantees (De Cecco, n.d.).

'Too-big-to-fail' policies involve a socialization of risk that is inherently asymmetrical in nature, since access to its benefits is conditional on the degree of market power that actors already enjoy. The interests that can count on public backing are those that have already become leveraged to such an extent that, if they were to collapse, would bring entire segments of economic life down with them. Since the onset of the subprime crisis, 'too-big-to-fail' policies have been portrayed as a very recent development and a departure from the hegemony of neoliberalism, as a kind of pathological 'moral hazard'. However, public bailouts have been a consistent feature of US financial policy since the early 1980s, and it is crucial to see that the state's willingness to selectively socialize risk has never just been a moral problem: the ability of financial elites to externalize the risks associated with their strategies has been a consistent driving force behind financial innovation and to the market expansion from which the US state benefited so much.

Much of the neoliberal period can be understood in terms of a publicly sanctioned and promoted unfolding of a highly symbiotic relationship between financial innovation and elites' market power on the one hand and social trends like growing inequality and stagnant wages on the other. In the wake of the S&L crisis, regulators and banks cooperated to expand the techniques and instruments for securitization (MacDonald, 1996, p. 298), and the Clinton administration's social policies were heavily based on improving access to financial services. The government-sponsored enterprises Fannie Mae and Freddie Mac increased their investments in mortgages for lower-income borrowers, and other financial institutions were given incentives to do the same. The availability of securitization techniques interacted with neoliberal social trends and policies to produce a massive expansion of asset-backed debt (Montgomerie 2007, Dymski 2007). While the integration of lower-income groups into the formal financial system was widely portrayed as promoting financial inclusion, intermediaries increasingly treated low-income households as a 'captured market' (Montgomerie, 2007, p. 21).

The nineties saw the steady expansion of an elaborate web of financial relations based on the mutually reinforcing further penetration of financial relations into everyday life and the accelerating gyrations of the wholesale capital markets. During this time 'too-big-to-fail' functioned as a background regime that, owing to the decade's relatively stable growth, did not have to be invoked very often. The infrastructural aspects of US state power were more immediately obvious in the very significant policy leverage that the Federal Reserve developed. Not entirely unlike an economist who can alter the parameters of a model on the basis of an understanding of its systemic properties, the Fed could set some of the institutional parameters of a system of highly liquid financial markets. Due to the growth of market depth and the consequent improvement in market arbitrage, the price of federal funds was now almost instantly transmitted across highly integrated financial markets, allowing the Fed an unprecedented degree of control over market interest rates (Krippner, 2007; Phillips, 1996). To be sure, the Fed's regulatory authority remained dependent on the networks of institutional linkages through which it had been constituted. Its policy autonomy was specifically a capacity to manage and stabilize financial expansion; it was not in a position to control the total quantity of money and credit created in the financial markets. Even if Federal Reserve chairman Greenspan's expression of concern regarding 'irrational exuberance' threw the markets off-kilter for a few weeks, this lamentation was itself testimony to the fact that the Fed was not in a position to reduce their dynamism on a structural basis (Parenteau, 2005).

This logic of financial expansion and governance survived the dot-com meltdown of the first years of the century largely intact. Owing to the Fed's liquidity-infusions, the effects of the stock market meltdown, while spectacular, were prevented from spilling over into the wider financial system and triggering a system-wide credit crunch. Banks quickly embarked on a new set of profitable strategies, with securitized mortgage and consumer debt the driving forces behind financial growth (Blackburn, 2008, p. 81). Lending practices took on increasingly predatory qualities. Many mortgage lenders found their way into poor neighbourhoods that in the past they had 'redlined', that is, designated as areas ineligible for loans.

The incorporation of new actors into the forms and relations of American finance produced contradictions that were more serious than financial authorities had imagined possible. As banks and brokers adopted lending strategies that in earlier times had been the preserve of loan sharks, they went well beyond enlisting subordinate actors into hegemonic patterns of control. Instead, by tightening the financial screws to the point of overstrain, they undermined their ability to function as competent social actors with access to the requisite set of capacities. Many poor Americans were less creditworthy than lenders and credit-rating agencies had hoped. And so it was that, in the summer of 2007, it became clear that many Americans had for some time been unable to service the debts they had taken on. Because much of this 'bad debt' was hidden in larger pools of asset-backed securities, uncertainty spread and markets froze.

Over the course of the following year, the gravity of the situation became fully apparent. When the Federal Reserve's attempts to restore confidence proved ineffective and several Wall Street giants teetered on the brink, authorities quickly signalled their willingness to extend financial guarantees. As it became clear that selectively rescuing firms was not going to hold the American financial system together, 'too-big-to-fail' policies assumed entirely new dimensions, beginning with the Troubled Asset Relief Program. Over the past years the US state has extended major public guarantees to financial institutions. This has reinforced the structural salience of the 'too-big-to-fail' logic: since post-crisis legislation has not in any meaningful way changed the configuration of incentives facing American financial institutions, they will still be able to take on risks that will have to be socialized when they go sour. The question is how this continued redistribution of financial pressure will be managed and what kind of responses it will provoke.

CONCLUSION

The US state's recent crisis management efforts have been highly non-neoliberal in spirit. However, we should exercise considerable caution when depicting the highly visible role of the state in the present situation as a break with a preceding neoliberal era. For, as this essay has argued, neoliberal practices have *never* been very neoliberal in spirit. If we see the disjunction between neoliberal theory and practice as a constitutive aspect of the construction of power relations and political capacities over the past three decades, then the recent deployment of political capacities appears less as the breakdown than as the provisional culmination of the neoliberal era and its distinctive practices. Like all episodes of intense strategic manoeuvring, these strategies generate contradictions and will be affected by a range of unforeseen consequences and unacknowledged interdependencies. Yet they are not without foundation, as they operate on the basis of capacities rooted in the institutional construction of the American financial system.

If, as a result of the severity of the crisis, the discrepancy between theory and practice has now become so flagrant that it has actually undermined the credibility of neoliberal free market myths, we should bear in mind that that myth has only ever been the tip of the iceberg of neoliberal patterns of power. We are not just dealing with neoliberal policies and ideas but with a much wider infrastructure of power that involves organically rooted norms, institutions and actor capacities (Cahill 2009).

A conventional perspective that aims to re-assert the state *against* financial markets is profoundly inconsistent with developments of the past years. The current strategies of the American government, far from representing a classic instance of direct state intervention or a return to Keynesianism, are profoundly imbricated with and reliant on the financial institutions and connections that have proliferated throughout social life during the neoliberal era. The sheer degree of infrastructural control that is involved in the bailout packages goes well beyond the kind of intervention mechanisms that were available to Keynesian welfare state planners during the post-WWII period. The state's tentacles have been wrapped around the heart of economic life, and it is now wielding these to reconfigure the institutional parameters of financial growth and in such a way as to restore systemic properties that allow for stable expansion. The progressive potential of this will be slim, unless we can muster the political agency to effect such change.

REFERENCES

Aitken, R. (2005) 'A Direct Personal Stake': Cultural Economy, Mass Investment and the New York Stock Exchange. *Review of International Political Economy* 12 (2): 334-363.

Altvater Eltmar, 2009. "Postneoliberalism or Postcapitalism? The Failure of Neoliberalism in the Financial Market Crisis", *Development Dialogue*, 51.

Beckert, J. (2003) Economic Action and Embeddedness: How Shall We Conceptualize Economic Action? *Journal Of Economic Issues* 37 (3): 769-787.

Best, J. (2003) From the Top Down: The New Financial Architecture and the Re-Embedding of Global Finance. *New Political Economy* 8 (3): 363-384.

Blackburn, R. (2008) The Subprime Crisis. *New Left Review* 50: 63-106.

Blyth, M. (2002) *Great Transformations: Economic Ideas and Political Change in the Twentieth Century*. Cambridge: Cambridge University Press.

Cahill, D. (2009) 'The end of neoliberalism?', *ZCommunications*, http://www.zcommunications.org/the-end-of-neoliberalism-by-damien-cahill

Calder, L. (1999) *Financing the American Dream. A Cultural History of Consumer Credit*. Princeton: Princeton University Press.

De Cecco, M. (n.d.) The Lender of Last Resort. CIDEI Working Paper No. 49.

Degen, R. A. (1987) *The American Monetary System. A Concise Survey of its Evolution Since 1896*. Massachutts/Toronto: D.C. Heath And Company/Lexington.

Dymski, G.A. (2007) From Financial Exploitation to Global Banking Instability: Two Overlooked Roots of The Subprime Crisis. URL (consulted on 17 July 2009): http://www.soas.ac.uk/economics/events/crisis/43938.pdf.

Gamble Andrew (2009) *The Spectre at the Feast. Capitalist Crisis and the Politics of Recession*. New York: Palgrave.

Gemici, K. (2008) Karl Polanyi and the Antinomies of Embeddedness. *Socio-Economic Review* 6 (1): 5-33.

Greider,W. (1987) *Secrets of the Temple: How the Federal Reserve Runs The Country*. New York: Simon and Schuster.

Helleiner, E. (1994) *States and the Reemergence of Global Finance. From Bretton Woods to the 1990s*. Ithaca, NY: Cornell University Press.

Jones, A. (2008) Beyond Embeddedness: Economic Practices and the Invisible Dimensions of Transnational Business Activity. *Progress In Human Geography* 32 (1): 71-88.

Krippner, G. (2002) The Elusive Market: Embeddedness and the Paradigm of Economic Sociology. *Theory & Society* 30 (6): 775-810.

Krippner, G. (2007) The Making of US Monetary Policy: Central Bank Transparency and the Neoliberal Dilemma. *Theory & Society* 36 (6): 477-513.

Langley, P. (2008) *The Everyday Life of Global Finance. Saving and Borrowing in Anglo-America*. Oxford: Oxford University Press.

Macdonald, H. (1996) Expanding Access to the Secondary Mortgage Markets: The Role of Central City Lending Goals. *Growth & Change* 27 (Summer): 298-312.

Mann, M. (1984) 'The Autonomous Power of the State: Its Origins, Mechanisms and Results', *Archives Europeennes de Sociologie*, 25 (2).

Mitchell, T. (2005) Economists and the Economy in the Twentieth Century. G. Steinmetz (ed.) *The Politics of Method in the Human Sciences: Positivism and its Epistemological Others*, pp.126-141. Durham: Duke University Press.

Montgomerie, J. (2007) Financialization and Consumption: An Alternative Account of Rising Consumer Debt Levels in Anglo-America. CRESC Working Paper Series No. 43, University of Manchester.

Panitch, L. and Gindin, S. (2005) Finance and American Empire. L. Panitch And C. Leys (eds.) *Socialist Register 2005*, pp. 46-81. London: Merlin.

Parenteau, R. (2005) The Late 1990s' US Bubble: Financialization in the Extreme. In G.A. Epstein (ed.) *Financialization and The World Economy*, pp. 111-148. Cheltenham: Edward Elgar.

Phillips, S. M. (1996) The Place of Securitization In The Financial System: Implications for Banking and Monetary Policy. L. T. Kendall and M. J. Fishman (eds.) *A Primer on Securitization*, pp. 129-138. Cambridge, MA/ London: MIT Press.

Polanyi, K. (1957) *The Great Transformation*. Boston: Beacon Press.

Ruggie, J.G. (2007) Global Markets and Global Governance. The Prospects for Convergence. S. Bernstein and L. Pauly (eds.) *Global Liberalism and Political Order*, pp. 23-48. New York: SUNY Press.

Vogel, S.K. (1996) *Freer Markets, More Rules. Regulatory Reform In Advanced Industrial Countries*. Ithaca: Cornell University Press.

Wade, R. (2008) 'Financial Regime Change?', *New Left Review*, 53 (September–October).

Power, the State and Global Politics After the Great Freeze:Towards a New Articulation?

Randall Germain[1]

INTRODUCTION

In the social sciences, scholarly disciplines can be prompted to re-evaluate the analytical traction of their central concepts by abrupt changes in how the object of their scholarship is organized. The disciplines of International Relations (IR) and International Political Economy (IPE) have long faced such pressure. For example, some see the interwar years and the Great Depression as the precursor not only to the empirical development of American hegemony, but also as a key spur to the emergence of realism as a central method of apprehending power (Carr, 1946; Schmidt, 1998; Cox, 2000). Several decades later, scholars took the breakdown of the Bretton Woods system as a prompt both to re-evaluate the utility of realism as a theoretical lens for IR and IPE, and as a signal that the post-war structure of the global political economy was itself entering a period of 'after hegemony', to use the title of a significant text from that era (Keohane and Nye, 1977; Keohane, 1984). This last debate over American decline of power was seemingly resolved in the closing years of the 20th century, amid the aftermath of the end of the Cold War, the collapse of the Soviet Union and the re-assertion of American power (Cox, 2001). The uni-polar era had arrived even as governance was becoming increasingly globalized (Scholte, 2000; Ikenberry, Mastanduno and Wohlforth, 2009).

The financial crisis of 2007-2009 has brought this paradoxical resolution into question. The central features of the crisis include both domestic and international dynamics: regulatory failure among leading

---

1 Randall Germain is Professor and Chair of the Department of Political Science at Carleton University (Ottawa, Canada). He is the author of *Global Politics and Financial Governance* and *The International Organization of Credit: States and Global Finance in the World-Economy*. He can be reached at: randall_germain@carleton.ca

financial powers (most critically the United States (U.S.) but others as well); financial innovation among banks, investment banks and non-bank financial institutions that built up significant systemic risk; macro-economic imbalances at the global level that included trade and capital account disequilibria alongside currency misalignments; inappropriate monetary policies; high sovereign debt loads; and ultimately massive institutional failure. I have elsewhere labelled this crisis the Great Freeze, because one of its principal consequences was a steady constriction of credit markets from the summer of 2007 that ultimately resulted in a near total blockage–or flash freeze–after Lehman Brothers went bust in September 2008 (Germain, 2010). The twelve months following this spectacular bankruptcy saw the harshest contraction of global economic activity since the worst days of the Great Depression. Indeed, 2009 is the only year since 1945 that the global economy as a whole has been in recession (IMF, 2009).

This article uses this crisis as the occasion to explore the changing global articulation of power. Power in IR and IPE is usually viewed in relational terms, as the ability to effect change in actor's behaviour, where actor A gets actor B to do what it might not otherwise would (Baldwin, 2002; Schmidt, 2005). Power here is understood as the capacity–derived most often from control over material capabilities that translate into instruments of pressure–of one actor to influence (directly or indirectly) the decisions of another actor. In contrast, I deploy an understanding of power that is more structural in orientation, derived from the work of Susan Strange, who argues that it is the structural determinants of power that are more important to understand than the relational determinants (Strange, 1988b). On this basis, Strange disagreed with those who, in the mid-1980s, viewed the global political economy to be entering a period marked by American decline (Strange, 1987).

The argument I advance below takes it cue from her framework to argue that the new global articulation of power suggested by the Great Freeze is both highly fluid and relatively opaque or ambiguous. This is so because even as some key structural determinants of power have become hollowed out, other elements remain intact while yet more have yet to emerge fully. The result will be a period of struggle waged around and through the principal organizational pillars of the global political economy for control over the very foundations of political order. The outcome of this struggle will not be resolved any time soon.

POWER, THE STATE AND GLOBAL POLITICS

The idea that we can measure power in global politics has long been attractive to scholars, even as they have acknowledged the immense difficulties of the task (Knorr, 1975; Kirshner, 1995; Hardt and Negri, 2000; Andrews, 2006). Here I wish to follow the British IPE scholar Susan Strange in asking how changes in the structural determinants of power help us to understand select contemporary trends. Strange developed her understanding of power against prevailing views, largely American in origin, that saw in the 1980s a sharp and steep decline in the ability of the U.S. to shape the international economic order. At the time, IR and IPE scholars were concerned primarily with the ability of the U.S. to compel its long-time allies to follow American preferences and accommodate themselves to American interests as they had for much of the Bretton Woods period. From across the theoretical spectrum, this was most often articulated as the erosion of international regimes, whose main cause was a decline in American power (Block ,1977; Gilpin, 1981; Krasner, 1983).

In contrast, Strange argued that such measurements of American power were at the very least inaccurate, and at worst entirely misleading (Strange, 1983; 1987). She noted that even as the share of American gross domestic product (GDP) in relation to global GDP had declined, the control of American corporations over key international markets remained high and was even (in certain industries such as services) growing. For Strange, the key question was not the weight of the American economy in the global economy, but the control exerted by American corporations and lawmakers over global markets (Strange, 1988; cf Nizan and Bichler, 2009). Here she pointed out that this control was not under threat from global competition; in fact, global competition was defined and shaped inexorably by the demands, preferences and resources of American corporations. In short, the structure of global competition was determined (or controlled) by American interests, even if these interests were themselves no longer expressly related to the territorial borders of the U.S. She sometimes styled these interests in the form of a 'Transnational' or 'American' empire' (Strange, 1988b; 1989). It was this structural capacity to control the global economic agenda which counted in the power sweepstakes, not where widgets were actually produced. And such power at its heart was constituted by a complicated amalgam of public and private authority.

At one level, for Strange, the global articulation of power in the 1980s was constituted by an iron triangle of inordinate (American) military power, an inter-state system that refracted and radiated America's governmental power throughout its most important elements, and the dominance of an ideational framework that privileged American principles and ideals. Here Strange disagreed with two of the strongest proponents of the argument that America was no longer ascendant. From a realist perspective, Robert Gilpin argued that American power, measured as its ability to compel its allies to make contributions to the *Pax Americana,* was in terminal decline (Gilpin, 1981). And from a critical historical materialist perspective, Robert Cox argued that the U.S. was no longer able to direct a hegemonic structure of world order (Cox, 1987). Both Gilpin and Cox, albeit for quite different reasons, pointed to the inability of the U.S. to fashion consensus or accommodate its allies' needs as part of the negotiations necessary to maintain a benevolent (from an American point of view) global economic system. For them, a neo-liberal (or hyper-liberal, to use the term initially coined by Cox) world signalled the end of American dominance.

Strange had a different answer to the question of American decline, relying instead on a careful distinction between relational and structural power. Relational power was of course above all about the U.S. being able to coerce or compel its allies and competitors to undertake particular courses of action. Here she acknowledged that this form of power waxed and waned with global economic circumstances, and was entirely dependent upon very specific and particular contexts. On this reading, from the early 1970s until the late 1980s it did appear that U.S. relational power was in retreat. The instrumental capacity of the U.S. to exert its willpower seemed to have eroded, or at the very least to be under severe stress.[2]

However, what was significant for Strange's counter-intuitive analysis was the capacity of some states to set the rules by which others would have to play the 'great power' game. In other words, for Strange the key to understanding who actually 'had' power lay not in determining who could prevail in specific decisions, but who could set the rules by which such decisions were made in the first place (Strange, 1988b). In her estimation at the time, it was still American political leaders who had it within their grasp to provide such leadership. Even though not all decisions went America's way, they were made under American rules that reflected American interests. This social fact also called attention to the global reach of American domestic political conflicts, which had a disproportionate impact on international regulatory developments. Beyond

---

[2] For Strange, however, this decline in relational power was predominantly caused by U.S. domestic politics, by an inability on the part of the American political system to organize itself effectively so as to project and use its (structural) power appropriately (Strange, 1987).

this, there were also some decisions that were simply not taken because the U.S. in effect blocked the way; such 'non-decisions' as she called them were also the product of American structural power (Strange, 1986).

In Strange's view, this ability to set the rules derived from several sources, some public or state-centred and some centred more in the operation of the (capitalist) economic system. The American state still maintained a considerable military edge over its closest rivals, which was bolstered by the continued reluctance of European states to devote adequate resources to defending themselves. But equally importantly, American corporations continued to dominate transnational production systems, which were a principal source of high value profits. The superior innovative capacities of these firms, bolstered by state-sponsored military research, bestowed onto certain segments of America's 'private' economy an unalloyed competitive advantage. As well, American ideas about how to organize economic activity (and its associated set of political values and ideals) complemented these advantages, and held a global appeal. And finally, and for her critically, the U.S. (through its government, its markets and its private institutions) had a lock-grip over the organization and operation of the world's monetary and financial system (Strange, 1987; 1988; cf May, 1996). For Strange, all that was required for America to actually exercise its structural power was a willingness to act politically in a manner congruent with its underlying power capacities.[3]

This understanding of power ties together the capacity of the state with the operation of private institutions and the inter-state system to provide for Strange a structural reading that suggests where power actually resides in the global political economy. Because power is about the capacity to decide agendas, it is not directly related to the ability of A to compel B to undertake a particular course of action; rather, it is related to the context of agency, which has two levels: (1) the capacity of A to convince B that its menu of choice involves X, Y and Z and nothing else; and (2) the capacity of A to influence this menu of choice either directly, through its own ability to compel the acceptance of the menu, or indirectly, because the majority of the elements of the menu remain in a dependent relationship to A. This kind of power, which she called structural power, belonged as a property to the U.S. throughout the period of supposed American decline.

To highlight the exercise of such power, Strange (1988b) considered the example of the international debt crisis of the early 1980s, when several countries ran into significant debt repayment problems. Instruc-

3 By the end of her life, Strange had finally concluded that the U.S. was in fact unwilling to act in a manner congruent with its own 'structural' interests (Strange, 1998).

tively for her, only those countries with close ties to the U.S. were able to work towards a resolution that involved creditors booking losses on their assets within the framework of an overall IMF-sanctioned debt recovery scheme. Crucially, it was the U.S. which was able to dictate these rules of engagement, and it was these rules which all indebted countries had to follow if they wanted debt relief on a multilateral scale. American power here was omnipresent but structural, reflecting its pole position within the inter-state system rather than a calculated exploitation of its own instrumental power.

Strange's view of structural power–and indeed power in general–is not of course without problems, many of which are connected to her idiosyncratic view of theory in IR and IPE. Some of these are noted in a volume dedicated to engaging with the corpus and legacy of her work (Lawton, Rosenau and Verdun, 2000). We could, for example, take her to task for developing taxonomies rather than theoretical insights (Cohen, 2000); for not working through the tension in her work between materialism and idealism (Guzzini, 2000); for failing to overcome the *de facto* analytical barriers between economics and politics (Cutler, 2000); and for refusing to socialize adequately her fundamentally empiricist reading of knowledge, ideology and ultimately power itself (Tooze, 2000). What these critiques of Strange's view on power suggest is that she offers an insightful but yet truncated conception of power, which only partially connects the foundations of power to the way in which it is exercised. Most importantly, Strange seems oddly reluctant to reflect theoretically on her insights, and determined to restrict her theoretical reflections to the terrain of empirical falsification. This is perhaps due to her ambiguous acceptance of the place of positivism within the social sciences, and to her ultimate unwillingness to modify its evidence-based evaluative precepts (May, 1996; Palan, 1999; Cutler, 2000; Tooze, 2000).

Even with these caveats, however, her conception of structural power offers a useful framework to consider how the global articulation of power has been affected by the Great Freeze. This is because it directs our attention to two key developments: (1) the changing role of the state in regulating financial markets; and (2) the rise of emerging market economies and their new role in setting the agenda of global economic decision-making. On both counts, what emerges from such a consideration is a recognition that established patterns of decision-making are unravelling, even if new patterns have yet to be firmly established. Each development will be reviewed below.

POWER AND THE STATE: FINANCIAL REGULATION

The key authorities involved in global financial regulation are American and European officials together with their counterparts in international regulatory institutions. This should not be surprising, as historically these states sit astride the world's deepest and most liquid financial markets. What is noteworthy from the perspective of considering the effects of the Great Freeze is to observe how systematically these states are moving forward to intervene more forcefully in the operation of financial markets under their jurisdiction. States are renewing their authority to set the agenda of global finance.

In the U.S., two major directions of change are developing: in the organization and logic of supervision; and in the range and extent of supervision. Each of these regulatory changes will increase the degree of state intervention in its financial system, and thereby encourage other states to intervene more forcefully in their financial systems. The first major change concerns the organization of financial supervision and in particular the question of whether such supervision should be sectoral or unified in scope and scale. While the U.S. may be an extreme case with its plethora of financial regulatory bodies, the logic of sectoral supervision has a considerable historical record (Russell, 2008).[4] The Great Freeze has brought into sharp relief how problematic such a fragmented regulatory apparatus is when set within the context of an integrated set of financial markets.

Here the Great Freeze has unquestionably tipped the balance in favour of a more strongly unified supervisory framework. In the U.S., the Obama Administration's efforts to recalibrate U.S. financial regulation have resulted in the passage of the Dodd-Frank bill, which among other things identifies the Federal Reserve Board (Fed) as the principal overseer of systemic risk. A combined council of regulators will further close many of the remaining gaps within the U.S. system. Equally important are new powers given to regulators to wind-up insolvent firms, and to compel banks to limit or restrict their proprietary treading units under the so-called Volcker Rule. This rule prescribes how banks are to capitalize their special investment vehicles, and how much they are allowed

4 Financial markets have historically been differentiated by the kinds of instruments that comprise them and their institutional makeup. Regulation has evolved in line with how these markets operate and what kinds of products they generate. This has traditionally been understood in terms of key pillars, most importantly banking, equities, insurance and pensions. Almost everywhere each pillar has spawned its own regulatory apparatus, together with a few more recent developments such as organized futures markets. See Germain (2010) and Porter (2005) for an historical account.

to invest in hedge funds and private equity firms. Together with the vetting powers which the new Consumer Protection Agency will have for financial instruments, the Dodd-Frank bill will push the government to cast a much heavier footprint over the organization and operation of the American financial system.[5]

A heavier footprint is also taking shape in Europe, where British and E.U. authorities are moving to give the state a much stronger presence within their respective financial systems. In the U.K., a major reorganization of financial supervision has been undertaken to strip the Financial Services Authority of its supervisory role and to relocate it within the Bank of England.[6] This has been further supported by the recommendations made by an independent commission struck by the new British government to examine how to strengthen the British financial system in light of the Great Freeze (*Economist* 2011: April 16th–22nd). This commission–known as the Vickers' Commission–has recommended that British banks organize themselves to insulate or ring fence their domestic U.K. retail arms from their investment and commercial banking operations. In other words, the (British) state looks set to intervene more forcefully in how financial institutions active in the U.K. are actually run. Similar albeit weaker trajectories are underway in the E.U.[7]

Of course, none of these developments have yet to be fully implemented as of the time of writing of this manuscript, and there are some who doubt that their impact will be as argued here. Such scepti-

---

5 Other provisions in the 'Wall Street Reform and Consumer Protection Act' include bringing all major financial institutions–whether bank or non-bank–within the purview of federal regulation, more closely regulating derivatives trading and hedge funds, limiting the proprietary trading prerogatives of banks, and providing the federal government with a more clearly specified way of closing down insolvent financial institutions. See http://www.opencongress.org/bill/111-h4173/show (accessed August 6th, 2010).

6 Among the proposals published by the British government in July 2010 were to return both macro- and micro- prudential supervisory responsibilities to the Bank of England, and to create a new consumer protection agency to absorb the institutional responsibilities of the Financial Services Authority (which will effectively be gutted). These proposals arise out of the Turner Review–the official enquiry into how the UK's supervisory arrangements failed to contain the fallout from the Great Freeze–as well as the political preferences of the Conservative and Liberal-Democrat partners in the new coalition government. See http://www.fsa.gov.uk/pubs/other/turner_review.pdf (accessed May 04, 2009) and http://www.hm-treasury.gov.uk/consult_financial_regulation.htm (accessed August 06, 2010).

7 The E.U. struck a high-level committee to examine the crisis and how to respond to it, chaired by Jacques de Larosière, a former Managing Director of the IMF who also played a leading role in preparing the E.U. for monetary union. In addition to proposing E.U.-wide risk and supervisory councils, this panel recommended reviewing accounting standards and Basel II (especially its capital adequacy requirements), tighter regulation of derivatives trading and the shadow banking system, and the harmonization of deposit insurance schemes on an E.U.-wide basis. See http://ec.europa.eu/internal_market/finances/docs/de_larosiere_report_en.pdf (accessed on July 29, 2009).

cism however should be treated with caution, for two reasons. First, across Europe and the U.S., banks have been recapitalized and are being forced to hold much more capital in relation to their lending and proprietary operations than prior to 2008. Swiss banks, for example, are being compelled by their government to hold nearly 20% capital buffers whereas prior to 2008 they were capitalized at nearer to 7%.[8] The British and Dutch governments are arguing strenuously with the E.U. that they should be allowed to impose higher capital requirements than the new Basel III rules. Here, minimum Tier 1 capital ratios are being raised from a pre-crisis requirement of 4% to at least 7%, with a further tranche of easily accessible capital at 3%. Furthermore, somewhere between 20 and 30 globally-active financial institutions are about to be categorized by the Basel Committee on Banking Supervision as 'Systemically Important Financial Institutions', or SIFIs, which will need to hold extra capital buffers above and beyond normal operating guidelines of between 1.5-2.5%, due to their perceived systemic importance. No one should doubt that increased capital ratios, which influence how much banks can lend, are on the way, and that these will have an impact on banking operations. It is through the mechanism of increased capital ratios that major banks are having their activities more closely supervised, and similar consequences are in train for other regulatory developments.[9]

The second reason why sceptics should be cautious relates to the politics of financial regulation. For much of the post-war period, financial regulation in the rich economies has been debated and conducted in a kind of segregated, insulated bubble, removed for the most part from popular (and democratic) pressures (Helleiner, 1994; Strange, 1998; Porter, 2005; Wood, 2005; Germain, 2010). This is no longer the case. From the Tea Party phenomenon in the U.S. to the role played by populist and nationalist political parties in Scandinavia in addressing the 2010-2011 European debt crisis to the refusal of Icelandic voters to sanction an IMF bailout, financial supervision and the politics of finance have moved to centre stage in national politics. And while this development has yet to fully play itself out, all indications are that the relatively insulated nature of financial politics has for the moment become impossible to maintain (Thirkwell-White, 2009).

8 See http://online.wsj.com/article/SB10001424052748704631504575531222507779044.html (accessed October 15, 2010).

9 A summary of the Basel III can be found at http://www.bis.org/press/p100912.htm (accessed October 15, 2010).

And yet a word of caution is in order. The state that is at the centre of this reassertion of authority is not itself entirely distinct from private authority. In all three jurisdictions examined here, private financial institutions have over the 1990s won a strengthened degree of involvement in the debate over how the financial system should be regulated. In the U.S. this is because of the porous and fragmented nature of the American political system, which has long been open to lobbying efforts from private firms. In the U.K. this is because of the historic ties between the City, the Exchequer and the Bank of England, and the single-minded determination of successive governments to maintain London's role as a leading international financial centre. And in the E.U., although the influence of the private sector is not as strong as in the U.S. or U.K., it has grown over the years due to the sheer increase in the weight of financial affairs in the overall economy of Europe, as well as the organizational efforts of Europe's leading banks to lobby on their own behalf in Brussels (Underhill and Zhang, 2008; King and Sinclair, 2003). Geoffrey Underhill (2000) is surely correct to note that there is a growing *condominium* between state and market in today's global political economy.

Here, it is helpful to follow Susan Strange's understanding of the intimate relationship between public and private forms of authority, as she recognizes that this relationship is part of a continuum whose balance changes over time. In her last major publication, she argued that markets and private authority had outrun state authority to the point where only an almost complete collapse of confidence in the capacity of private authority to effectively organize global finance could catalyze state authorities to reassert their traditional grip on financial systems (Strange, 1998, p. 190). This collapse came upon us in 2008, when it fell to public authorities alone to stem the tide, which was estimated by one respected analyst to cost nearly US$14 trillion (Haldane and Alessandri, 2009). So, while the precise nature of the new balance between public and private authority has yet to be stabilized, there should be no questions about the direction of change: in each of the world's major financial markets, the role of the state is being up-scaled, with the result that state authority is being re-articulated to exert more structural power over how financial markets are organized. We may say that the agenda-setting capacity of the state has been re-asserted over financial markets, even if this reassertion is uneven and subject to private sector push-back.

POWER AND THE STATE SYSTEM: EMERGING MARKET ECONOMIES AND THE BALANCE OF POWER

Many scholars and commentators have observed that global politics, understood primarily through the lens of the inter-state system, has been in a period of transformation (e.g. Jacques, 2009; Halliday, 2009). On the debit side of this ledger is the weakening grip of western powers, symbolized by the economic troubles of the U.S. On the credit side of this ledger are the emerging market economies, symbolized most importantly by the rise of the BRIC countries but including other non-G7 countries whose economies and international profiles have been growing rapidly. For these countries the early years of the 21st century have at last brought dynamic economic growth and public sector reform that has enabled them to acquire the material vestiges of real power: their economies have hummed; their trade has skyrocketed; their companies have gone global; their reserves have been bolstered; and their armies have become better equipped. In short, enough emerging market and other non-G-7 economies have grown in relation to the historically-powerful countries that talk of a new and emerging international balance of power is warranted.

Following from our earlier analysis, however, we can ask whether scholars are not committing the same analytical error that Strange reprimanded her peers for making over two decades ago? A critical example is the accumulation of international reserves by the BRIC countries, which is often considered a key barometer of the growing power of emerging market economies. For Strange, this would be a clear example of how structural power works, because the stockpiling of foreign currency reserves denominated in U.S. dollars confirms three important features of American structural power: (1) America still has the world's confidence as the pre-eminent provider of global liquidity; (2) there are at this time no serious rivals to accumulating and using U.S. dollars as an international reserve currency, even if those accumulating such reserves complain about the injustice of it; and (3) whereas BRIC and other countries have to *earn* their liquidity (which are what such reserves represent), America can simply *create* its liquidity. It is hard to think of a better indicator of structural power than this, what Strange (1987, p. 569) in her own time called *super-exorbitant privilege*.

Nevertheless, since 2009 Chinese officials (often but not always supported by other BRIC countries) have stepped up calls for the development of a non-dollar-denominated international reserve currency unit. What would be needed for such a development to occur? On the government side, it would require holders of large dollar-denominated reserves to make their own currencies completely convertible in order to allow for their use abroad as trade and investment vehicles. In other words, emerging market economies such as China, Russia, India and Brazil need to liberalize their current and capital accounts to the point where others will have the necessary confidence to diversify into these currencies and use them as genuine reserve currencies. As these governments tighten their hold on undesired movements of capital into and out of their economies (as indeed many emerging market economies are doing), such a possibility seems more remote today than at any time in the past twenty years.[10] Indeed, one only has to look back to the experience of Japan during the 1980s and its antipathy towards internationalizing the yen to understand the deep political forces that constrain governments which otherwise might challenge existing reserve currencies.[11]

But on the private or market side of the equation the forces supporting the continuing use of the U.S. dollar are equally powerful. Private firms and market actors demand not just that governments relinquish control over currencies in order that they may be used for purposes dictated by the interests of private accumulation, but also that there be ample liquidity in order that the temporary use of a currency (as a store of value, for example) does not become a permanent and unwanted long-term investment. For this condition to obtain, governments need to adopt a *liberal* view of their currencies, most importantly by freeing their use abroad and by abjuring their use as a developmental tool. There also needs to be an adequate supply of the currency in question. Absent suitable liberalization and an ample supply, private firms and markets will not have the confidence to use a currency (or facilitate its use), and will therefore minimize how they employ it.

10 Over the past two years, countries including China, South Korea, Singapore, Brazil and Turkey have joined Russia and India to implement controls on the inflow of capital as an important tool in the battle to protect their economies from currency appreciation and, to a lesser extent, over-heating. These controls are now supported by the IMF, which has shifted its long-standing blanket opposition to capital controls. See for example http://www.nytimes.com/2010/11/11/business/global/11capital.html?_r=1&ref=business (accessed December 5, 2010).

11 The basic problem faced by a country possessing an international reserve currency is that it loses its ability to hold onto direct control of its exchange rate, and thereby the ability to use its currency as a developmental tool. By its very nature an international reserve currency is widely dispersed and intensely traded, and this compromises the ability of its issuing government to control its value. Of course, there are significant advantages to the issuer of an international reserve currency, most importantly the ability to fund its government's activities cheaply because of the international demand for its government bonds (which are the chief component of international reserves). To most developing and emerging market countries, however, the benefits of issuing a reserve currency are far outweighed by the disadvantages, hence their reluctance to allow their currency to act as such.

And this is where we are in 2011 with respect to the future of the American dollar as an international reserve currency. Many countries (and not just BRIC countries) are uncomfortable with the international role of the U.S. dollar. By making it cheap for the U.S. to fund its budgetary and current account deficits (what economists often call *seigniorage*), using the dollar as the international reserve currency retards the adjustment process the U.S. needs to undertake to bring its trade, current and capital accounts into a more sustainable balance. It also prolongs the vulnerability other countries experience with respect to having to follow or react to America's monetary policies. Yet, the world is not rushing out to adopt the rouble or the rupee or the yuan as reserve currencies, simply because they cannot. And neither can they freely use the pound sterling, Japanese yen, Swiss franc or, most significantly, the euro. There are simply not enough of the former to be thrust into this role, while the political mismatch between the issuance of euro-denominated debt and who controls its value ultimately means that an enormous question mark hangs over precisely how robust an international role the euro can play. By default, the dollar will be required for use as an international reserve currency until well into the middle decades of the 21st century.[12]

So, the accumulation of a mountain of U.S. dollar-denominated reserve assets by BRIC and other countries such as Japan does not *prima facie* indicate the decline of American power. In relational terms, to return to Susan Strange's argument, it may indeed appear that the U.S. now has serious rivals to its monetary power. However, in structural terms, its challengers are hobbled by the framework of practices that have developed over the past decades that have been entirely cantered on American interests and needs. The U.S. has held a firm grasp on monetary and financial power since 1945, and this has allowed it to build up

12 The problems of the euro zone in 2010-11 have clarified how significant the political mismatch is in Europe, possibly dealing a fatal blow to a global role for the euro. Two developments could conceivably undermine the future role of the U.S. dollar. One development might be a genuine budgetary (and therefore political) crisis in the U.S., involving both default and devaluation. If this happens all bets are off. The August 2011 downgrade U.S. debt by Standard and Poor's sets up an interesting confrontation between the U.S. government and American credit rating agencies in this respect, but it is difficult to see quite what the practical outcome of this move will be, since a large part of these agencies' role in the global financial system derives in part from their explicit (American) government sanctioned role in rating government and private debt (Sinclair 2005). Moreover, it is difficult to identify America's budgetary woes as a 'debt' problem when in fact its effective tax rate is less than 25% of GDP, well below the OECD average of 35%. The other development might be the development of SDRs into a kind of proper international reserve currency. Even if this were to happen it would still not address the needs of private firms and market actors for an internationally-tradable currency, which an SDR is most manifestly not. International reserve currencies need to be accepted and used by both public and private agents; this accounts for how difficult they are to establish as well as why they take so long to fade.

an historic reservoir of influence and power that will not be easily dislodged.[13] Yet, the balance of economic power has not been entirely static over the post-war era, and even though American firms and indeed the American government together constitute a significant element of the world's monetary and financial system, they are not as ubiquitous an element as they once were. The U.S. has been to a certain extent decentred from the structure of financial governance over the past decade and a half, so that even though it is still an immensely powerful actor it must now negotiate the framework of this structure with other actors and their concerns (Germain, 2010). It is this political fact which marks out the salience of current governance developments, where the interaction of international political relations with the demands of regulatory change are generating a set of issues whose importance is both novel and potentially long-lasting.

STRUCTURAL POWER AND POLITICAL ORDER

Two important sets of long-term structural consequences have been set in motion. One set of consequences revolves around the role of the state in the global financial system. As states–in both the developed and developing economies–move to re-calibrate how they intervene in the organization and operation of financial systems, their centrality within the globalized structure of financial governance will grow. The nation-state is not simply important here because it is the instrument through which all regulation actually gets implemented. Even more critically, it is the only institution which can generate financial regulation that is appropriate and suitable for its own economy. Emerging market economies–and the BRIC countries in particular–will here take their cue from what the U.S. and E.U. states actually do to impose tighter regulations on financial institutions; a slightly less globalized financial system is most likely to be the outcome. This is so because higher capital requirements, more capital controls and more tightly circumscribed operating environments will inevitably generate a global financial system less hospitable

13 Many of the themes canvassed in the above paragraphs can be found also in a recent volume on the future of the U.S. dollar (Helleiner and Kirshner, 2009). Interestingly, the experts in that volume agree to disagree on the future of the dollar.

to what I elsewhere describe as *deep globalization*.[14] This does not mean that globalization as we know it is coming to an end, merely that there will be less of it going forward. We will move from a highly globalized world to a world in which the pull of the nation-state away from deep globalization is more clearly felt.

Intersecting with the strengthening of the state is the second set of consequences, namely the refashioning of the inter-state balance of power. We have seen how this works in terms of the role of the U.S. dollar as an international reserve currency: its role is being eroded and brought into question, yet with no alternative in sight. In other words, one of the critical foundations of political order for the global political economy is entering a period of intense uncertainty. We have not witnessed such a situation since the inter-war period. Strange might have observed here that the structural power of the U.S. is changing only very slowly, while its instrumental power to shape decisions directly is increasingly haphazard, reflecting the volatility of circumstances (including significantly an increasingly unstable domestic political landscape). What is especially important at the current moment, however, is that the global economic decision-making agenda does not yet appear to have ceded substantial power to emerging market economies, despite for example their accumulation of enormous reserves of U.S. dollars. Structural power remains asymmetrically concentrated in American institutions and subject to American rules.

How much longer will this remain so? If we return to Strange's conceptual formulation of structural power, we can recall that it relied on American military dominance, the continuing dominance of American ideals and values, and the place of American financial institutions, markets and government in the global financial system. If these fundamental elements of the global political order become further constrained or even undermined, then those adopting Strange's position would have to concede that the structural power of the U.S. is weakening. What is the status of these elements of global political order?

The U.S. continues to outspend the rest of the world combined on defence, and it continues to be the only state with the military capacity

---

14 Deep globalization here refers to the intensity of liberalization efforts which have driven economic growth since the end of the Bretton Woods era in the early 1980s. Globalization–understood as increasing levels of economic integration among major economies together with the emergence of a global political consensus organized around neo-liberal principles–has been sustained by the global reach of liberalization, and it is precisely this which is coming unstuck as a consequence of the Great Freeze. This theme is explored below and in some detail in Germain (2010: ch. 6).

to fight a two-front war. Yet, its military might is no longer unrivalled, and the build up of military assets by China could be viewed by some as a significant challenge. But it must be acknowledged that the only potential military rival to the U.S. is China, and so long as European states continue to rely disproportionally on American security via NATO it is unlikely that the military dominance of the U.S. will collapse any time soon. While the idea of a uni-polar moment may be overstating the case, we are in many respects well short of a genuine multi-polar inter-state system (Ikenberry, Mastanduno and Wohlfarth, 2009).

What should be of more concern to scholars of global power is the condition of American values and ideals, which support in so many ways the entrenched American-centred global economic agenda. Here it is interesting that one of the consequences of the Great Freeze has been the severe questioning of liberalization as the default ideational template for global capitalism. There are still no serious alternatives to organizing the global economy along capitalist lines. What has changed, however, is the degree to which capitalism needs to be organized along liberal (or neo-liberal) lines. Here liberalization as an ethos is now subject to two important charges: (1) it is unsustainable as a form of economic regulation; and (2) that state-organized capitalism is in fact more stable than liberal capitalism. And while neither of these charges are categorical or themselves without controversy, they have undermined the persuasive power of liberalization's ideologues to spread their gospel. From Europe to Asia to Latin America and Africa, liberalism is in retreat, and this has undermined the ideational supports for the operationalization of American structural power.

Finally, the Great Freeze began in the U.S. financial system, even if it was aided and abetted by global forces and dynamics. Has it also challenged the centrality of the American financial system to the global financial system? This question is difficult to assess at this moment in time. On one hand, even with the carnage wreaked by the Great Freeze, American financial markets remain the deepest and most liquid in the world. And while American banks and financial institutions no longer remain the world's largest by many ratios, they continue to be among the most profitable and innovative, and equally important they continue to provide unparalleled access for foreigners to American capital markets. Their centrality to the organization and operation of the global financial system will not soon disappear. And because both U.S. markets and financial institutions remain key components of the global financial system, so too does the American government. Its image and halo may be tarnished and dented, but it continues to possess a definite and considerable weight in how the global financial system runs.

This sets up an interesting scholarly debate between those, like myself, who now emphasize the extent of change in the landscape of global political economy, and those who remain impressed by the continuity of capitalist relations as the key factor that explains current trajectories. At one level this is a debate about the relative weight to assign to competing explanatory variables: are we focusing on state versus class; public versus private; or global versus national? At another level it is about the grounds of adjudication: does more regulatory control also mean that state authorities are somehow in ascendancy, when in fact the dividing line between public and private authority may be impossible to identify? And at still another level, it is about the means used to understand and verify the categories we are using: do we appeal to 'evidence' or 'theory' ('beliefs'?) when it comes to establishing the fundamental basis of our arguments? There are no easy or clear answers to these questions; thus such debates will long maintain their traction.

Yet here again it is worthwhile to return to the work of Susan Strange, for she offers at the very least a way of negotiating some of the hurdles thrown up by these debates. For Strange, who understood that there were several ways of apprehending all important events, the question of the significance of current changes would need to be addressed within the context of *cui bono*, or for whose advantage? This context almost always provides a clear causal chain to follow, even if the measurement of 'advantage' can be a bit messy. In the case of changes to financial regulation, it appears that the biggest beneficiaries of higher capital requirements, increased capital controls and less liberalization are states in general and major developed states in particular, because it is they who will have to spend less to bail out their financial institutions if regulatory reforms are successful. Of course, private financial institutions should also benefit from these reforms, but the weight of advantage lies with states. Similarly, the unevenness of the changes outlined above regarding the inter-state balance of power, while not directly challenging the structural power of the U.S., certainly begin to undermine the ideational core of that power. Over time, this will have the effect of eroding from within the dominant position of the U.S. in the global political economy.

It is for these reasons that I can argue that the global articulation of power within the global political economy is entering a period of uncertainty as established patterns of power erode and new patterns emerge unevenly. There is no question that the relational power of the U.S. is eroding: firms from emerging market economies are challenging American firms in some areas, while the ability of the U.S. state to dictate its preferences onto a pliant world no longer holds. At the same time, the agenda setting ability of American authorities, both public and private, has not entirely deteriorated, and in some areas remains substantial. This is what continues to generate America's continuing structural power. The interesting aspect of this situation, from the perspective of scholars of IR and IPE, will be how it plays out over the medium term, when the economic and security capabilities of the U.S. seem to be moving in opposite directions. The prediction I would make in late 2011 is that as nation-states reassert their authority over their financial systems and intervene to blunt the advance of globalization, the entire fabric of the global political economy is becoming rebalanced, ushering in a new inter-state balance of power and a new era in the history of global politics that is no longer centrally defined by the hegemonic position of the U.S.

REFERENCES

Andrews, David M., (ed). (2006). *International Monetary Power*. Ithaca: Cornell University Press.

Baldwin, David. (2002). "Power and International Relations," in Walter Carlsnaes, Thomas Risse and Beth A. Simmons (Eds.), *Handbook of International Relations*. London: Sage.

Block, Fred. (1977). *The Origins of International Economic Disorder*. Berkeley: University of California Press.

Carr, E.H. (1946). *The Twenty Years Crisis*. London: Macmillan.

Cox, Michael (Ed.) (2000). *E.H. Carr: a critical appraisal*. Basingstoke: Palgrave.

___________. (2001). "Whatever happened to American decline? International relations and the new United States hegemony," *New Political Economy*, 6 (3), 311-340.

Cutler, A. Clair. (2000). "Theorizing the 'No-Man's-Land' Between Politics and Economics," in Lawton, Rosenau and Verdun (2000). *Economist*. London: various dates.

Germain, Randall. (2010). *Global Politics and Financial Governance*. Basingstoke: Palgrave.

Gilpin, Robert. (1981). *War and Change in World Politics*. Princeton: Princeton University Press.

____________. (1987). *The Political Economy of International Relations*. Princeton: Princeton University Press.

Guzzini, Stefano. (2000). "Strange's Oscillating Realism: Opposing the Ideal- and the Apparent," in Lawton, Rosenau and Verdun (2000).

Haldane, Andrew and Piergiorgio Alessandri. (2009). "Banking on the State," *BIS Review*, no. 139. Accessed at www.bis.org/review/r091111e.pdf on November 17 2009.

Halliday, Fred. (2009). "International Relations in a Post-hegemonic Age," *International Affairs*, Vol. 85, no.1: 37-51.

Hardt, Michael and Antonio Negri. (2000). *Empire* Cambridge: Harvard University Press.

Helleiner, Eric. (1994). *States and the Re-emergence of Global Finance*. Ithaca: Cornell University Press.

____________ and Jonathan Kirshner (Eds.). (2009). *The Future of the Dollar*. Ithaca: Cornell University Press.

Ikenberry, John G., Michael Mastanduno and William C. Wohlforth. (2009). "Unipolarity, State Behaviour and Systemic Consequences," *World Politics*, Vol. 61, no. 3: 1-27. IMF. 2009 *World Economic Outlook*, July. Washington: International Monetary Fund.

Jacques, Martin. (2009). *When China Rules the World: the end of the western world and the birth of a new global order*. London: Penguin Press.

Keohane, Robert O. (1984). *After Hegemony: cooperation and discord in the world political economy*. Princeton: Princeton University Press.

Keohane, Robert O. and Joseph S. Nye, Jr. (1977). *Power and Interdependence: world politics in transition*. Boston: Little, Brown.

King, Michael R. and Timothy J. Sinclair. (2003). "Private actors and public policy: a requiem for the new Basle capital accord," *International Political Science Review*, Vol. 24, no. 3: 345-62.

Kirshner, Jonathan. (1995). *Currency and Coercion: the political economy of international monetary power*. Princeton: Princeton University Press.

Knorr, Klaus. (1975). *The Power of Nations: the political economy of international relations*. New York: Basic Books.

Krasner, Stephen (Ed.). (1983). *International Regimes*. Ithaca: Cornell University Press.

Lawton, Thomas, James Rosenau and Amy Verdun (Eds.). (2000). *Strange Power: shaping the parameters of international relations and international political economy*. Aldershot: Ashgate.

May, Christopher. (1996). "Strange Fruit: Susan Strange's Theory of Structural Power in the International Political Economy," *Global Society*, 10 (2), 167-89.

Nitzan, Jonathan and Shimshon Bichler. (2009). *Capital as Power: a study of order and creorder*. London: Routledge.

Palan, Ronen. (1999) "Susan Strange 1923-1998: A Great International Relations Theorist," *Review of International Political Economy*, 6 (2), 121-32.

Porter, Tony. (2005). *Globalization and Finance*. Cambridge: Polity Press.

Russell, Ellen D. (2008). *New Deal Banking Reform and Keynesian Welfare State Capitalism*. London: Routledge.

Schmidt, Brian C. (1998). *The Political Discourse of Anarchy: a disciplinary history of International Relations* Albany: State University of New York Press.

____________. (2005). "Competing Realist Conceptions of Power," *Millennium*, 33 (3), 523-549.

Scholte, Jan Aart. (2000). *Globalization: a critical introduction*. Basingstoke: Macmillan.

Sinclair, Timothy. (2005). *The New Masters of Capital: American bondrating agencies and the politics of creditworthiness*. Ithaca: Cornell University Press.

Strange, Susan. (1983). "*Cave! hic dragones: a critique of regime analysis,*" in Krasner (1983).

___________. (1986). *Casino Capitalism*. Oxford: Basil Blackwell.

___________. (1987). "The Persistent Myth of Lost Hegemony," *International Organization*, Vol. 41, no. 4: 551-74.

___________. (1988a). "The Future of the American Empire," *Journal of International Affairs*, 42 (1), 1-17.

___________. (1988b). *States and Markets*. London: Pinter.

___________. (1989). "Towards a Theory of Transnational Empire," in Ernst-Otto Czempiel and James Rosenau, eds, *Global Changes and Theoretical Challenges: approaches to world politics in the 1990s*. Lexington: Lexington Books.

___________. (1998). *Mad Money*. Manchester: Manchester University Press.

Thirkwell-White, Ben. (2009). "Dealing with the Banks: populism and the public interest in the global financial architecture," *International Affairs*, Vol. 85, no. 4: 689- 711.

Tooze, Roger. (2000). "Ideology, Knowledge and Power in International Relations and International Political Economy," in Lawton, Rosenau and Verdun (2000).

Underhill, Geoffrey R.D. (2000). "State, market and global political economy: genealogy of an (inter-?) discipline," *International Affairs*, 76 (4), 805-24.

__________________ and Xiaoke Zhang. (2008). "Setting the Rules: private power, political underpinnings, and legitimacy in global monetary and financial governance," *International Affairs*, Vol. 84, no. 3: 536-54.

Wood, Duncan. (2005). *Governing Global Banking: the Basel Committee and the politics of financial globalization*. Aldershot: Ashgate.

The Ottawa and Gatineau Museum Workers' Strike: Precarious Employmentand the Public Sector Squeeze

Carlo Fanelli and Priscillia Lefebvre[1]

Nearly five years removed from what would later come to be known as the Great Recession, a large amount of critical writing has sought to show how a private sector-led economic crisis has been thoroughly displaced into the public sphere (McNally, 2011; McBride and Whiteside, 2011; Panitch *et al.*, 2010; Fanelli *et al.*, 2010). Having taken on private capital's debts, supplied new subsidies and undertaken a stimulus program in order to offset the recession, the economic downturn has been redefined as one originating in overgenerous social services, an inefficient government bureaucracy, unions and just about any user or producer of public services. Paradoxically, but perfectly logical in capitalist terms, the banks, corporations and capitalist classes that caused the crisis are now demanding austerity.

As David Camfield (2011, p. 96) has recently written: "There is evidence that governments and other public sector employees are beginning to conduct an intensified offensive against public sector unions. This offensive will likely feature not only freezes for wage and benefit costs but also other concessionary demands and job cuts, along with new efforts to restructure the public sector." In line with Camfield's contention, in this paper we seek to add to the growing body of literature examining the changing nature and content of government political economic intervention, social welfare provision, growing attacks against labour unionism and general restructuring of the federal public service.

1 Carlo Fanelli is a Ph.D. Candidate at the Department of Sociology & Anthropology, Carleton University, with interests in critical political economy, labour studies, Canadian public policy, social movements, urban sociology and education. Carlo serves as editor of *Alternate Routes: A Journal of Critical Social Research, and recently co-edited Capitalism & Confrontation: Critical Perspectives.* Priscillia Lefebvre is a collaborative Ph.D. student at the Department of Sociology and Anthropology/Institute of Political Economy, Carleton University.

We overview the transition from Keynesian to neoliberal public policy prescriptions, with a focus on precarious work and shifting labour market conditions. Our research is empirically grounded in an analysis of striking museum workers in the Ottawa and Gatineau region. As will be shown, the Public Service Alliance of Canada (PSAC) Local 70396's efforts in achieving job security and fair wages for its members offer valuable insights from which to learn in the continued struggles against precarious work and neoliberal public policy. The PSAC strike illustrates how increasing trends in non-standard, temporary, and contract work are making inroads into the public sphere. We conclude with some cursory projections as to the hardening relationship between employers and employees, particularly those unionized and in the federal public service, followed by some general observations on the in/adequacy of union responses.

CANADA'S KEYNESIAN COMPROMISE

As the political economic malaise and social devastation wrought by the Great Depression and WWII came to an end, decades of strife had transformed the class dynamics of Canadian society. Describing the Depression years of the 1930s, an excerpt from Pierre Burton's (2001, p. 9) study of the period is quite informative: "Nobody could tell exactly when it began and nobody could predict when it would end. At the outset they didn't even call it a depression. At worst it was a recession, a brief slump, a "correction" in the market, a glitch in the rising curve of prosperity. Only when the full import of those heartbreaking years sank in did it become the Great Depression." As rampant financial speculation, plunging primary resources extraction and industrial production coalesced in the turmoil of the 1930s, nearly one-third of Canadians were out of work and half the population had become reliant on some form of social relief. As Berton (2001, p. 10) noted, "Balancing the budget was more important than feeding the hungry. The bogey of deficit was enlisted to tighten the purse strings," while "[t]he bondholders enjoyed a free ride on the backs of the people." Unfortunately, it was only with Canada's entrance into WWII that the Canadian economy began to see some so-called recovery.

With social turmoil mounting, the Canadian state began introducing and expanding welfare provisions assuming a greater responsibility for social reproduction (McKeen and Porter, 2003). Indeed, the following years were an intense period of labour-capital disputes, marred by ideological, political and philosophical contestation. Panitch and Swartz (2003) suggest that due to swelling union membership and mass political mobilization, the 1940s represented an unparalleled shift in the balance of class forces. Commonly referred to as the 'Keynesian compromise', Harvey (2005, p. 10) describes the period thus:

> "States actively intervened in industrial policy and moved to set standards for the social wage by constructing a variety of welfare systems (health care, education and the like)...[M]arket processes and entrepreneurial and corporate activities were surrounded by a web of social and political constraints and a regulatory environment that sometimes restrained but in other instances led the way in economic and industrial strategy. State-led planning and in some instances ownership of key sectors (coal, steel, automobiles) were not uncommon" (Harvey, 2005, p. 10).

This social pact formed the basis from which the Canadian state enlarged and developed its active and interventionist provision of social services, while laying the groundwork for rising real wages and improved working conditions. Symbolic of the newfound 'compromise' was Privy Council Order 1003 which 'recognized the rights of private sector workers across Canada to organize, bargain collectively and strike... and backed these rights with sanctions against employers who refused' (Panitch and Swartz, 2003, p. 3). Canada's experiment with Keynesian demand-side macroeconomic policy was guided by certain key commitments: full employment; active fiscal and monetary policy; public works projects (e.g. roads, bridges, general infrastructure); progressive taxation (particularly income and corporate); universal social programs; some degree of capital controls and a commitment to domestic reinvestment (McBride, 1997; Evans and Shields, 1998; Burke *et al.*, 2000). As Canadian governments and their provincial counterparts implemented–to varying degrees–the aforementioned policies, two federal programs were central to the development of Canada's welfare state: Unemployment Insurance (1940) and Family Allowances (1944). This was followed over the next two decades with the expansion of pension and health care coverage, for example, as well as the introduction and extension of federal-provincial cost-sharing arrangements and direct income transfers to individuals.

In the quarter-century following the Second World War, growing militancy on the part of labour unions, anti-racist and women's' movements radically revamped the contours of work, labour market conditions and social reproduction. What has come to be known as the Standard Employment Relationship (SER) became the normative "white male breadwinner/family wage" model upon which legislation, labour laws, public policy and union organizing strategies were based (Vosko, 2006, 2007; Pupo, 1997. The SER refers to a work arrangement based on a single employer, full-time, year-round employment, often under direct supervision with benefits and expectations of indefinite employment. Throughout this period, inequities along the lines of race, gender, sexuality and ethnicity marred the shifting landscapes of work, with many of those deviating from the white male breadwinner model excluded from the SER (Teelucksingh and Galabuzi, 2005; Bezanson and Luxton, 2006; Das Gupta, 1996). As the 1960s progressed, most federal and provincial employees were finally granted the right to strike with the passage of the *Public Service Staff Relations Act,* something most private sector workers obtained more than a decade earlier (Panitch and Swartz, 2003). However, just as many gained these rights, economic recession would once again put many workers, working conditions and general labour market security under duress. After three decades of uneven, though gradual improvement in the provision of social entitlements and working conditions, growing regional uncertainty and international economic turmoil would come to radically halt the expansion of Canada's social programs and public goods and works investments. As inflation and unemployment mounted, postwar Keynesianism began to unravel in the 1970s "re-exposing all that had been learned about market failures and monopoly provision a century ago" (Albo, 2009, p. 5).

NEOLIBERALISM WITH CANADIAN CHARACTERISTICS

The 1970s would witness a significant transformation in the form and function of public policy, labour relations and social services. As the making of global capitalism stumbled amid the deep recession of the 1970s, collective efforts on the part of the capitalist classes would seek to refashion the institutional configurations and social provisions of the previous thirty years. Neoliberalism emerged in this context as a means to discipline the growing power of labour militancy and return to capitalist profitability. As three decades of unprecedented economic growth came to a standstill, social expenditures increasingly came under attack as unaffordable. The 1970s saw rising unemployment and inflation, increased foreign competition, the doubling of international oil costs and rising resource prices (McBride, 1992; Carroll and Shaw, 2001). Contending that the Keynesian welfare state cultivated dependency on the government for social security and interfered with the so-called natural machinations of the free market, emerging neoliberal models reoriented public policy toward fiscal restraint, the cultivation of a competitive business climate, enhanced capital mobility and individual responsibility. The state's role came to be seen as ensuring the institutional preconditions for free trade, private property and "flexible" labour market conditions. Neoliberal work arrangements sought to intensify the profit motive with the use of shift work, short-term contracts, workplace speed-ups, evening and overnight work, part-time labour, weekend work, rotating and split shifts, variable schedules, as well as casual and seasonal employment (Shalla and Clement, 2007; Pupo and Thomas, 2010). It was at this point, roughly in the mid-1970s, where the SER began to crumble. In its place has arisen what some have identified as atypical, non-standard, contingent and casualized forms of work, but which we prefer to characterize as "precarious" (Vosko, 2006, 2007; Pupo and Thomas, 2010; Braedley and Luxton, 2006; Camfield, 2011).

Four key indicators are often taken as measures of precarity: the degree of certainty in employment; control over the labour process (linked to the absence or presence of trade unions); the degree of regulatory protection through union representation or law (e.g. against unfair dismissal, discrimination); and income level (as even 'secure' jobs can be low-paying) (Rogers and Rogers, 1989). However, not all contract or part-time work is precarious: "sometimes it is progressive, sometimes regressive, and it can be both precarious and permanent" (Clement *et al.*, 2010, 57). As such, the concept of precarious employment remains a multidimensional and heterogeneous concept (Vosko, 2006). In an effort to reduce production costs and maximize profitability, many employers have adopted a neoliberal approach to employment, which is achieved through union-busting, the temporary and discretional use of employment, layoffs, labour intensification, the denial of benefits and retrenchment of wages. The results of which have brought median real wages to a near stand-still for more than three decades amid the growing discrepancy between the intensification of worker productivity and the compensation that follows (Clement, 2007). For instance, it is estimated that real median wages in Canada peaked in 1982, while productivity grew more than 35 percent between 1981-2008 (Gonick, 2009; IOW, 2009). Businesses now openly regard workers as disposable commodities. For example, take a senior manager at AT&T: "In AT&T, we have to promote the whole concept of the workforce being contingent, though most of our workers are inside our walls. "Jobs" are being replaced by "projects" and "fields of work" are giving rise to a society that is increasingly "jobless but not workless."...

People need to look at themselves as self-employed, as vendors who come to this company to sell their skills" (cited in Perelman, 2011, p. 31). As such, central to the new reality of work in the twenty-first century are insecure labour arrangements, low-pay, the absence of benefits or entitlements, and growing work-life incongruities.

In this regard, central to Canadian neoliberalism was a deepening integration with American economic policy; the de- / re-regulation of foreign direct investment, including a steadfast emphasis on free trade agreements, particularly with the U.S. and later Latin America; corporate and personal income tax reductions; new subsidies to capital in the form of loans, grants and tax exemptions; increases in consumption taxes; public sector reform through New Public Management strategies; the replacement of welfare with workfare; and the movement away from universal social programs toward market-based models (Broad and Hunter, 2010; McBride, 2001; Evans and Shields, 1998; Workman, 2009; Burke et al., 2000; McKeen and Porter, 2003). This was joined by an increasingly authoritative turn by corresponding Canadian governments, notably the Liberal government of Trudeau (1968-79, 1980-84) and Conservative government of Mulroney (1984-1993), which sought to dismantle the regulatory gains and protections afforded by Keynesian-era social protections. Both the Trudeau and Mulroney governments intensified neoliberal policy prescriptions by serving injunctions on unions, jailing prominent union leaders (notably the federal government's showdown with the Canadian Union of Postal workers and Public Service Alliance of Canada), freezing wages for federal workers, the increasing designation of unionized workers as "essential", and the growing use of back-to-work legislation, while laying off workers under the auspices of fiscal responsibility. For some commentators this signaled a return to a more open reliance of the state and capital on coercion to secure the subordination of labour, including the consolidation of a state of "permanent exceptionalism" (Panitch and Swartz, 2003, p. 25).

But it was in the 1990s with the election of the Chretien Liberals, who "adopted the neoliberal fiscal agenda much more vigorously than Mulroney" (McBride, 2001, p. 99), that the most sustained welfare state restructuring took place. McBride (2001) has come to describe this period, particularly the 1995 federal budget, as one when erosion ended and demolition began. The primacy of deficit reduction over social welfare coupled with inflation-targeting over full-employment, characterized this period as expenditure restraint and supply-side arguments dominated the political economic arena. A wave of privatization measures also swept over the federal and provincial landscapes as the most lucrative Crown corporations were dismantled and sold off piecemeal. Social services also became increasingly subject to public-private-partnership (P3) delivery models, as in health care and education (Armstrong et al., 2001; Fisher et al., 2006; Loxley and Loxley, 2010). The notion that unemployment was more a result of individual failure as opposed to market failure came to dominate public policy debates, as the principle of private responsibility over collective responsibility transformed the parameters of the welfare state. Neoliberal policies also reproduced and intensified patterns of racialized and gendered labour market segmentation and inequality by ignoring socio-historical structural relations and transformations in the breadth and depth of protective regulations. For instance, as social services became ever-more market-dependant, the burden increasingly fell on historically racialized groups, women and immigrants to occupy the most precarious labour market positions (Braedley and Luxton, 2010; Teelucksingh and Galabuzi, 2005; Arat-Koc, 1997; Bakan and Stasiulus, 1997).

By the mid-2000s, the neoliberal project had thoroughly remodeled the Canadian welfare state. The election of Conservative Prime Minister Stephen Harper in 2006 is perhaps the most comprehensive attempt to embed a particularly aggressive form of neoliberal market dogma. Since his election in 2006, Prime Minister Harper has methodically worked to entrench a market-led revamping of the federal public service. This includes: cutting federal social services programs, especially those that would fall under the auspices of the provinces; freezing federal wages; cutting the federal Goods and Services tax (GST) from seven to five percent; mandating provinces to consider the P3 route in order to receive federal grants; increasing defense spending by nearly 40 percent; allocating $9 billion to build new 'super jails'; easing environmental regulations in the Arctic for oil and mining companies; fast tracking development project's in the Alberta tar sands; weakening Canada's internationally admired long-form census; defunding equity seeking groups; intensifying free trade talks with the European Union; and leading the largest militarization, and subsequent mass arrests, in Canadian history at the June 2010 G20 summit in Toronto (Evans and Albo, 2010; Fanelli and Hurl, 2010; Hussey and LeClerc, 2011; McBride and Whiteside, 2011).

Despite being found in contempt of parliament, Stephen Harper has been clear about his intensions "to make conservatism the natural government philosophy of the country" (Whittington, 2011). Moreover, although already one of the most tax-friendly regimes for corporations in the world, Harper's Conservatives will provide over $10 billion in corporate welfare for 2011-12. While corporate tax rates were 30 percent in 2000, they had fallen to 21 percent in 2004, 19.5 percent in 2008, 16.5 percent in 2011 and 15 percent by 2012 (ibid). In just twelve years corporate tax rates will have been cut exactly in half, with Prime Minister Harper's Conservatives overseeing the bulk of corporate subsidies and the undermining of federal revenue streams. Altogether, tax cuts enacted by the Conservatives since 2006 will result in $220 billion in foregone revenue by 2013-14; that's money that could have gone toward expanding and improving health care and education, pension plans, early learning and child care programs, tackling poverty and fighting climate change. Such changes in the nature and content of public policy have had significant implications for the transformation of labour market conditions with some important differences in the public and private sectors. As Stinson (2010, 94) has argued: "The key difference is that casualization in the public sector has taken place primarily through the growth of temporary full-time employment between 1997-2007, whereas in the private sector the growth in casualization has been mainly in temporary part-time work. Over this period, temporary full-time work has squeezed out permanent part-time employment as the main form of casualized labour in the public sector." Given significant structural forms of discrimination, such as those historically linked to the female gender wage gap and racialized exclusions, transformations in the quality and form of work and working conditions remains important given that nearly one in four Canadians, 61 percent of which are women, work in the public sphere.

Moreover, these transformations will also have grave implications for the strength and vitality of Canada's highly unionized public sector (75 percent), and its relationship to the shrinking union density of the private sector (19 percent) (ibid). Recent scholarship regarding the growing spread of precarious work is also revealing new insights. Lewchuck *et al.* (2011) propose that we may be in the early stages of a major shift in the interrelationship between production and social reproduction in the last century. Their data suggests that men and women's employment experiences are becoming increasingly similar, due in part to the downward convergence of wages and working conditions –i.e. those historically associated with "feminized labour"– characterized by dual precarious earner households. As they argue (Lewchuck *et al.*, 2011, p. 94), "White male workers can no longer assume that secure labour market positions are theirs, while new opportunities for hidden forms of both gender and racial privileging/discrimination have merged in the less secure segments of the labour market, in the pay differences, constant scheduling, and rehiring/firing of temporary and contingent work." On the whole, then, while in the preceding Keynesian period the public sector often set the general standards for working conditions and wages, due in good part to unionization, under neoliberalism the weakened private sector has become the benchmark, often at the detriment of public sector workers today. As our analysis of the 2009 strike by museum workers in PSAC Local 70396 illustrates, their struggle over decent working conditions and fair wages may be a sign of things to come as neoliberal public policy seeks to undermine free collective bargaining in a renewed age of austerity.

PREPARING FOR A STRIKE: BACKGROUND AND CONTEXT

After seven months of negotiations without a contract, on September 21, 2009, 375 Public Service Alliance of Canada (PSAC) members with Local 70396 took job action against the Canadian Museum of Civilization Corporation (CMCC), which operates both the Canadian Museum of Civilization (CMC) and Canadian Museum of War (CMW). [2] PSAC Local 70396 is separated into two main groups: (1) the floor staff, public hosts, tour guides, client services and animators, (2) and about one-third work in administration, collections and exhibition (PSAC, 2009a). The union is composed of approximately 60 percent women, with 5 percent from historically racialized groups, 2 percent from First Nation communities, and 6 percent persons with disabilities. At the time of the strike there were only 6 permanent tour guides at both museums, while 49 positions remained temporary and part-time. With 92 percent of the voting membership choosing to exercise their right to strike, members took to the picket lines over job security, wages and contracting-out. As one of the striking workers stated, "This is a frightening time in which people who have full-time, permanent status still feel they could be laid off or replaced by a private firm at any time. It's incredibly difficult on the psyche" (Personal Communication, 2009).

Using the recession as an excuse to freeze wages and contract-out employees, the strike pitted the Crown corporation against PSAC workers striking in the bordering cities–one in Ontario and the other in

---

2 Since its beginning in 1966, PSAC has grown into one of the largest labour unions in Canada representing over 172,000 Canadian workers, many from the federal public sector. With representation in the private sector also growing, the majority of PSAC members remain federal government workers in agencies such as Postal Communications, Agriculture, Customs and Immigration, National Defense, and Heritage Canada. PSAC also represents workers in the broader public sector including teaching and lab assistants in universities, casino workers, and employees in women's shelters.

Quebec–of Ottawa and Gatineau. Central to the strike was the Crown's efforts to increase the use of contractual and temporary work, which already accounted for nearly 38 percent of the workforce. As part of maintaining this level of casual employment, the CMCC regularly terminated temporary positions days before they would reach the level at which they would become eligible for a permanent position as then stated by the collective agreement. After enforcing a three-week waiting period, the employer would unashamedly offer the former employee a new contract. The newly re-hired worker was then forced to start from the bottom of the pay scale without any seniority. Where lay-offs and promotions were concerned, management possessed the power to terminate temporary contracts at their discretion thus making it impossible for casual workers to become permanent employees and union members. One such termination involved an employee who had twenty years of employment experience with the CMCC. Examples are abound of workers with nearly two decades of experience still considered temporary by the corporation, and could therefore be let-go at any time. Likewise, an important element of the strike was significant pay differences among workers. It was not uncommon for employees in similar positions to make anywhere from twenty to forty percent less than their colleagues working at other Crown museums, despite similar levels of training, education and experience. For example, at the time of the strike a host working at the Museum of War was paid an hourly wage of $13, while one at the Museum of Nature was paid $24 per hour, despite near equal levels of experience, training and education. Similarly, in an effort to avoid providing benefits to its employees, the CMCC sought to extend benefit eligibility requirements for sick leave and vacation pay from a six month probationary period to twelve. In fighting to end the unfair treatment and casualization of labour at the museums, job security, control over the labour process and wages on par with other workers at CMCC museums was a sticking point throughout negotiations (ibid).

ON STRIKE

Throughout the first four weeks of the strike few discussions were held between PSAC Local 70396 and the CMCC bargaining committee. Aware of the impasse, then-Minister of Labour Rona Ambrose offered to send the labour dispute to binding arbitration; however, while Local 70396 was open to the idea, the CMCC refused, perhaps fearful that an arbitrator would rule in the union's favour given precedent at other CMCC museums. Seeking to avoid arbitration, and after nine weeks of refusing to meet with PSAC members unless their demands for job security and the end of casualization were taken off the table, the corporation finally agreed to meet with the union on November 20, 2009. However, bargaining failed to provide any concrete movement as censorship and intimidation became the preferred approach of the CMCC. For instance, PSAC was presented with a letter from CMCC's legal counsel threatening that immediate action would be taken if so-called defamatory comments and photos were not deleted from a Facebook page set up to provide strike support entitled "Fairness and Justice for Museum Workers." PSAC responded by saying that they were not of the opinion that the material on this page was offensive or inaccurate and in turn accused the Corporation of attempting to suppress the voice of the workers who were exposing the unfair work practices and experiences they had endured. Maria Fitzpatrick, the Regional Executive Vice-President for the National Capital Region, described this attempt at censorship as "acts of desperation" and went on the say at the time that "we are appalled that a Crown corporation is spending taxpayers' money to attempt to intimidate workers into silence, rather than getting back to the bargaining table to negotiate a fair settlement" (Blatt, 2009).[3]

Nevertheless, the CMCC's bargaining committee refused to address issues related to workplace insecurity, staffing procedure and wage disparities, using the rationale that the public service needed to be "flexible" like their private sector counterparts. Private security surveillance was subcontracted by the CMCC to constantly videotape the strikers, at times from only a few feet away. Also, Records of Employment were sent to the homes of those on strike without explanation as part of a rather bold intimidation strategy. PSAC did not take kindly to such tactics and indicated that their lawyers would be demanding an explanation for this offense. This proved to be the first time an employer has ever sent such documents to the homes of striking employees in the forty four years of the union's existence. In

3 PSAC also presented the CMCC with a letter of their own referring to a web publication entitled "Union Activities Counterproductive to Negotiations." In an attempt to sway public support away from the strikers, the CMCC document stated: "The Public Service Alliance of Canada and some of the strikers have taken their labour dispute from the work site to the private residences of employees of the Canadian Museum of Civilization Corporation. These employees, their spouses and children were frightened, and felt intimidated and harassed by these questionable tactics. We believe that the majority of striking staff and Canadian citizens would find such activities reprehensible and not conducive to a timely resolution of the current labour dispute". The "reprehensible" activity in question was a pancake breakfast, which PSAC describes as "in no way intimidating, frightening, harassing or otherwise improper or questionable." If the corporation refused to remove the document PSAC was ready to pursue legal action for damages and sue for defamation on grounds of its own.

response, PSAC reassured its members that there was no legal cause for the sending out of such documents and advised them to ignore the Records of Employment. At the time, PSAC (PSAC, 2009b) reminded management that "Section 94 of the Canada Labour Code clearly states that no employer may terminate, layoff, discipline, transfer, suspend, intimidate, threaten or otherwise discriminate against an employee for participating in a legal strike" and threatening to do so would result in charges of unfair labour practices. Yet, despite the corporation's attempts to scare workers into concessions and forcefully impose upon them a state of permanent precarity, striking PSAC workers held the line. Strong bonds were formed while picketing and a newfound sense of courage amongst workers left them anxious for talks to resume. Throughout, strikers stressed that the dispute was not with the public, but with the CMCC.

Unlike the resentful memory of the Ottawa public transit strike over late 2008 and early 2009, including bitter civic workers' strikes in nearby Windsor and Toronto (Fanelli and Paulson, 2010; Noonen, 2009), striking museum workers in Gatineau and Ottawa continued to gain public support as the strike went on. Walking a picket line for weeks with no obvious end in sight can be extremely demoralizing. As anyone who has ever been on strike or been effected by a strike can attest, the financial and personal/familial strains this puts on picketers can easily fracture a common front. One useful way museum workers fought this was by putting together regular cultural events that normally would have taken place inside the museum, but holding them outside on the picket line instead. These events were open to the public and provided the workers with an opportunity to organize and work together on the picket line in a fulfilling way. The successful execution of these events, such as one honouring veterans on Remembrance Day (CBC News, 2009a) and picket line tea parties held in celebration of Prince Charles' visit to Canada (PSAC, 2009c) contributed in a substantial way to workers' ability to maintain their spirits throughout the strike. The events also demonstrated to the public an effort on the part of workers to make the best out of a difficult situation while informing them of their issues. This was especially evident when the Museum of Civilization opened the "Afghanistan: Hidden Treasures" exhibit and workers on the picket line created their own exhibit featuring 200 photographs of museum workers engaged in strike action entitled "Striking Treasures." To quote a striking employee who worked on this project, "The purpose was to show people the real treasures of the museum… unfortunately on the sidewalk" (CBC News, 2009b).

Holding events such as these on the picket line made workers extremely visible to the community and showcased the skills of the striking workers and their work as valuable contributors to the community. It encouraged dialogue between the picketers and the public, providing an opportunity for workers to express their legitimate concerns and reasons for being on strike, as well as garnered positive media attention and political support. Picketers were also visited by fellow artists and musicians as every bit of encouragement counted. This included the support of politicians Marcel Proulx (Member of Parliament Hull-Aylmer, Liberal Party) and Paul Dewar (Member of Parliament Ottawa-Centre, NDP), public supporters and other prominent figures such as Barry Blake (National Councilor for the Alliance of Canadian Cinema, Television and Radio Artists) and Douglas Cardinal (architect of the CMC), which provided the workers with positive reinforcement and confidence (PSAC, 2009d).

Other unions and labour affiliates also came forward in support of PSAC Local 70396, such as the Professional Institute of Public Service and the Canadian Union of Public Employees. At the same time, the Canadian Labour Congress (CLC) met in Ottawa and agreed that the CMCC "has blatantly abandoned their responsibility by failing to negotiate a fair collective agreement" (CLC, 2009). The CLC also asked the Canadian government, then a Harper minority, for a public showing of support for the employees in their struggle by applying pressure to the CMCC, and in particular its Chief Executive Officer Victor Rabinovitch, to begin a new round of talks that would put an end to the strike. Cognizant that back-to-work legislation would not make it passed a Conservative minority government, the Harper government did not intervene.

OUTCOME

Negotiations with the CMCC finally resumed on December 11, 2009, but it took a meeting between Victor Rabinovitch, then PSAC president John Gordon, the Deputy Minister of Labour Canada, and a Senior Official of the Federal Mediation and Conciliation Service to make it happen. To sum a long and bitter labour dispute, in the end some important improvements to the working conditions of PSAC Local 70396 employees were won. Four improvements were central: first, the CMCC agreed to provide full-time temporary workers with the opportunity of permanent status; second, internal applicants were granted preference to available jobs, providing they possess the necessary skills and experience; third, new language was introduced in the collective agreement that guarantees no existing temporary position will be involuntarily eliminated as a result of the contracting out of the same position; and fourth, improvements in maternal and parental leave benefits were gained, which are now on par with the Quebec Insurance Plan (Emploi et Solidarité Sociale Québec, 2011).[4] Also, gained in negotiations were salary protections for those who are reassigned to different positions. As a step toward recognizing seniority among casual employees, the CMCC offered seven newly created permanent part-time positions filled internally based on experience and years of service. After 86 days on strike, on December 15 2009, PSAC Local 70396 workers voted to accept the tentative agreement reached with the CMCC (PSAC, 2009e).

Of course, there are other aspects of the strike that were not quite as successful. For instance, workers with PSAC Local 70396 were unsuccessful in their quest for wage parity with museum workers at other Crown corporations, such as the Museum of Nature. Likewise, after nearly three months on strike, relations with management remained obviously strained, as do tensions between non-union and union members who crossed the picket lines. Rather than resorting to unjust terminations, the CMCC now uses attrition as a way of reducing staff numbers, while in the event of layoffs employees are offered a severance package that both the employee and the union Local must approve.

The above aside, however, reflecting on the strike's relative success, one striking worker mused that building solidarity among the rank-and-file of the two museums and the bargaining executive played a major role in PSAC's optimism over the long haul (Personal Communication, 2009). Tensions among the classic divide between Francophone and Anglophone workers were few, if any, perhaps due to the recognition that they were–as one striker remarked–"in this together." All union communications were issued in French and English, ensuring the free flow of necessary information. Regular updates were communicated to the membership by the negotiating team and the demands of the workers were presented in a clear and consistent way. Feelings of camaraderie were fostered within the union throughout the negotiating process. Also, important to striking workers was support from other PSAC Locals and unions. Indeed, some workers attributed the overwhelming refusal of the CMCC's "final offer" by the membership to their new-

4 The Quebec Parental Insurance Plan is perhaps the strongest in the country providing paid leave for wage-earning birth or adoptive parents. Benefits can be shared by parents or taken separately as maternal/paternal leave and include a 55-70% income replacement for a maximum of 18 to 37 weeks depending on the chosen option. See: http://www.rqap.gouv.qc.ca/travailleur_salarie/choix_en.asp

found politicization and solidarity. In interviews conducted during and after the strike, they suggested that their resounding "no" sent a clear message to the corporation that "workers remained fiercely united, were not prepared to back down, and were to be taken seriously" (PSAC, 2009f; PSAC, 2009g).

A SIGN OF THINGS TO COME

Even though the strike ended in what may be considered a relatively small victory with gains in the protection of employees against contracting-out and improvements to parental leave, the spectre of increased private sector penetration into the CMCC looms large. For instance, shortly after the strike the CMCC's CEO Victor Rabinovitch stated that he intended to focus his energies on "attracting private sector support to supplement government funding" (CMCC, 2009). As disconcerting as such comments are, the PSAC Local 70396 strike over the Winter of 2009 is one small success in what may, unfortunately, be an increasingly aggressive Federal Conservative, now majority, government. Workers at the National Gallery of Canada and Museum of Civilization are once again being threatened with continued cuts to heritage institutions. Without a contract since June 2010, the Gallery's management has announced plans to trim its budgets by privatizing its book store and terminating nine employees. Commenting on the situation, Local 70397 President David Bosschaart said: "We just want a fair contract that provides service pay, improved job security and some protection against inflation" (PSAC, 2011). Since gaining a majority in the House of Commons, the Conservatives have been unhesitant in their quest to remake the public sector in the image of the private sector. For instance, over the next three years 6000 full-time jobs in the public service are set to be cut. National vice-president of PSAC, Patty Ducharme, commenting on the cuts, said: "They are chipping away at services they consider have no value. Arts, culture, heritage, language [and the] environment..." (Cobb, 2011). Likewise, in an effort to further shrink public sector employment, workers are being offered buyout packages, the option of taking early retirement and, ultimately, layoffs should attrition fail to produce the desired results. Indicative of this trend, from 1990 to 2009, as a percentage of the total labour force government employment experienced a decline from 21 percent to 18 percent (McBride and Whiteside, 2011). In addition to making the public sector market-dependent, the Federal Conservatives are flexing their majority power with the growing use of back-to-work legislation.

After seven months of negotiations without a contract, on June 2, 2011, nearly 50,000 workers at the Canada Post Corporation (CPC) took job action against employer efforts intent on downgrading their wages, benefits and working conditions.[5] Rather than launching an all-out strike, the Canadian Union of Postal Workers (CUPW) decided on rotating job action, while continuing to deliver pension and social assistance cheques. Canada Post's intentions were unambiguous: introduce new machinery and workplace reorganization in an effort to intensify productivity; increase the volume of mail carried by each letter carrier; cut well-paying, full-time positions; introduce more evening and overnight shift work; replace sick leave rights with an inferior Short Term Disability Plan; and, most contentiously, introduce a lower pay scale and replace the defined benefit pension plan with the unstable fluctuations of a market-dependent defined contribution plan. After twelve days of rotating job action, however, on June 14, 2011, the CPC locked out the workers. Just one-day later Labour Minister Lisa Raitt tabled back-to-work legislation imposing a wage scale that was lower than the CPC's last offer (CTV News, 2011). But, as David Camfield (2011b) has written, that wasn't the worst part:

> "The law dictates that the new collective agreement for urban postal workers will be determined by an arbitrator appointed unilaterally by the Minister of Labour, using a method called final offer selection (FOS). FOS is uncommon in Canada, and is very rare in back to work legislation. In this case, the union and the employer are each required to submit a final offer covering the many disputed issues. The arbitrator will then select one offer or the other in its entirety. In addition to allowing the Conservatives to handpick whoever they want as the arbitrator, the law includes guidelines that the arbitrator must follow in choosing a settlement...This puts intense pressure on CUPW officials to submit a final offer that includes concessions they would never have agreed to in bargaining, in the hope that the arbitrator will pick their offer rather than an even-worse one from the employer."

Like Canada Post workers, on June 14, 2011, 3,800 call-centre staff and check-in workers unionized with the Canadian Automobile Workers (CAW) at Air Canada took job action against employer efforts to reduce

5 The impending commentary on the 2011 Air Canada strike and Canada Post lockout were written just as the strikes were coming to an end and are therefore cursory at best.

wages, benefits and the quality of working conditions. Central to the job action was Air Canada's efforts to implement a two-tiered wage system, increase the minimum retirement age by five years and, like the CPC, impose a defined contribution pension plan over the much more secure defined benefit plan. A private company, unlike the CPC, it must be recalled that for the majority of Air Canada's rank and file workers, wages had been cut and frozen in 2003 amidst bankruptcy proceedings. This has not, of course, stopped executive compensation from rising excessively. In 2010, for example, Air Canada's CEO pay increased forty percent for a total compensation worth $4.5 million. Nevertheless, just two hours into the strike Labour Minister Lisa Raitt, vowing not to put at risk "Canada's fragile economic recovery," motioned that she would be tabling back-to-work legislation (Kane, 2011). With the threat of back-to-work legislation looming large, Air Canada and the CAW were able to reach an agreement soon after the Minster of Labour tabled legislation forcing striker's back-to-work. Details of the agreement are few at the time of writing, but the contract includes a nine percent wage increase over four years, while the contentious issue of pensions will be dealt with through arbitration (Murphy and Godfrey, 2011). The newfound aggressiveness of the Harper Conservatives in employing coercive back-to-work legislation signals what is likely a disturbing precedent for future collective bargaining. The question moving forward, then, is whether or not unions, social justice and community activists can match the aggressiveness and organization of their counterparts?

TOWARD A MILITANT, CLASS UNIONISM

Writing in an era much different than the twenty-first century, though in many ways similar, it is worthwhile recalling the words of one of the U.S.'s most celebrated labour activists who reminds us that "...the struggle in which we are engaged today is a class struggle; and labour unionism to be of any real value to the working class must be organized, not along craft lines, but along class lines" (Debs, 1905, n.p.). Current labour struggles under the new Conservative majority of Prime Minister Harper are about more than workers' rights to job security, health and safety, benefits and pensions; it is also about defending public services, democratic control over resources and decision-making power, and the rights of all persons to chart out a future without the ever-present fear that capital will at any moment abandon them. In short, it is about recognizing the Tory attacks as acts of class war.

Like Debs, Marx and Engels recognized long ago that improvements in working conditions for those organized also helped raise the basic legislative floor for others. But they also recognized that the benefits accrued through unionization and legislation would always be under attack and likely provisional. Consequently, they stressed that "*The unions must convince the world at large that their efforts, far from being narrow and selfish, aim at the emancipation of the downtrodden millions*" (Marx, 1866, n.p). If unions were to become a substantive force of movement–rather than reactionary, even if defensive, opportunists–this meant building unions as expressions of working class unity. All in all, for Marx and Engels, as for Debs, if organized labour was going to have a progressive future it would need to be anchored in a politics that oriented its struggles toward the emancipation of the working class as a whole and, therewith, the abolition of class privileges. This ineradicably meant challenging the very existence and legitimacy of capitalism.

While striking PSAC workers in Local 70396 were certainly not, on the whole, anti-capitalist in their aims and efforts, important seeds were revealed in the strike toward a turn to class-struggle unionism. This included, as we outlined above, generalizing their specific qualms into broader social issues, connecting with the general public, seeking to break down the arbitrary distinction between public and private sector workers, challenging the division of labour within the employment structure, communicating with their members and the public in a clear and consistent manner, and confronting management prerogatives. As workers learned and struggled together confidence and optimism became contagious among members. Indeed, while the Ottawa and Gatineau museum workers' strike may be one, albeit relatively small but successful trade union struggle, it is becoming ever-more apparent that trade unions must go beyond their role as mediators between workers and management. This requires, in our view, transforming trade unionism into class-struggle unionism.[6] As likewise argued by Panitch and Swartz (2003, 237), "Union activists and leaders would need to engage directly–not just as surrogates who issue statements to support the vital issues taken up today by social movements–in many spheres of working people's lives, from education and housing to racism and sexism, and the nature of the work they do... Unions need to open themselves up to the broader community to become centres of working-class life and ultimately vehicles through which working people develop

6 There is valuable research examining the importance of union renewal. However, just what such changes are required is a matter of continuing discussion. While we do not have the space to provide an exhaustive literature review, for strong starting points see Kumar and Schenk, 2006; Ross, 2008; and Camfield, 2011c.

the capacity and confidence to lead society." Furthermore, a call to a more inclusive working class resistance model brings attention to the "false logic of competitiveness" of neoliberal capitalism as the collective fight takes place at the community level, which requires the cooperation of those who live and work in shared spaces (Radice, 2010, p. 39). For this strategy to be effective, cooperative efforts must be made between unions representing working people as well as renewed union outreach to people without jobs and non-unionized labour with the goal of building class consciousness. To do so requires that unions step beyond formal membership and offer support to the broader community of working class people including the unemployed, non-unionized, migrant labour, the disabled and the poor. Considering the brashness of Prime Minister Harper's newfound Conservative majority, and the coordinated responses of the capitalist class, it is conceivable that the worst for Federal public service workers (and the users of those services) is yet to come. As PSAC Local 70396 members showed, fighting back matters.

CONCLUSION

To conclude, in this paper we have sought to trace the trajectory of neoliberalism in Canada, with a focus on precarious labour and public services through an analysis of the Ottawa and Gatineau museum workers' strike over late 2009. We situated in historical perspective the coercive mechanisms employed by consecutive Federal governments' since the 1980s, drawing attention to the most recent maneuverings by the current government of Stephen Harper. As we have argued, unions and oppressed persons generally can no longer, if they ever could, put their unbridled faith in the courts, laws or governments to enforce and protect workers' fundamental human rights. Since at least the 1970s, Canadians have witnessed the progressive dismantlement of Keynesian-era social programs amidst an increasingly militant and recalcitrant capitalist class offensive. While PSAC Local 70396's struggle with the CMCC may be considered a victory, scores of losses in the decades preceding and since then mar the political landscape. The attacks against the collective bargaining rights of workers should unmistakably be understood as acts of class war. A twenty-first century unionism, then, must come to terms with an increasingly aggressive capitalist class-state nexus and the limits of unionization as an end in itself; only then may the political potential of a working class unionism rekindle the struggle for realizing a world without capitalism.

REFERENCES:

Albo, G. (2009). *Challenges for Urban Social Justice Movements, Neoliberal Urbanism, the Canadian City and Toronto*. Toronto: Centre for Social Justice.

Albo, G. (2010). The 'New' Economy and Capitalism Today. In N. Pupo and M. Thomas (Eds.), *Interrogating the New Economy: Restructuring Work in the 21st Century*. Toronto: University of Toronto Press.

Armstrong, P., Carol Amaratunga, Jocelyne Bernier, Karen Grant, Ann Pederson and Kay Wilson (Eds.). (2001). *Exposing Privatization: Women and Health Care Reform in Canada*. Aurora, ON: Garamond Press.

Arat-Koc, S. (1997). From Mothers of the Nation to Migrant Workers. In A. Bakan and D. Stasilus (Eds.), *Not One of the Family: Foreign Domestic Workers in Canada*. Toronto: University of Toronto Press.

Bakan, A and D. Stasilus (Eds.). (1997). *Not One of the Family: Foreign Domestic Workers in Canada*. Toronto: University of Toronto Press

Berton, P. (2001). *The Great Depression: 1929-1939*. Toronto: Anchor.

Bezanson, Kate, and Meg Luxton (Eds.). (2006). *Social Reproduction: Feminist Political Economy Challenges Neoliberalism*. Montreal & Kingston: McGill-Queen's University Press.

Blatt, S. Legal communication, October 30, 2009. http://www.psac-afpc.org/documents/bargaining/oct30letter_facebook_issue-e.pdf

Braedley, S., and M. Luxton (Eds.). (2010). *Neoliberalism and Everyday Life*. Montreal & Kingston: McGill-Queen's University Press.

Brassard, R. (2009). Interview with Priscillia Lefebvre on November 15, 2009.

Brenner, N. (1999). Globalization as Reterritorialization: The Rescaling of Urban Governance in the European Union. *Urban Studies* 36, 3, 431-451.

Broad, D. and G. Hunter. (2010). Work, Welfare, and the New Economy: The Commodification of Everything. In N. Pupo and M. Thomas (Eds.), *Interrogating the New Economy: Restructuring Work in the 21st Century*. Toronto: University of Toronto Press.

Burke, M., C. Mooers and J. Shields. (2000). *Restructuring and Resistance: Canadian Public Policy in the Age of Global Capitalism*. Halifax: Fernwood.

C News. Murphy, J. & Godfrey, T. Air Canada workers back at work Friday. *Canoe.ca,* June 16, 2011, http://cnews.canoe.ca/CNEWS/Canada/2011/06/13/18277961.html

Camfield, D. (2011). The 'Great Recession', the Employers' Offensive and Canadian Public Sector Unions. *Socialist Studies,* 7 (1/2), 95-115.

Camfield, D. (2011b). Lessons From the Canada Post Lockout. *Rabble,* http://rabble.ca/blogs/bloggers/behind-numbers/2011/07/lessons-canada-post- lockout

Camfield, D. (2011c). *Canadian Labour in Crisis: Reinventing the Workers' Movement.* Halifax, NS: Fernwood Publishing.

Carroll, W. K., & Shaw, M. (2001). Consolidating a Neoliberal Policy Bloc in Canada, 1976– 1996. *Canadian Public Policy*, 27, 195–217.

CBC News. (2009a, November 12). "War museum pickets honour Remembrance Day." *CBC.ca,* http://www.cbc.ca/news/canada/ottawa/story/2009/11/11/war-museum.html

CBC News. (2009b, October 22). "Striking museum workers spoof exhibit." *CBC.ca,* http://www.cbc.ca/news/canada/ottawa/story/2009/10/22/ottawa-museum-workers-spoof-exhibit.html

Clement, W. (2007). "Methodological Considerations: Thinking about Researching Work" in *Work in Tumultuous Times*. V. Shalla and W. Clement (Eds.). Montreal, QC: McGill-Queen's University Press.

Clement, W. and G. Williams (Eds.). (1989). *The New Canadian Political Economy*. Montreal & Kingston: McGill-Queen's University Press.

Clement, W., S. Mathieu, S. Prus and E. Uckardesler. (2010). Restructuring Work and Labour Markets in the New Economy: Four Processes. In N. Pupo and M. Thomas (Eds.), *Interrogating the New Economy: Restructuring Work in the 21st Century*. Toronto: University of Toronto Press.

CLC. "CLC supports striking museum workers." *Canadianlabour.ca,* October 28, 2009, http://www.canadianlabour.ca/national/news/clc-supports-striking-museum-workers-asks-union-members-not-visit-civilization-and-war

CMCC. "Dr. Victor Robinovitch renewed as head of the Canadian Museum of Civilization Corporation." *Civilization.ca,* December 18, 2009, http://www.civilization.ca/cmc/media/press-releases/2009/dr-victor-rabinovitch-renewed-as-head-of-the-canadian-museum-of-civilization-corporation

Cobb, C. "PSAC to mount campaign against federal job cuts." *The Vancouver Sun,* June 17, 2011, http://www.vancouversun.com/news/PSAC+mount+campaign+against+federal+cuts/4966648/story.html

CTV News. "Angry postal workers rally before returning to work." *CTV.ca,* June 27, 2011, http://www.ctv.ca/CTVNews/TopStories/20110627/strike-canada-post-mail-delivery-resuming-tuesday-110627/

Das Gupta, T. (1996). *Racism and Paid Work*. Toronto: Garamond Press.

Debs, E. (1905). *Class Unionism*. Retrieved June 21, 2011 from, http://www.marxists.org/archive/debs/works/1905/classunionism.htm

Engels. F. (1881). *Trade Unions*. Retrieved June 22, 2011 from, http://www.marxists.org/archive/marx/works/1881/05/28.htm

Evans, B. and G. Albo. (2010) "Permanent Austerity: The Politics of the Canadian Exit Strategy From Fiscal Stimulus." In C. Fanelli, C. Hurl, P. Lefebvre, and G. Ozcan *(Eds.) Saving Global Capitalism: Interrogating*

Austerity and Working Class Reponses to Crises (pp.7-28). Ottawa: Red Quill Books.

Evans, B. and J. Shields. *Shrinking the State: Globalization and Public Administration.* Halifax: Fernwood.

Fanelli, C. and C. Hurl. (2010). "Janus-Faced Austerity: Strengthening the 'Competitive' Canadian State." In C. Fanelli, C. Hurl, P. Lefebvre and G. Ozacan (Eds.), *Saving Global Capitalism: Interrogating Austerity and Working Class Reponses to Crises* (pp.29-49). Ottawa: Red Quill Books.

Fanelli, C. and J. Paulson. (2010). Municipal Malaise: Neoliberal Urbanism and the Future of Our Cities. *The Bullet,* 357, http://www.socialistproject.ca/bullet/357.php

Fanelli, C. and M. Thomas. (2011). Austerity, Competitiveness and Neoliberalism Redux: Ontario Responds to the Great Recession. *Socialist Studies,* 7 (1/2), 141- 170.

Fisher, D., Rubenson, K., Bernatchez, J., Clift, R., Jones, G., Lee, J., MacIvor, M., Meredith, J., Shanahan, T., & Trottier, C. (2006). *Canadian Federal Policy and Post- Secondary Education.* Vancouver: Centre for Policy Studies in Higher Education and Training.

Galabuzi, G.E. (2006). *Canada's Economic Apartheid: The Social Exclusion of Racialized Groups in the New Century.* Toronto: Canadian Scholars Press.

Gonick, C. (2009). "A Great Leap Forward?" In J. Guard and W. Antony (Eds.), *Bankruptcies and Bailouts* (pp. 8-17). Halifax: Fernwood.

Government of Canada. (2011). *A Low-Tax Plan for Jobs and Growth.* Retrieved June 12, 2011 from, http://www.budget.gc.ca/2011/plan/Budget2011-eng.pdf

Harvey, D. (2005). *A Brief History of Neoliberalism.* Oxford: Oxford University Press.

Hussey, I. and P. Leclerc. (2011). "The Big Smoke" Screen: Toronto's G20 Protests, Police Brutality, and the Unaccountability of Public Officials. *Socialist Studies,* 7 (1/2), 282-302.

Institute of Wellbeing. (2009). "How are Canadians Really Doing?" Retrieved June 17, 2011 from, www.ciw.ca/en/TheCanadianIndexofWellBeing.aspx

Kane, L. "Feds table legislation to end Air Canada strike." *The Vancouver Sun,* June 15, 2011, http://www.vancouversun.com/business/Feds+table+legislation+Canada+strike/4948582/story.html

Kumar, P. and Chris Schenk (Eds.). (2006). *Paths to union renewal: Canadian experiences.* Peterborough: Broadview

Langille, D. (1987). *The Business Council on National Issues and the Canadian State.* Studies in Political Economy, 24, 41-85.

Lewchuk, W. M. Clarke and A. De Wolff. (2011). *Working Without Commitments: The Health Effects of Precarious Employment*. Montreal and Kingston: McGill-Queen Press.

Loxley, J. and S. Loxley. (2010). *Public Service Private Profits: The Political Economy of Public-Private Partnerships in Canada*. Halifax, NS: Fernwood Publishing.

Marx, K. (1866). *The Different Questions*. Retrieved June 11, 2011 from, http://www.marxists.org/archive/marx/iwma/documents/1866/instructions.htm#06

— (1871). *R. Landor, Interview with Karl Marx*. Retrieved June 22, 2011 from, http://www.marxists.org/archive/marx/bio/media/marx/71_07_18.htm

— (1990). *Capital. Vo.1*. London: Penguin.

Marx, K. and F. Engels. (2002). *The Communist Manifesto*. London: Penguin.

McBride, S. (2001). *Paradigm Shift: Globalization and the Canadian State*. Halifax: Fernwood.

McBride, S. and H. Whiteside. (2011). *Public Austerity, Private Affluence: Economic Crisis and Democratic Malaise in Canada*. Halifax: Fernwood.

McBride, Stephen, and John Shields. (1997). *Dismantling a Nation: The Transition to Corporate Rule in Canada*. Halifax, NS: Fernwood.

McKeen, W. and A. Porter. (2003). Politics and Transformation: Welfare State Restructuring in Canada. In W. Clement and L. Vosko (Eds.), *Changing Canada: Political Economy as Transformation* (pp. 109-134). Montreal & Kingston: McGill-Queen's University Press.

McNally, D. (2011). *Global Slump: The Economics and Politics of Resistance*. Oakland:

PM Press.

Noonen, J. (2009). The Windsor CUPE Stike: Implications for the Labour Movement and the Left. *The Bullet*, 236, http://www.socialistproject.ca/bullet/bullet236.html

Panitch, L. and S. Gindin. (2004). *Global Capitalism and American Empire*. London:

Merlin Press.

Panitch, L., G. Albo and V. Chibber (Eds.). (2010). *The Crisis This Time, Socialist Register 2011*. London: Merlin Press.

Panitch, Leo and Donald Swartz. (2003). *From Consent to Coercion: The Assault on Trade Union Freedom, 3rd Edition*. Toronto: Garamond.

Peck, Jamie. (2001). *Workfare States*. New York & London: The Guilford Press.

Perelman, M. (2011). *The Invisible Handcuffs of Capitalism: How Market Tyranny Stifles the Economy by Stunting Workers*. New York: Monthly

Review Press.

Personal Communication. (2009). Interview with Priscillia Lefebvre on November 22, 2009.

PSAC. (2009a, August 21). "Museum workers deserve respect on the job." *PSAC.com*, http://www.psac.com/news/2009/bargaining/20090821-e.shtml.

PSAC. (2009b, October 10). "Update for Striking Museum Workers Concerning Unusual Correspondence from CMCC." *PSAC.com*, http://psac.com/news/2009/bargaining/20091010-e.shtml

PSAC. (2009c, November 9). "Striking museum workers to throw picket line tea party in honour of Prince Charles." *PSAC.com*, http://www.psac-afpc.com/news/2009/releases/72-1109-e.shtml

PSAC. (2009d, December 11). "Rally and concert to support striking museum workers." *PSAC.com*, http://www.psac-afpc.com/news/2009/releases/84-1209-e.shtml

PSAC. (2009e, December 15). "Museum strike is over." *PSAC.com*, http://www.psac-afpc.com/news/2009/releases/87-1209-e.shtml

PSAC. (2009f, November 26). "Negotiated settlement impossible Museum reject final offer." *PSAC.com*, http://www.psac-afpc.org/news/2009/releases/77-1109-e.shtml

PSAC. (2009g, December 2), "Why We Voted No." *PSAC.com*, http://www.psac-afpc.org/documents/bargaining/why_we_voted_no-e.pdf

PSAC. (2011, June 15). "PSAC members show support for their negotiating team at the National Gallery of Canada." *PSAC.com*, http://www.psac-afpc.org/news/2011/bargaining/20110615-e.shtml

Pupo, N. (1997). Always Working, Never Done: The Expansion of the Double Day. In A. Duffy, D. Glenday and N.Pupo (Eds.), *Good Jobs, Bad Jobs, No Jobs: The Transformation of Work in the 21st Century* (pp. 144-165). Toronto: Harcourt Brace & Company

Pupo, N. and M. Thomas (Eds.), *Interrogating the New Economy: Restructuring Work in the 21st Century*. Toronto: University of Toronto Press.

Québec Parental Insurance Plan. (2011). *Emploi et Solidarité sociale Québec.* Retrieved June 21, 2011, from http://www.rqap.gouv.qc.ca/index_en.asp

Radice, H. (2010). Confronting the Crisis: A class analysis. In L. Panitch, G. Albo, and V. Chibber (Eds.), *Socialist Register 2011: The Crisis This Time* (pp. 21-43). Halifax, NS: Fernwood Publishing.

Rogers, G. and J. Rogers (Eds.). (1989). *Precarious Jobs in Labour Market Regulation: The Growth of Atypical Employment in Western Europe.* Belgium: International Institute For Labour Studies.

Ross, S. (2007). Varieties of Social Unionism: Towards a Framework for

Comparison. *Just Labour*, 11, 16-34.

Ross, S. (2008). Social Unionism and Membership Participation: What Role for Union Democracy? *Studies in Political Ecomony, vol.81.* Retrieved from http://spe.library.utoronto.ca/index.php/spe/article/view/4957

Shalla, V. and W. Clement (Eds.). (2007). *Work in Tumultuous Times: Critical Perspectives*. Montreal & Kingston: McGill-Queen's University Press.

Siltanen, J. (2007). "Social Citizenship and the Transformation of Paid Work: Reflections on Possibilities for Progressive Change" in *Work in Tumultuous Times*. V. Shalla and W. Clement (Eds.). Montreal, QC: McGill-Queen's University Press.

Stinson, J. (2010). Labour Casualization in the Public Sector. In N. Pupo and M. Thomas (Eds.), *Interrogating the New Economy: Restructuring Work in the 21st Century*. Toronto: University of Toronto Press.

Teelucksingh, Cheryl, and Grace-Edward Galabuzi. (2005). "Working Precariously: The Impact of Race and Immigrants Status on Employment Opportunities and Outcomes." In T. Das Gupta, C. James, R. Maaka, G.E. Galabuzzi and C. Andersen (Eds.), *Race and Racialization: Essential Readings* (pp. 202-208). Toronto: Canadian Scholar's Press.

Vosko, L (Ed.). (2006). *Precarious Employment: Understanding Labour Market Insecurity in Canada*. Montreal & Kingston: McGill-Queen's University Press.

Vosko, L. F. (2007). "Gendered Labour Market Insecurities: Manifestations of Precarious Employment in Different Locations" in *Work in Tumultuous Times*. V. Shalla and W. Clement (Eds.). Montreal, QC: McGill-Queen's University Press.

Warskett, R. (2007). "Remaking the Canadian Labour Movement: Transformed Work and Transformed Labour Strategies" in *Work in Tumultuous Times*. V. Shalla and W. Clement (Eds.). Montreal, QC: McGill-Queen's University Press.

Whittington, L. (2011, January 19). Tax Cuts Drive Harper's Right-wing Agenda. *Toronto Star*, http://www.thestar.com/news/canada/article/924121–tax- cuts- drive-harper-s-right- wing-agenda?bn=1

Workman, T. (2009). *If Your In My Way, I'm Walking: The Assault on Working People Since 1970*. Halifax, NS: Fernwood.

Québec Solidaire: A Québécois Approach to Building a Broad Left Party

Richard Fidler[1]

A number of attempts have been made in recent years to launch new parties and processes, addressing a broad left or popular constituency, that are programmatically anti-neoliberal if not anti-capitalist, some of them self-identifying as part of an international effort to create a "socialism of the 21st century." They vary widely in origins, size, social composition, and influence. The process has gone furthest in a number of Latin American countries; among the best known are the United Socialist Party of Venezuela (PSUV), led by Hugo Chávez, and the Bolivian Movement Towards Socialism–Political Instrument of the Sovereignty of the Peoples (MAS-IPSP), led by Evo Morales.

Efforts in Western Europe, such as Italy's Refoundation Party, Germany's Die Linke, or France's Parti de Gauche originated in part in splits in the traditional parties of "20th century socialism," in avowed rejection of both Stalinism and Social Democracy. Many of these parties include members who in the past were associated with one or another of the Marxist currents identified historically with Trotsky's anti-Stalinist legacy. In France, the Nouveau Parti Anti-capitaliste (NPA) was initiated under their aegis. Parallel developments have not yet occurred in the United States or Canada, where anticapitalist ideas and movements have less presence in the political landscape today than they had a century ago. However, as it does in so many respects, Quebec constitutes something of an exception. A new left party, Québec Solidaire, created during the past decade, is attracting considerable interest and growing support as an anti-neoliberal alternative to Quebec's three capitalist parties. While not explicitly anti-capitalist or socialist, it defines itself

1 Richard Fidler is an independent researcher and writer who publishes the blog Life on the Left (www.lifeonleft.blogspot.com). He is based in Ottawa and can be reached at: rfidler_8@sympatico.ca. Thanks are due to John Riddell and David Mandel for their critical comments on an earlier draft. The usual caveats apply.

as a party "resolutely of the left, feminist, ecologist, altermondialiste,[2] pacifist, democratic and sovereigntist." This paper will outline how this party originated, describe how it functions, and explore some major challenges it faces and how it is confronting them.

THE QUEBEC EXCEPTION

Quebec's political evolution has always followed a distinct trajectory within the Canadian social formation. A crucial determinant has been the province's character as the homeland of a distinct nation, with its own territory, language, culture, historical tradition and a well-defined national consciousness as a minority people within Canada and North America. Until well past the mid-20th century, French-Canadian nationalism was essentially defensive, focused on protecting the autonomy of Quebec, the last major enclave of the Francophone presence in Canada, against involvement in imperialist wars and the increasing encroachment on the province's constitutional jurisdiction by the federal state with its expanding economic and social functions. Industrialization and the concomitant urbanization and growth of trade unions aggravated these tensions, disrupting the social and political culture of a Francophone population long dependent on church and parish for the provision of basic social and community services.

In the 1960s a new, more assertive nationalist dynamic gained force as Quebec rapidly moved to modernize its industrial infrastructure, nationalized hydro-electric power resources and expanded and secularized its education, health and social welfare systems. A large provincial state bureaucracy developed, increasingly directed to stimulating the expansion of a skilled labour force and the growth of a Francophone bourgeoisie through the provision of financial and other assistance. Quebec pushed increasingly — but unsuccessfully — for constitutional changes that would give it greater autonomy within the federation, especially in areas crucial to its national identity and development. Union membership expanded exponentially. A veritable cultural revolution occurred with the appearance of many new radical publications and other media, many of them raising the demand for Quebec autonomy, political sovereignty or independence. On the left, pro-independence movements sprouted, their members inspired by the post-war Afro-Asian decolonization and, closer to home, the socialist ideology of the Cuban revolutionists.

2 In French, those who advocate "another world" of global justice and solidarity.

National consciousness and class consciousness have maintained a close and reciprocal relationship in Quebec in recent decades. But this social ferment, both a product and promoter of rising Québécois national consciousness, largely bypassed the parties of the existing "20th century" Canadian left. Their historical failure to sink mass roots in Quebec was directly related to their programmatic orientation toward strengthening the Canadian state and their indifference to Quebec's national oppression and/or hostility to Québécois nationalist sentiment. The Regina Manifesto, the founding document of Canadian social-democracy, omitted any reference to the Quebec national question.[3] The Communist party expelled Québécois members who developed a pro-autonomy interpretation of the party's formal support of Quebec's right to self-determination.[4]

The labour-based New Democratic Party, founded in 1961, has been unwilling to embrace any fundamental alteration to Canada's existing institutional structure that would reflect Quebec's national character, or even to develop a coherent approach that differed significantly from the constitutional priorities of the federal government of the day.[5] Soon after its founding, its Quebec section voted to form a distinct Parti Socialiste du Québec (PSQ). The PSQ advocated that Quebec and Canada be constitutionally recognized as "associated states." If such an agreement proved impossible, it said, "Quebec should declare its independence."[6] But the PSQ was upstaged on its nationalist flank by the pro-independence Rassemblement pour l'Indépendance Nationale (RIN), while the Quebec trade unions were still unprepared to drop their longstanding support of the Quebec Liberals in favour of independent labour political action. The PSQ dissolved in the late 1960s.

In the absence of a viable left-wing alternative sympathetic to Québécois national aspirations, this consciousness was politically channeled into support for the pro-sovereignty Parti Québécois. Founded in the late 1960s, the PQ came to hegemonize the national movement as its political expression. Moreover, its increasing attraction for the leaderships of Quebec's three big union centrals — which gradually shifted to seeing the PQ, and not the Liberals, as their preferred vehicle for political

3 Regina Manifesto, 1933. The Manifesto was adopted by the first "national" convention of the Co-operative Commonwealth Federation (CCF).

4 Henri Gagnon, n.d.

5 For a summary of NDP positions in this regard, see Cooke, 2004. For a critique of the NDP's Sherbrooke Declaration, its most complete and recent statement on the Quebec national question, see Fidler, 2011b. See also Fidler, 2011d.

6 Parti Socialiste du Québec, 1966

influence and reform — tended to eclipse early attempts by some union militants to found independent and anticapitalist political formations. A notable effort, the Front d'action politique (FRAP), a radical municipal party initiated in part by the Montréal section of the CSN, foundered in the wake of the October 1970 crisis and repression. An upsurge in mass nationalist and pro-sovereignty sentiment fueled a radicalization in the labour movement that in the early 1970s saw all three labour centrals[7] issue and debate anticapitalist manifestos. But the capitalist PQ was the primary political beneficiary, although a nationalist left within the party that included some prominent union officials often had a problematic relationship to the party hierarchy.

The PQ project was, and remains, to achieve a bourgeois-nationalist form of state sovereignty associated — the political context permitting — with Canada outside Quebec, or if necessary functioning as a fully independent (but thoroughly capitalist) Quebec state. The PQ's popular support derived from its advocacy of sovereignty, its strong defense of the French language, culture and national identity and, initially at least, its promise of social reforms.

During its first term in office, the PQ enacted some important reforms, particularly in the area of French-language rights, although its legislation in this regard has been subject to constant challenges and adverse court rulings over the years. But after a total of 18 years in government (1976-1985, 1994-2003), the party no longer inspires the hopes for change that it once did. PQ governments have on occasion viciously attacked unions, as in 1982 when the Lévesque government legislated a 20% reduction in the salaries of government workers. The PQ has consistently supported anti-worker "free trade" and investment agreements and its governments have imposed harsh austerity programs.

Although opinion polls have registered high and remarkably consistent support for Quebec independence,[8] the PQ has failed to win its two sovereignty referendums. Equally important, ongoing developments in bourgeois politics — such as the 1982 unilateral patriation of Canada's constitution without Quebec's consent; the 1990 defeat of the Meech Lake Accord; or the federal Parliament's enactment of the Clarity Act in the wake of the narrow 1995 referendum defeat — have signalled the

---

7 The three centrals were the Quebec Federation of Labour (FTQ), the Confederation of National Trade Unions (CSN) and the teachers' union, the CEQ (now the Centrale des syndicats du Québec, or CSQ).

8 Opinion polls indicate that even today more than 40% of Québécois support independence (more than those who declare support for the PQ), and a substantial majority favour greater autonomy for Quebec.

lack of sympathy in Canada's ruling circles not only for Quebec sovereignty but for any meaningful constitutional recognition of Quebec's national identity, let alone unfettered provincial autonomy in jurisdictions essential to that identity.

The new Francophone bourgeoisie that has developed since the Sixties, with state support (both provincial and federal), functions largely as a subset of the Canadian bourgeoisie and no major component favours Quebec sovereignty. Today the Parti Québécois has less appetite for independence, although the goal of "sovereignty" is still article one in its program. Doubts are growing about the party's ability to capture enough popular support for its program to create the "winning conditions" for a successful referendum vote on sovereignty.

The PQ's commitment to working within the neoliberal order, which has often brought it into sharp conflict with the unions, has fueled disenchantment with the party among the very social layers that are the driving force of the national movement. However, a credible left alternative to the Parti Québécois was slow to emerge within the broad Québécois nationalist and left milieu. Until the early 1980s, when they unceremoniously collapsed, the Mao-Stalinist currents that largely dominated the far left for a decade opposed Quebec sovereignty, which they regarded as a purely bourgeois objective dividing the "Canadian" working class. And although they opposed the PQ, they also opposed proposals within the trade unions in favour of establishing an independent working-class party, advocating instead, in true sectarian fashion, the constitution of their own "proletarian party."[9] Like the CCF and pro-Moscow CP before them, this "far left" was ideologically defined around international events and alliances that had little or no resonance in the conditions of Quebec, where the class struggle tends to unfold within a nationalist framework of opposition to linguistic and cultural oppression.

There was always, of course, a smaller left that favoured independence and rejected the PQ and its capitalist program. Sporadic attempts were made in the 1980s to build new parties of the left, but without lasting success. The trade unions remained resistant to proposals to engage in political action independent of the PQ. And during the 1980s and 1990s, the major labour centrals initiated — with political support and generous tax breaks from both levels of government — investment funds that have enmeshed the unions in the financial industry, company management structures and other strategic "partnerships" with capital.

9 For a critical analysis of this experience, see Moreau, 1986. For a more extended analysis, see Dubuc, 2003, especially chapters 3 and 4.

During the late 1990s, however, some cracks began to appear in the edifice of bourgeois sovereigntist hegemony in the left. Feminists, the one broadly-based social movement that had largely survived the neoliberal onslaught of the 1980s — waging a successful defense of abortion rights, for example — organized a mass "march for bread and roses" that directly challenged Lucien Bouchard's PQ government and its "zero deficit" austerity program. They followed up with further demonstrations and, in 2000, sponsored a World March of Women that mobilized tens of thousands in Quebec and elsewhere. When the government rejected their modest demands for an increase in the minimum wage, women's federation leader Françoise David publicly mused on the need to create a "feminist left-wing political alternative" to the Parti Québécois.

Then, in 2001, tens of thousands mobilized at the Quebec Summit in opposition to the proposed Free Trade Area of the Americas. Opponents of neoliberal globalization — "altermondialistes" as they are known in Quebec — were soon joined by hundreds of thousands more in massive demonstrations in the lead-up to the 2003 U.S. invasion of Iraq, the largest antiwar mobilization in Quebec history. For the first time in decades, there was now a realistic potential for a new configuration of progressive forces.

REGROUPMENT AND FUSION

The initiative was taken — first separately, then in combination — by three far-left groups:[10]

The Parti de la démocratie socialiste (PDS) originated as the Quebec section of the federal NDP. In 1995 it broke definitively from the NDP; adopted its new name; defined itself as "anti-capitalist, anti-neoliberal, feminist, internationalist and independentist"; and campaigned for a Yes to sovereignty in the referendum. The PDS was joined by some independent left-wing nationalists who had left the PQ. Members of Gauche socialiste, a section of the Trotskyist Fourth International, were prominent in the PDS leadership.

The Rassemblement pour une alternative politique (RAP) was founded in 1998, in response to a public appeal for a "political alternative" issued in November 1997 by prominent left-wing personalities including former PSQ leader and union militant Michel Chartrand; Pierre Dubuc (editor of the popular independentist monthly L'aut'journal); and Paul Cliche, a journalist who in 1970 had led the left-wing municipal party

10 The following chronology borrows in part from Dostie *et al.*, 2006. See also Lavallée, 2011, p. 202-14.

FRAP in Montréal. The RAP later (in November 2000) voted to change its name to Rassemblement pour l'alternative progressiste.

The Parti communiste du Québec (PCQ), the Quebec section of the Canadian CP, now led by individuals who had once been prominently associated with Quebec's Mao-Stalinist parties.[11]

In the 1998 general election, the RAP ran seven candidates while the PDS contested 97 ridings; their overall vote was small (36,000), although in Jonquière the RAP candidate Michel Chartrand took 15% of the popular vote against the PQ's Premier Lucien Bouchard.

In 2000, a joint public meeting in Montréal organized by the PDS, RAP and PCQ attracted some 650 persons to discuss "unity of the political left and progressive forces." A liaison committee was set up by the three groups along with the Bloc Pot (a marijuana legalization group) and the Quebec section of the Green Party of Canada, with the objective of establishing common positions and actions. In April 2001, just days before the huge protest demonstrations at the pro-free trade Québec Summit of the Americas, independent candidate Paul Cliche won 24% of the popular vote in a by-election in Montréal's Mercier riding. His campaign, supported by the liaison committee, some trade unions and community organizations, indicated the positive potential of left unity. The liaison committee then became the coalition of the Union des forces progressistes (UFP). In December 2001 the RAP voted by a narrow majority at its congress to join the UFP.[12]

At a convention in June 2002 the UFP was founded as "a federated party that seeks to become a mass alternative to the parties of neoliberalism." Those attending included a large number of independent activists in addition to members of the PDS, RAP and PCQ.[13] At a subsequent policy convention in February 2003 the new party adopted a radical platform opposing free-trade agreements and calling for international solidarity (Palestine, Cuba, Iraq), cancellation of third-world foreign debts,

---

11 The PCQ separated from the Canadian CP in 2005 when a majority of its members voted to support Quebec independence. Some members of the reconstituted Quebec section of the Canadian CP are members today of Québec Solidaire, but they do not constitute a recognized "collective" within QS.

12 RAP founder Pierre Dubuc, in the minority, abandoned the project of building a political alternative to the PQ. In June 2005, he joined with some trade union leaders and "left" PQ members (péquistes) to found Syndicalistes et Progressistes pour un Québec Libre (SPQ-Libre), which for a time was officially recognized as a "club" within the PQ.

13 According to an internal UFP study cited by Amir Khadir, 56% of the members were under the age of 35 and 29% were under 29; 50% of them were first-time party members; there was a minor yet real presence of Anglophone activists as well as several members of Montreal's cultural communities (Amir Khadir, interview by Pascale Dufour, March 2006), cited in Dufour, 2003.

defence of the environment, extensive social and educational reforms, electoral reform, labour rights, First Nations self-determination, and a constituent assembly to draft a constitution for a "progressive, republican, secular and democratic Quebec."[14]

The UFP adopted a pluralist structure recognizing the right of organized tendencies ("political entities") to "promote specific orientations compatible with the platform and statutes of the UFP." The PDS was now a political entity called Démocratie socialiste (later Québec socialiste), although it soon dissolved as such. The RAP, for its part, simply dissolved into the UFP, while the PCQ became a recognized political entity within the new party.

In the April 2003 general election the UFP, now registered as an official party, ran 73 candidates (26% were women) and obtained just over 40,000 votes — barely attaining the 1% of the popular vote required to qualify for partial rebate of expenses under the Elections Act. The highest vote was Amir Khadir's 18% in Mercier riding. This campaign was considered a success; some UFP candidates were endorsed by unions, and a post-election report noted that a considerable number of students had been recruited. The party now claimed a membership of some 1,800 members, almost double its membership in 2002.

At a June 2003 meeting, the UFP Council adopted an ambitious agenda of social movement participation, antiwar mobilizing, unification talks with the Parti Vert (a resuscitated Green party), and fighting for an electoral regime of proportional representation to help overcome Quebec's "democratic deficit." The members voted to investigate possible participation in municipal elections and creation of a "youth organization... both independent of and in solidarity with the UFP."

Meanwhile, during the fall and winter of 2002-03, D'abord solidaires, a "non-partisan collective" of activists from the women's and other social movements, had been formed independently of the UFP to mount a public campaign against a rise in right-wing politics that was aimed primarily against Action démocratique du Québec (ADQ), a party that split from the provincial Liberals in the early 1990s on a pro-autonomy program and at one point in the months before the 2003 election was registering 40 percent support in public opinion polls on a platform centered on "family values" and "old-stock" Québécois identity issues. D'abord solidaires was officially indifferent between the governing PQ and the opposition Liberals, not opposing a vote for either as a "lesser evil" to the ADQ. As it turned out, the ADQ polled just 18%, the PQ was

14 See Fidler, 2003.

defeated — its vote dropped by 10 percentage points from its previous result — and the Liberals led by Jean Charest formed the government.[15]

In May 2004, one of the three component collectives in D'abord solidaires, led by feminist leader Françoise David and social housing activist François Saillant, founded Option citoyenne (OC–citizens' choice). It favoured political action to the left of the PQ but initially rejected an invitation to join the UFP.[16] David toured Quebec promoting her book Bien commun recherché ("seeking the common good") and probing support for a new left party. David encountered much support for uniting the political forces to the left of the PQ, and considerable openness to the idea of joining with the UFP in a new party — notwithstanding the reservations of many of her supporters, and David herself,[17] about the UFP's strong commitment to Quebec independence.

In December 2004 Option citoyenne began negotiations with the UFP to explore the possibility of forming "a single progressive, ecologist and feminist party." The year-long fusion process posed some major challenges to both groups. Each had its distinct constituency or corporate culture. The UFP's membership included young people from the global justice movement — internationalist and strong supporters of Quebec independence, which they saw as essential to their anti-capitalist politics — along with an older layer of members, many with long experience in left and far-left politics. OC members, on the other hand, were primarily active within feminist and community organizations (60% were women) and in local grass-roots organizing around tenants' rights, food and housing co-ops and the like, a milieu in which the politics of consensus and accommodation of conflicting views and interests are valued. OC members tended to radicalize around anti-poverty concerns, and were less likely to be concerned with Quebec's national question. But the UFP was adamant that the new party must advocate Quebec independence.

Over a year, beginning in November 2004, Option citoyenne held three "national [Quebec] meetings" of its membership to develop a programmatic basis for negotiations with the UFP. Draft position papers were circulated and resolutions adopted on feminism, democracy, plu-

15 In the 2007 election, the ADQ managed to displace the PQ as Official Opposition until the following year's election, when it was reduced to 7 seats.

16 UFP leader Pierre Dostie later explained that his party would have preferred that OC simply join the UFP. "But reality is very often more complex than we imagine. Once we found that this political movement, given its composition and what it represented, had to comply with its own process, we sought areas of convergence and we entered into a dialogue." *À Bâbord !*, February-March, 2005.

17 David was once a member of En Lutte, a Mao-Stalinist group that opposed Quebec independence.

ralism and economic questions.[18] A typical resolution declared that "a party of the common good, inspired by feminism" should be oriented around "values of social justice, equality, peace, solidarity, respect for the integrity of individuals and the environment, while recognizing the importance of struggles against forms of exclusion, racism, discrimination and violence, including those that continue to be exercised against women in the private and public sphere."

A resolution on economic issues, adopted unanimously, proposed that the "private-public" economic model be replaced by a "plural model" based on "the domestic economy" of family and gratuitous or volunteer services, the "social economy" of non-profit community or cooperative agencies, in addition to "private undertakings... that agree to function in accordance with collective (social, environmental, etc.) rules," and a "public, state and parastate" sector providing equal and accessible services to the entire population. These positions differed substantially from the explicit anti-capitalism of the UFP's program.

The most contentious issue among OC members was the national question, and it was not resolved until the last OC national meeting in October 2005, when the 300 delegates voted overwhelmingly in favour of Quebec sovereignty, thus fulfilling a key condition for UFP consent to a merger. The coordinating committee's position paper justified its position largely on the basis that there was no credible or workable perspective for a renewed federalism that would allow Quebec the additional powers it needed in order to resolve its social problems, but insisted that the defining characteristic of the new party should be its "social agenda" (projet social) and not its position on the national question. The delegates then voted unanimously to join with the UFP to form a new pro-sovereignty party.

Just three days earlier, on October 19, a right-wing manifesto had been published by former PQ premier Lucien Bouchard, some other prominent péquistes, and equally prominent Liberals. Entitled Pour un Québec lucide (For a clear-eyed vision of Quebec), it castigated "big unions" and called for lifting the freeze on university tuition fees, raising electricity rates and consumption taxes, focusing on debt reduction, opening the doors further to private sector investment in public infrastructures and ending the "unhealthy suspicion of private business that has developed in some sectors." The important challenges facing Quebecers, it proclaimed, were declining demographics and increasing global competition from Asia — not sovereignty. The manifesto reflected

18 Option Citoyenne, 2004.

a strong rightward drift of both the neoliberal PQ and its federal counterpart the Bloc Québécois.[19]

Thus, while the traditional pro-sovereignty parties were shifting further to the right and some prominent péquistes like Bouchard were retreating from their previous commitment to a sovereigntist perspective, there was a perceptible trend developing in the opposite direction on the left, which now tended overwhelmingly to see a sovereign Quebec as the framework for its social agenda.

During 2005 Option citoyenne and the UFP participated in some common actions and published joint briefs on sustainable development and electoral reform. And in response to the lucides' manifesto, they initiated a counter-manifesto, Pour un Québec Solidaire, that garnered more than 2,500 signatures.A special convention of the UFP in November 2005 voted unanimously in favour of a fusion with Option citoyenne, and in February 2006 the two organizations held a joint congress to establish the new party, Québec Solidaire. The founding declaration of principles defined it as a party "resolutely of the left, feminist, ecologist, altermondialiste, pacifist, democratic and sovereigntist." It was an impressive achievement — uniting leading activists in the women's movement, some prominent trade-union militants, grassroots community organizers and long-standing leftists around a project to build a new Québécois political movement based on popular and national sovereignty grounded in general principles of solidarity with the oppressed and exploited.

A WORK IN PROGRESS

Québec Solidaire celebrated its fifth anniversary in February 2011. How has it fared? The balance sheet is uneven. During its first year, Québec Solidaire's membership rose from 3,000 to just over 5,000, about 50% of them women, but since then has remained fairly stable. The party has just over 70 local associations organized on the basis of their respective electoral ridings as well as some university campus sections. About one third of these associations are considered "very active," another one third less so, while the remainder function only minimally.[20] In the last

19 At its convention in October 2005, the Bloc voted to support NATO membership, an EU free-trade (and investment) agreement, and the development of a Quebec army and air force that would participate actively in international "peacekeeping", as in Canada's occupation of Haiti. At about the same time, Pierre Dubuc, the left-wing SPQ-Libre candidate, received barely 1% support in his campaign for the PQ leadership.

20 Information provided at the party's Fifth Convention, November 2009.

election, in 2008, the party nominated candidates in almost all of Quebec's 125 electoral counties, or ridings.

Québec Solidaire strives for male-female parity in its structures and representation at all levels, and is headed by two "co-spokespersons": Françoise David, the party president, and Amir Khadir, currently its sole member of the Quebec legislature, the National Assembly. The party has an office with a small full-time staff, a web site and members' intranet, and makes ample use of modern communications media such as Twitter, Facebook, blogs and videos. However, it has no newspaper, although this deficiency is partially compensated by various independent alternative media published by members and sympathizers of the party.[21] The party lacks an internal discussion bulletin or email list, so there is little horizontal communication at the general membership level apart from organized pre-convention discussions, which are held in general assemblies in areas of greater membership density such as Montréal and Quebec City.

A national (i.e. Quebec-wide) Policy Commission is composed of a dozen or so theme committees, responsible for drafting papers and proposals for program development. A national Women's Commission is composed of delegates from the various regions of Quebec, and is charged with ensuring adherence by the party to the values of feminism. In the December 2008 general election, Québec Solidaire scored a major breakthrough. Despite an undemocratic first-past-the-post electoral system, it managed to elect a member to the National Assembly. The election of Amir Khadir in Mercier riding brought welcome media attention to the party. His effective interventions in the National Assembly have given the party considerable media exposure, and he has been able to speak out on many issues not previously associated with the left.[22] However, his high media profile and popularity — opinion polls recently rated him the "most popular" MNA in Quebec! — have not translated into corresponding support for the party as a whole. Although some recent polls have attributed 8-10% or more support to QS among the electorate, the overall score of its candidates in the two general elections since its founding (2007 and 2008) has been just under 4%. A handful of individual candidates, including David, have won electoral scores of between 10% and 30%, however; in each such case they are well-known activists in trade unions or other social movements.

21 Presse-toi a gauche, http://www.pressegauche.org/ (on-line webzine), À Bâbord! http://www.ababord.org/ (bimonthly magazine), and Nouveaux Cahiers du Socialisme, http://www.cahiersdusocialisme.org/ (semi-annual journal, which also hosts a webzine).

22 To see Khadir's interventions in the Assembly (there are hundreds of them since his election), see: http://www.assnat.qc.ca/fr/deputes/khadir-amir-25/interventions.html.

Although it styles itself "a party of the ballot-box and the streets" — a party of mass action as well as elections — this has not been an easy balance to establish or maintain. The political context, at least until Khadir's election, has been a difficult one in which to find opportunities to establish a visible presence in Quebec's political landscape.

As in other parts of North America, Quebec experienced a general downturn in extra-parliamentary mobilizations after 9-11, with the notable exception of the massive antiwar actions prior to the Iraq war. Added to this was the political demoralization of many militants following almost a decade of neoliberal austerity under a Parti Québécois government that for many discredited the very idea of Quebec "sovereignty" as envisaged by the PQ. The trade union movement has suffered major defeats in the face of an antilabour offensive orchestrated since 2003 by the Liberal government. The student movement has been relatively quiescent since a successful mobilization against tuition fee increases in 2005. Although antiwar sentiment remains high, mass actions are fewer and smaller. Thus, Québec Solidaire has had to build itself in a period of general retreat for the very movements that generated its existence.

In addition, Québec Solidaire has found its attention, energy and finances absorbed by election organizing, often to the detriment of extra-parliamentary mobilization. In its first three years the party faced two general elections and more than a half-dozen by-elections. Besides meeting the demanding legal requirements of a registered party, it had to find and train candidates, raise funds, and hold successive delegated conventions to cobble together interim election platforms.

The 2007 election platform,[23] was limited to modest reforms that (as the party admitted) could be implemented within the "neoliberal and provincial framework." It featured proposals for modest social reforms, free education, a publicly-owned pharmacare (prescription drugs insurance) agency, repeal of antilabour legislation, electoral reform through institution of proportional representation, tax reform, nationalization of wind power and expansion of public transit. However, this platform did not even reflect the minimal basis of agreement between the party's founding components. For example, it called for a constituent assembly to determine Quebec's political and constitutional future, but did not call for sovereignty or independence.

23 http://www.quebecsolidaire.net/files/25EngagementsQS.pdf. Summarized in Fidler, 2006.

The 2008 platform[24] was much more elaborate. It called for "making Quebec a country by way of popular sovereignty," and included detailed proposals on language rights, intercultural secularism and international solidarity (for example, replacing free trade agreements with "new international treaties based on individual and collective rights, respect for the environment and a widening of democracy (such as the ALBA[25])." But it also contained some notable omissions; for example, it opposed "Canadian imperialist intervention" in the war in Afghanistan but did not mention NATO or Canada's other military alliances.

In the 2008 election, more than half of Québec Solidaire's 122 candidates were women — a first for a party in Quebec and possibly in Canada. The party was endorsed by the Montréal Council of the CSN, and some candidates were endorsed by other unions.

ADOPTING A PROGRAM

In 2009 the party launched a lengthy process aimed at producing a formal program setting out Québec Solidaire's proposals for a "democratic transformation of the whole of society over the medium and long term." The program is distinguished from an election platform, which applies to a single government mandate, or an emergency program, a plan of action addressed to a specific context or issue.[26]

Over a three-year period, culminating before the next Quebec election, a series of delegated conventions are being held, each to debate and adopt sections of the program organized according to subject matter. The first convention, in November 2009, adopted resolutions on the national question, electoral reform, immigration policy and secularism. A second convention, held in March 2011, was addressed to the economy, the environment, and labour. Other topics — health and social services, education, social and formal justice, culture, agriculture, and international solidarity and altermondialisation — will be addressed in subsequent conventions.

Under the complex procedure the party has chosen for conducting its program debates, initial written submissions by the members (or by "citizens' circles" composed of both members and non-members) must

---

24 http://www.quebecsolidaire.net/files/QS-Commitments-2008.pdf (in English). Discussed in Fidler, 2008.

25 Alianza Bolivariana para los Pueblos de Nuestra América (Bolivarian Alliance for the Peoples of Our America), a progressive economic and social alliance for fair trade and mutual assistance initiated by Venezuela and Cuba, which now comprises eight countries of Latin America and the Caribbean.

26 See Québec Solidaire, 2009b.

not exceed 800 words in length. The policy commission then compiles a "perspectives booklet" presenting concise demands based on what it considers the "principal orientations" in these submissions. These are discussed and amended or added to by QS local associations and general assemblies, following which the policy commission produces a "synthesis booklet" that arranges the revised demands by topic and, where appropriate, lists differing resolutions addressed to a particular issue as "options" (a half-dozen or so, in some cases) for debate and decision at the convention — first in topic workshops, then in plenary session, where delegates are limited to two or three minute interventions from the floor.[27]

At each stage the draft documents are published on the members' intranet. (In the lead-up to the first convention, written contributions to the debate by individual members or groups of members were published on the QS web site; however, it appears this practice is no longer being implemented.) Whatever the democratic merits of this procedure–and there are some, to be sure–it effectively precludes lengthier written contributions within the party structures that could outline a general strategic or programmatic framework on the given subjects and allow a broader debate among opposing approaches. As noted earlier, the party has no public or internal discussion bulletin or even an email discussion list that would allow such debates.

The main topics for debate at the first program convention, in November 2009, were the national question and reform or creation of "democratic institutions." The three hundred delegates agreed, by large majorities:[28] that the Quebec "nation" includes all residents of Quebec, and is based not on ethnic origin but on voluntary membership in the political community, with French as the common language of public communication; this nation being composed historically by the successive integration of people originating from other communities, including the Anglophone community. QS also acknowledges the sovereignty of "the ten Amerindian peoples and the Inuit people who also inhabit Quebec territory," and their fundamental right to national self-determination, however they choose to exercise that right.

27 In the most recent discussion, prior to the Sixth Convention held in March 2011, the policy commission received about 150 submissions. Following publication of the perspectives booklet, members submitted about 600 amendments and new proposals or comments from about 40 local associations or committees entitled to representation at the convention. (Introduction to the *Cahier Synthèse–Programme*) This suggests that most of the internal preconvention discussion was on the basis of the perspectives document, with its succinct specific demands.

28 For a full report, see Fidler, 2009.

that "Canadian federalism is basically unreformable. It is impossible for Quebec to obtain all the powers it wants and needs for the profound changes proposed by Québec Solidaire." A new relationship with the rest of Canada can only be negotiated once the Québécois have clearly established their intent and ability to form an independent state.

that independence should be achieved through a process of participatory and representative democracy, through election of a Constituent Assembly composed equally of women and men, with "proportional representation of tendencies and the various socio-economic milieus within Quebec society." The Assembly would conduct an extensive consultation of opinion and, following its debates, its conclusions — in effect, a draft Constitution — would then be put to a popular vote in a referendum.

These positions mark a major advance in the party's understanding of the national question, when compared with the minimal agreement on this question at its founding. And they clearly delimit it from the PQ's sovereignty-association and ethnic nationalism, as well as its referendum strategy which limits popular input to a vote on a question negotiated between the parties in the National Assembly.

The convention also addressed another of Québec Solidaire's founding "values" — laïcité, or secularism — basically, separation of church and state. This is a hot-button issue in Quebec, where right-wing ideologues, narrow nationalists, and some leftists and feminists have campaigned in recent years against "reasonable accommodation" of ethnic minority practices. Those particularly targeted include Muslim women wearing "ostentatious symbols" of their religious faith such as the hijab, or scarf, which are deemed threats to national identity or challenges to women's rights. The QS delegates ratified the party leadership's concept of "open" and "intercultural" secularism and opposed proposals for state-enforced dress codes that would effectively outlaw the wearing of symbols of religious belief. Debate continues in the party on some related issues such as the growing demand by many nationalists and feminists that the government adopt a "Charte de laïcité," a charter to control more generally the expression of religious beliefs in the public sphere.

The convention also adopted progressive proposals on measures to integrate immigrants into Quebec society and on democratic reform of electoral institutions. In regard to the latter topic, QS advocates a system of proportional representation that would elect 60% of MNAs as individual riding representatives, the other 40% of the seats being allocated to the various parties in proportion to their respective shares of the popular vote.

The second program convention, held in March 2011, focused on environmental, economic and labour issues.[29]

Environment. The 350 delegates voted for a major turn to "green energy," including:

A reduction in greenhouse gas emissions by at least 40% by 2020 compared with 1990 levels, and by 95% by 2050. Abandonment of fossil fuels by 2030.

Opposition to carbon taxes, carbon trading and storage schemes, biofuels, and geo-engineering.

"Public control" over energy firms, defined as majority participation of the state up to and including 100% nationalization as needed.

Prohibition of any new hydro-electric development. Production of renewable energies: solar, geothermal, wind, to limit to the maximum any supplementary resort to hydro-electricity.

An end to all exploration and development of fossil fuels, such as petroleum in the Gulf of St. Lawrence (Old Harry), shale gas, and LNG ports. Elimination of Quebec's nuclear reactor system, and an end to the exploration and development of uranium mines.

Development of electrified transportation to ensure the accessibility, universality "or even gratuity" of public transit.

Support for a new, legally binding international agreement, and participation in the world movement linking climate and social justice. It was noted that this movement is inspired by the alternative peoples' summit on the environment held at Cochabamba, Bolivia in April 2010.

Natural resources. The convention voted by large majorities that the mining and forestry industries should be placed under "public control," with up to 100% nationalization "as needed." In addition:

All resource industries to be subject to strict environmental regulations, and no project to be approved without meaningful public consultation in the communities concerned and a veto by local or regional authorities over development plans. Mining royalties to be increased and shared equitably between the resource region and the government.

In the forest industry, elimination of laws allowing clear cutting and cutting in the boreal forest north of the 49th parallel. A reduction in disparities between natural and managed forests, and a need for prior agreements with the indigenous people in all regions under aboriginal treaties or land claims.

Fresh water, whether surface or underground, to be considered a

29 See Fidler, 2011a.

"non-commodified common good accessible to all but the property of no one," with the state as guardian. Water used by industry and businesses to be considered a "loaned" public property subject to royalties and post-treatment controls.

Trade union and labour rights. Among the programmatic demands adopted by the convention — usually by large majorities, in some cases unanimously — are the following:

Constitutional protection of the right to join unions, bargain and strike, including the right to political and solidarity strikes (strikes for political objectives and in solidarity with striking workers and students).

Prohibition of lockouts, and strict controls on layoffs and shutdowns — including mandatory justification before a government agency, protection of company pensions, compulsory retraining and re-employment in similar jobs, etc. State assistance to employees wishing to form local worker coops when companies relocate.

Union rights for farmworkers and self-employed workers, and the right to multi-employer certifications.

Right of full employment in safe, stable, socially useful, ecologically sound work free of discrimination, with social protection in case of loss of employment, incapacity and ageing. Affirmative action for women, disabled, visible minorities and indigenous.

Immediate reduction in the workweek to 35 hours, and "gradual" transition to 32 hours with no loss of pay, compensatory hiring and no speed-up in workload or pace. Legal restrictions on the use of overtime work.

An immediate increase in the minimum wage to the low-income (poverty) threshold for a person working full time, with a "gradual" increase to 50% over this threshold, indexed to the cost of living. This would mean a gradual increase from $10.66 to $15.99 per hour.

Expanded public employment in social services, construction, infrastructures maintenance and environmental clean-up.

Accessible programs for job retraining, free and funded by employers and government.

Virtually all of these demands have been raised by the unions and social movements; Québec Solidaire sees itself as their political and electoral representative.

BEYOND CAPITALISM?

Introducing the preconvention debates, the policy commission asked QS members to consider a question that goes to the very heart of the party's conception of its overall objective:

"As we work on our program, we should spell out the nature and limits of the system, and ask ourselves the following question: isn't the capitalist system, based as it is on maximizing profit and irresponsible exploitation of nature, the main obstacle to social progress and a healthy relationship to the environment? We need a serious debate on the question so we can determine whether our social problems can be corrected by reforms that respect the logic of the system or if we need to adopt the perspective of going beyond the system."[30]

This was also the question put by the Québec Solidaire leadership in a Manifesto issued for May Day 2009, entitled "To emerge from the crisis, should we go beyond capitalism?"[31] The Manifesto's anticapitalist rhetoric met with a very favourable response in QS ranks.This defining issue was debated briefly during the preconvention period, although not in official party publications. Some members argued that QS should remain a "rainbow coalition," fighting "for immediate changes realizable within the framework of the present capitalist state and system." Others, however, argued for a more radical perspective: "ecosocialism," and an explicit attention to "the class interests of the workers' movement."[32]

Judging from the debates at the March convention, these questions remain open for "serious debate" in Québec Solidaire. In the plenary session on "general orientations," delegates voted by a large majority for a statement declaring that "QS ultimately intends to go beyond capitalism," and calling for a "plural economy" and "an eventual socialization of economic activities, based on a strengthened public economy (state-owned companies and nationalization of major enterprises in some strategic sectors), a greater role of the social economy (cooperatives, community-owned firms), and a controlled private sector, with much greater emphasis on promoting small and medium enterprises (SMEs)."

No relative weight was assigned to any of these sectors. A number of delegates objected that many SMEs are low-wage sweatshops, the proprietors being bitter opponents of trade unions. Their alternative motions were outvoted after brief debate.

Delegates voted as well that:

Nationalized enterprises are to be operated in a framework of national and democratic planning, with decentralized management including

30 Québec Solidaire, 2010, p.5
31 Québec Solidaire, 2009a.
32 For excerpts, see Fidler, 2011a.

representatives of employees, the community, and First Nations where applicable. Forms of self-management are to be promoted in place of bureaucratic oversight.

Economic growth must cease to be considered an objective in itself. A QS government will take immediate legal, regulatory, fiscal or other measures to discourage over-production, over-indebtedness, and over-consumption.

The emphasis on the "social economy" is not surprising, perhaps, given the traditional prominence within Quebec society of farming co-operatives, the caisses populaires (originally, parish-based credit unions), and similar service-based not-for-profit organizations, with self-defined "social missions" and relatively democratic decision-making structures.[33] The attention to the "domestic economy" reflects as well the traditions and roots of many QS members in the feminist movement and its recognition that many important economic functions of society go unpaid or underpaid relative to other economic sectors.

However, many of these undertakings operate in low-wage ghettos, and they often serve to legitimize the privatization of public services. And although some sectors, as in the childcare industry, have managed to unionize, some major proponents of Quebec's "social economy" are heavily implicated in collaborating with the trade union-sponsored investment funds such as the FTQ's Solidarity Fund or the CSN's Fondaction, which have served as a major economic and ideological bulwark for the conservative union bureaucracy.[34] The "social economy," as it actually functions in Quebec society, is an integral part of its capitalist economy. And some of its components, such as the massive Desjardins Movement, a dominant player in retail banking and insurance in the province, are major institutions of "Québec Inc.," the new Francophone corporate elite.

A packed agenda did not allow time for debate on important resolutions on banking and the financial industry — where some draft proposals called for complete expropriation — and taxation, where pro-

---

33 In Quebec as a whole, the "social economy" comprises more than 7,000 "collective enterprises (cooperatives and non-profits)" employing 125,000 workers and accounting for 8% of the province's GDP. See: http://www.chantier.qc.ca/?module=document&uid=871. A recent study of the "social economy" in Montréal alone lists close to 4,000 establishments with $2 billion in revenues and employing more than 65,000 salaried workers (women occupying about 59% of full-time and 66% of part-time jobs). They encompass a wide variety of undertakings: housing cooperatives, child-care centres, caterers, domestic care agencies, as well as some major operations in the retail, finance and insurance sectors. See Université du Québec à Montréal, 2008.

34 See, for example, Neamtam,2010.

posals included, inter alia, rejection of consumption taxes and radically shifting the tax burden from individuals to corporations. These topics were left for future debate and decision.

A PARTY OF THE BALLOT BOXES... AND THE STREETS?

Aware that "politics" is conventionally viewed as electoral and parliamentary activity, Québec Solidaire has established itself as an officially recognized party under Quebec law. Since its founding, and particularly since Khadir's election in 2008, the focus has been increasingly on a strategy of building the party through the ballot box, to the neglect of extra-parliamentary action "in the streets." A "development plan" adopted at a National Council meeting, in June 2010, summarized the objectives for the next two years as "advancing our ideas in the population, gaining a greater presence in public debates, electing more MNAs and appreciably increasing our percentage of the vote in the next general elections."

A draft resolution of the QS policy commission, still to be debated and adopted in a future convention, addresses "the relations between Québec Solidaire, the trade-union movement and the social movements in general." The draft text outlines a strategy by which QS, "as a party and as a government, should seek to strengthen the capacities of the social movements, encourage their unity in action and participate in them on the basis of a program of social transformation." It proposes that QS members who belong to the various social movements be encouraged to "network" within the party — that is, coordinate their activities within the unions and other movements around a strategy of reciprocal reinforcement of the movements and the party while respecting "the organizational and political autonomy of the social movements." This draft text addresses an important lacuna in Québec Solidaire's activities.

Québec Solidaire works alongside the unions and some social movements in a number of coalitions, such as the pro-independence Conseil de la Souveraineté. But its modest campaign in relation to the public-sector unions' negotiations with the Quebec government last year, labelled "Courage politique," failed to mount a clear defense of the unions' demands and was largely confined to arguments in support of existing social programs and opposition to privatization. The party has no organized presence as such in the unions.

As the policy commission puts it, the conquest of political power requires "a structured political organization whose program integrates the demands of the social movements and an overall projet de société [program for society]." And thus it is important to think in particular about the party's relation with "the trade-union movement, which occupies a central place within Quebec's social movements."

The undemocratic first-past-the-post system in Quebec (as in every other jurisdiction in Canada) poses some formidable obstacles to a new party with radical ideas facing a hostile mass media in a multiparty environment. Québec Solidaire promotes a detailed proposal for a system of proportional representation, but recognizes that there is no early prospect of its adoption. With this in mind, the party leadership asked delegates to the March convention to consider whether QS should seek electoral agreements with other parties under which each party would agree not to contest certain ridings in which the other stood a better chance of electing its candidate. Two options were on the table: (a) a possible tactical agreement with the Parti Québécois and/or the Verts (a small Green party); or (b) a possible tactical agreement with the Verts alone, a "strategic alliance" with that party being deemed conceivable if based on the Global Greens Charter, but ruled out for "practical reasons pertaining to internal decisions of the Verts in Quebec."

After an intense debate, the delegates rejected any such alliances, despite appeals from both Amir Khadir and Françoise David, among others, in support of either option. Opponents noted that such alliances would blur Québec Solidaire's programmatic differences from the other parties, particularly the PQ, and in any case were impractical — the PQ is apprehensive of the growing popularity of QS among many of its traditional supporters, and PQ governments have always resisted implementing any form of proportional representation. The vote also reaffirmed the members' determination to build Québec Solidaire as an independent left-wing political alternative to the Parti Québécois.

A 'COUNTRY OF PROJECTS'

The unexpected surge in support for the New Democratic Party in the May 2 federal election, and the sharp decline in the Bloc Québécois vote,[35] have underscored the volatility of the Quebec electorate and stimulated hopes in Québec Solidaire, which does not run for federal office, for major gains in the next provincial election. It has also given

35 The NDP took 43% of the popular vote in Quebec, electing 59 of the province's 75 MPs. In 2008 it had polled only 12.2%, electing one MP. The Bloc vote fell from close to 40% in 2008 to less than 24%, and it elected only 4 MPs, although it had elected a majority of Quebec's MPs since 1993. See Fidler, 2011b. The Bloc's collapse has touched off a profound crisis within the Parti Québécois and traditional pro-sovereignty movement: see Fidler, 2011e

a powerful boost to the party's campaign "for a country of projects," launched in mid-April of 2011 pursuant to a resolution adopted at its November 2009 convention.[36] The campaign web site sets out the party's vision of sovereignty and the approach it favours for achieving it. It also outlines the party's approach to strengthening the status of the French language, especially in Montréal. As the web site explains:

"Some of these projects can be achieved here and now, without affecting Quebec's constitutional status. However, the people's ambition to realize many other projects will soon be hobbled by the total or partial absence of any latitude for Quebec in areas as fundamental as the environment, foreign policy, foreign trade and even language. The full mastery of our destiny is therefore indispensable for achieving all of the projects of our dreams."

Associated materials (all on-line) include a historical survey that dates a Québécois quest for sovereignty back to the 18th century, a critique of Canadian federalism and the failure of past efforts to reform the system, and a critique of "the impasse of the PQ and its referendum strategy," to which it counterposes Québec Solidaire's proposed grassroots campaign to build support for sovereignty and, eventually, the election of a democratic non-partisan Constituent Assembly to adopt a constitution for an independent Quebec. Associated articles describe parallel "inspiring experiences" in Bolivia, Ecuador and, most recently, in Tunisia.

In the fall of 2011, the campaign will feature a tour of Quebec by QS president Françoise David and public meetings "on themes chosen by local party associations."

This campaign has the potential to boost Québec Solidaire's profile as the left wing of the independence movement, with a "project for society" and a "country of projects" that points toward an anticapitalist alternative vision that breaks sharply with the PQ-Bloc strategy for independence — a strategy "based on alienation from Canada," and "fuelled by resentment," as Amir Khadir described it in a recent analysis of the federal election results.[37]

21ST CENTURY SOCIALISM?

The rightward evolution of the traditional sovereigntist parties, the PQ and BQ, has left a very broad space to their left, one that Québec Soli-

---

36 See Fidler, 2009. The interactive campaign web site may be accessed at: Québec Solidaire 2011.

37 *Le Devoir*, May 14, 2011. Translated in Fidler, 2011c

daire aspires to fill. The party has managed to cast a wide net, encompassing leading activists from the women's movement and community social action groups, veterans of previous but unsuccessful attempts to found viable parties of socialism and a Marxist left, and some trade unionists.

It cannot (yet) be classified as anti-capitalist, or a party of 21st century socialism as that concept has generally been conceived. But it is clearly much more than a Québécois version of the federalist NDP, notwithstanding hopes expressed by QS leaders that the NDP will some day prove a valuable Canadian interlocutor for Quebec as it moves to independence.

Québec Solidaire's support of Quebec independence means that its strategic framework is not limited to the existing form of the state; it opens the party's imagination and perspectives to conceiving another, very different Quebec based on the "values" or principles upheld by the party. This is not a line of march that facilitates accommodation with the Canadian bourgeoisie or its Quebec component. This independentism is one of Québec Solidaire's strongest programmatic assets, offering it the potential to build a party that encompasses and represents the driving forces for progressive social transformation within the Quebec social formation.

There are other important features of the party, however, that underscore its sui generis nature in the Quebec, and indeed Canadian, political landscape and that offer hope for its evolution and development into a mass socialist party with deep roots among Quebec working people.

The party's strong commitment to feminist principles has given it a compass in navigating through the shoals of the public debate over Quebec identity and "reasonable accommodation." Despite some backsliding by the party leadership,[38] QS has generally stood firm behind its support of "open secularism" in the face of harsh criticism from some on the left. The near parity of women with men in the party's membership and structures is unique in Quebec, and in Canada.

Québec Solidaire's internationalism has been given limited expres-

38 QS has given critical support to the Charest government's Bill 94, which would deny government-funded health care, education and child care services to all whose clothing prevents disclosure of their face, and would bar them from government and public-service employment. The bill patently targets a tiny number of Muslim women who wear niqabs or burqas. And when some Sikhs sought to appear before a parliamentary committee to express their opposition to Bill 94, Amir Khadir added his vote on a PQ motion, supported by the other parties, to exclude them from the National Assembly because they were wearing their ceremonial dagger, the kirpan. This action is arguably inconsistent with the resolutions on laïcité adopted a year ago, mentioned in this paper.

sion in its opposition to capitalist trade and investment deals, its opposition to the war in Afghanistan, and in its sympathy toward progressive governments in Latin America. The party has been harshly attacked in the mainstream media for its participation in the Boycott, Divestment and Sanctions campaign against Israeli apartheid, which the delegates to its November 2009 convention voted unanimously to endorse — a position that demarks Québec Solidaire from the NDP's strong support of the Zionist state.[39]

The party's commitment to defence of the environment, if adhered to consistently, points it toward anti-capitalist solutions and the formulation of a radical ecosocialism that can link up with the worldwide movement developing in the wake of Bolivia's Cochabamba conference of 2010.

Last but not least, the pluralism of Québec Solidaire, its desire to include within its ranks all those in Quebec who wish to fight for another, better world, opens space for revolutionary socialists and Marxists to join the party and to fight for their perspectives within the party as organized "collectives" democratically recognized by the party's statutes although not represented as such in its leadership bodies. Although they have maintained a rather low profile so far, some of these collectives could play a leading role in helping to bring theoretical understanding and clarity to the evolving debates on the party's program and its activities. Perhaps more importantly, they could help to overcome a glaring deficiency in the party: its lack of any coherent organized educational effort among its members and the larger left constituency.

This paper has described in considerable detail the process of formation of Québec Solidaire because it has features that can serve as guides for other processes in other settings. The left groups that initiated the process recognized a shift in the objective situation — in this case the growing disillusionment with the PQ, the new vibrancy of the women's movement, and the appearance of a new altermondialiste movement mobilizing young people in opposition to capitalist oppression and injustice. They laid down a minimal set of principles for regroupment and consolidation: a strategic framework of striving for the independence of Quebec; feminism, both programmatically and organizationally (as in male-female parity in party structures); pluralism, inclusion of all who agreed to support and work to implement the party's "values" and general orientations, and respect for minority opinions including the right

39 Québec Solidaire was a strong supporter of the recent "Boat to Gaza" solidarity project, delegating a QS leader, Manon Massé, to participate personally on the party's behalf in the international attempt to breach the Israeli blockade of the Palestinian statelet.

of members with particular perspectives to organize within the party in support of their views; internationalism — placing anti-imperialism, solidarity and global justice at the core of the new party's politics.

And throughout, they were willing to let the process follow its own rhythm. As Pierre Dostie said, in describing the UFP's approach to fusion with Option citoyenne, the latter "had to comply with its own process, [so] we sought areas of convergence and we entered into a dialogue." (note 15, supra)

The goal is to build a party that encompasses and represents the leading militants in all those movements that are, in various ways, engaged in struggles against capital.

The future of Québec Solidaire is closely linked to its ability to become more integrated in Quebec's broad labour-radical subculture, and to develop the "reciprocal relationship" with the trade union and popular movements that is outlined in the policy commission proposal.

To the degree that it does this, the social and ethnic composition of the party will change. QS is still a "white" party, for example. Neither its membership nor its leading bodies reflect the diverse ethnic and immigrant composition of Quebec. It is no accident that its major achievements so far, the election of Amir Khadir, an Iranian-Quebecois with deep roots in the independence movement, was scored in one of Montréal's most ethnically diverse constituencies. Québec Solidaire cannot yet be characterized as an anticapitalist party. But it is fair to say that it is much more than a Québécois version of, say, the federal NDP. Some important features of the party underscore its sui generis nature and offer hope for its evolution and development into a mass socialist party with deep roots among Quebec working people.

REFERENCES

À Bâbord ! (February-March 2005). *Négociations UFP-Option Citoyenne: Go! Go! Gauche!*.

Chantier de l'économie sociale (March 28, 2011). *Définition*. Retrieved from http://www.chantier.qc.ca/?module=document&uid=871.

Cooke, M. (2004). *Constitutional Confusion on the Left: The NDP's Position in Canada's Constitutional Debates*. Retrieved from http://www.cpsa-acsp.ca/papers-2004/Cooke.pdf

Dostie, P. *et al. (2006).Quelques repères dans l'histoire de la gauche politique québécoise*. (website of the Union des forces progressistes, no longer available).

Dubuc, P. (2003). L'autre histoire de l'indépendance *(Éditions Trois-Pistoles,*

Éditions du Renouveau québécois).

Dufour, P. (2009). From protest to partisan politics: When and how collective actors cross the line. Sociological perspectives on Québec Solidaire, *Canadian Journal of Sociology/Cahiers canadiens de sociologie* 34(1), PAGE Range.

Fidler, R. (December 10, 2003). *Quebec's new united left party*. Retrieved from http://www.greenleft.org.au/node/28531

—. (December 10, 2006). *Québec Solidaire Adopts a Program for Government*. Retrieved from http://www.socialistvoice.ca/?p=142

—. (December 15, 2008). *Québec Solidaire scores major breakthrough in Quebec election*. Retrieved from http://lifeonleft.blogspot.com/2008/12/qubec-solidaire- scores-major.html

—. (December 4, 2009). *Quebec left debates strategy for independence*. Retrieved from http://lifeonleft.blogspot.com/2009/12/quebec-left-debates-strategy-for.html

—. (2011a). *Beyond capitalism? Québec Solidaire launches debate on its program for social transformation. Retrieved from http://www.socialistproject.ca/bullet/491.php*

—. (2011b). *The federal NDP's electoral breakthrough in Quebec: A challenge to progressives in Canada*. Retrieved from http://lifeonleft.blogspot.com/2011/05/federal-ndps-electoral-breakthrough-in.html

—. (2011c).*More on that election*. Retrieved from http://lifeonleft.blogspot.com/2011/05/more-on-that-election.html

—. (2011d). *Layton chooses Supreme Court, Clarity Act over NDP's Sherbrooke Declaration. Retrieved from* http://lifeonleft.blogspot.com/2011/05/layton-chooses-supreme-court-clarity.html

—. (2011e). *Behind those resignations from the Parti Québécois*. Retrieved from http://lifeonleft.blogspot.com/2011/06/behind-those-resignations-from-parti.html

Gagnon, H. (n.d.). *Les Militants socialistes du Québec*. Retrieved from http://www.pcq.qc.ca/Dossiers/PCQ/Histoire/LesMilitantsSocialistes.pdf

Lavallée, J, (2011). *Du parti de la démocratie socialiste à Québec Solidaire," in La gauche au Québec depuis 1945*, (Bulletin d'histoire politique, 19, 2, Winter 2011), p. 202-14.

Moreau, F. (1986). Balance Sheet of the Quebec Far Left. *Retrieved from* http://socialisthistory.ca/Docs/History/Bilan-Moreau-English.htm

Neamtam, N.. (2010). *Interview: Integration with trade unions is key to the success of Social/Solidarity Economy Initiatives*. Retrieved from http://www.chantier.qc.ca/?module=document&action=get&uid=1059

Option Citoyenne. (2004). *Document préparatoire à la rencontre nationale*. Retrieved from http://www.lagauche.com/lagauche/spip.php?article1078

Parti Socialiste du Québec. (1966). Programme 66. Longueil: Les Presses

Sociales.

Québec Solidaire (2009b). *Définition du programme politique.* Retrieved from http://programme.quebecsolidaire.net/definition

—. (2009a). *Pour Sortir de la Crise: Dépasser le Capitalisme? Manifeste de Québec Solidaire.* Retrieved from http://www.quebecsolidaire.net/files/2009-05- Manifeste-Crise.pdf

—. (2011). *Pour un pays de projets.* Retrieved from www.paysdeprojets.org

—. (2010). Pour une société solidaire et écologique....Cahier de participation au programme, Enjeu 2.Retrieved from http://programme.quebecsolidaire.net/documents/CAHIER_DE_PARTICIPATION corrige.pdf#page=5

Regina Manifesto. (1933). Title (italics) Retrieved from http://www.saskndp.ca/assets/File/history/manifest.pdf

Université du Québec à Montréal. (2008). *Chaire de recherche en économie sociale. Portrait statistique de l'économie sociale de la région administrative de Montréal.* Retrieved from http://www.credemontreal.qc.ca/Publications/Developpement%20Economique/P ortrait%20 statistique%20economie%20sociale.pdf

On Knowledge Production, Learning and Research in Struggle

Aziz Choudry[1]

[T]he most powerful, visionary dreams of a new society don't come from little think tanks of smart people or out of the atomized, individualistic world of consumer capitalism, where raging against the status quo is simply the hip thing to do. Revolutionary dreams erupt out of political engagement; collective social movements are incubators of new knowledge (Robin Kelley, 2002, p. 8).

INTRODUCTION

In his book, *Freedom dreams: The black radical imagination*, historian Robin Kelley (2002) points out that social movements generate new knowledge, questions, and theory.[2] He also emphasizes the need for concrete and critical engagement with the movements confronting the problems of oppressed peoples. In this article I discuss the politics of learning, knowledge production and research "from the ground up"–that which takes place in social action/social movement contexts. While on the one hand, scholarship on social movements owes significant intellectual debts to the learning, knowledge production and theorizing which occur in the course of social struggles, on the other, the intellectual work, ideas and analysis which emerge from concrete engagement in these struggles are often overlooked and undervalued by the dominant theorizing practices of the academy. Further, drawing firstly from the author's involvement with research and activism around Montreal's

---

1 Aziz Choudry is Assistant Professor, International Education, in the Department of Integrated Studies in Education, McGill University (Montreal, Canada). He recently co-edited *Organize! Building from the local for global justice, Learning from the Ground Up: Global Perspectives on Social Movements and Knowledge Production*, and *Fight Back: Workplace Justice for Immigrants*. He can be reached at: aziz.choudry@mcgill.ca

2 An earlier draft of this paper was presented at "Varieties of Socialism, Varieties of Approaches", organized by the Critical Social Research Collaborative (www.csrcproject.ca), Carleton University, Ottawa, 5 March 2011.

Immigrant Workers Centre and wider struggles for immigration/labour justice, and secondly from global justice/anti-colonial organizing in Aotearoa/New Zealand and the Asia-Pacific region, for this discussion, this paper argues that critical scholarship should strive to be engaged concretely with social struggles and the knowledge produced in these contexts for both political and intellectual reasons.

A growing interdisciplinary body of literature explores the politics and processes of knowledge production from within social movement and political activist milieus. In their article on "movement-relevant theory," Doug Bevington and Chris Dixon (2005) note that just as few activists read social movement theory, important debates inside movement networks often do not enter the scholarly literature about social movements. They contend that social movement scholars do not have a monopoly on theory about movements. They call for recognition of existing movement-generated theory and of dynamic reciprocal engagement by theorists and movement activists in formulating, producing, refining and applying research. They hold that: "[m]ovement participants produce theory as well, although much of it may not be recognizable to conventional social movement studies. This kind of theory both ranges and traverses through multiple levels of abstraction, from everyday organizing to broad analysis" (p. 195). As Flacks (2004) asserts, much social movement theory is being driven by attempts to define and refine theoretical concepts which are likely to be "irrelevant or obvious to organizers" (p. 147). Kelley (2002) notes that "too often, our standards for evaluating social movements pivot around whether or not they 'succeeded' in realizing their visions rather than on their merits or power of the visions themselves" (p. ix).

There are dominant tendencies–even among those on the left, within the university and outside–to make assumptions in relation to the relative value and significance of the location of intellectual work (in universities or in a myriad of everyday social action settings), what processes of knowledge production are recognized, and what counts as knowledge, theory or research. As Alan Sears (2005) puts it, deeper theoretical work is crucial, but "is not simply the property of specialized theorists with lots of formal education." (p.151). The historian Staughton Lynd (2011) reminds us that "of the principal luminaries of …Marxism, no one- not Marx, not Engels, not Plekhanov, not Lenin, not Trotsky, not Bukharin, not Rosa Luxemburg (who has a particular contempt for professors), not Antonio Gramsci, not Mao-Tse Tung–put bread on the table by university teaching…without exception the most significant contributions to Marxist thought have come from men and women who were not academics, who passed through the university but did not remain there" (p.144). In addition, there are many located outside of universities who, as Maori educationalist Linda Smith (1999) notes "are referred to as project workers, community activists or consultants, anything but 'researchers'. They search and record, they select and interpret, they organize and re-present, they make claims on the basis of what they assemble. This is research" (p.17).

The voices, ideas, and, indeed, theories produced by those engaged in social struggles are often ignored, rendered invisible, or overwritten with accounts by professionalized 'experts' or university-based intellectuals. In the realm of academic knowledge production, original, single authorship is highly valued, which can contribute to a tendency to fail to acknowledge the intellectual contributions of activism, or to recognize the lineages of ideas and theories that have been forged in struggles largely outside of universities, often incrementally, collectively, informally, and sometimes incidentally. An example of scholarly work which has explored the impact of anti-colonial struggles on an influential academic theoretical tradition is the attention that Tavares (1992) and Buck-Morss (2009) have brought to the way in which the Haitian revolution (the first and only successful slave revolution in the Americas) influenced Hegel's theorizing–in particular the master-slave dialectic. Marx (1984) rewrote his theory of the state under the impact of the Paris Commune. Raya Dunayevskaya (1958) points out that the spur to finishing the first volume of Capital came from the revival of the British working class movement in the context of the U.S. civil war. Many examples of feminist, anti-racist, and Indigenous scholarship have also arisen and benefited from mass mobilizations challenging patriarchal, racist, colonial–and often capitalist–relations. Yet within the university, there remains relatively little awareness of the many important debates and thinking occurring within those networks of activists, social movements, trade unions, community organizations and NGOs that take more critical stances in relation to state power and capital.

Further, we should be aware of the importance of drawing from those who have sought to extend Marx, firstly, in terms of thinkers who have emerged from, and been closely tied to anti-colonial and other left democratic struggles in the global south, such as Fanon (1968), Aijaz Ahmad (2000), C.L.R. James (1963), and many others. How, where and in which forms social struggles take place may differ greatly from context to context and challenge some of the dominant lenses applied to typologizing/categorizing them as both Bayat (1997, 2010) and Eschle (2001) remind us. In thinking through the challenges of theorizing social relations and struggles in both global south and north, Himani Bannerji (2011) contends that "historical and social realities of the world are neither macro-spaces of free-floating imaginaries and abstractions nor bounded within micro-formations and spaces of geographically discrete cultural identities" (p.3). Equally, these diverse contexts can be important sites of knowledge production and conceptual tools for other struggles. Biju Mathew (2005) suggests that "[m]aybe our collective task ...is to look carefully as the resurgent left social movements all across Africa, Asia and Latin America and comprehend the ideas of justice that inhere within these movements and the historical memory they are rooted in" (203). David Austin (2009) describes theory as being "congealed experience, which, in a concentrated form, can bring years of accumulated knowledge to bear on a particular issue or cause and help to prevent strategic mishaps" (p.115), while Kelley (2002) also reminds us of the importance of drawing conceptual resources for contemporary struggles from critical readings of histories of older movements.

Theorizing social movements, NGOs, community organizations and 'civil society' at a level which is too abstracted from the very real differences, contradictions and particularities on the ground, especially the geo-historical context, has severe limitations. As adult educationalist Paula Allman (2001, p.165) puts it, "our action in and on the material world is the mediation or link between our consciousness and objective reality. Our consciousness develops from our active engagement with other people, nature, and the objects or processes we produce. In other words, it develops from the sensuous experiencing of reality from within the social relations in which we exist (Marx and Engels, 1846)."

Analysis of social movements need to be situated in social dynamics and concrete conditions. Bannerji (2011) reminds us that "all meaningful, useful generalizations need to be shown as having a material, a social/existential and an historical ontology. To think otherwise is to indulge in the absurdity of separating human consciousness from existing human beings and detaching both from lived time. Thus micro-histories are part of history or history's mode of existence, they are inconceivable without each other, and subjugated knowledges are the pedestals of the dominant knowledge" (p.4). Thus, in order to understand social movements we need to carefully attend to the political, historical, cultural and economic forces that are at play in any one place, and explicate how they relate to the state, to capital, and to each other. The dominant strands of social movement theory tend to be reductionist, Eurocentric, and disconnected from the social movements and organizations that are the objects of its study. Some movements are overlooked or ignored simply because they do not conform to a model or typology through which the researcher approaches the subject (Eschle, 2001). Inadequate attention is given to questions of geo-history, political economy, and to the politics of knowledge production, both in terms of constructing theory, and of the knowledge(s) emerging from movements. I suggest that a sounder analytical framework might draw from knowledge and theory arising from movements themselves. It would recognize the importance of "history from below" rather than seeking to only interpret movements and mobilizations solely through an imposed interpretative framework or set of variables. Close attention must be paid to analyzing the trends of bureaucratization and professionalization in these movement and NGO networks.

So theory is not merely created from above to be imposed on material conditions of struggle–it is also born out of practice. Just as D. Smith (1987, p. 80) notes "the basis for a political economy from the standpoint of labour, according to Marx, is precisely that it is grounded in the work and activity of actual individuals producing their existence under definite material conditions," so too does theory and analysis about NGO and social movement networks require such a concrete grounding in our everyday activities in the world.

LEARNING FROM THE GROUND UP

In his work on social movements and radical adult education, John Holst (2002) refers to the "pedagogy of mobilization" to describe the learning inherent in the building and maintaining of a social movement and its organizations. Through participation in a social movement, people learn numerous skills and ways of thinking analytically and strategically as they struggle to understand their movement in motion.... Moreover, as coalitions are formed people's understanding of the interconnectedness of relations within a social totality become increasingly sophisticated (Holst, 2002, pp. 87–88). Both Holst and Griff Foley's (1999) work on learning in social action highlight and value the incremental learning and building of knowledge, which arises from actual and dialectical engagement in our everyday world.

Located in a historical materialist framework, Foley's (1999) book, *Learning in Social Action: A Contribution to Understanding Informal Education* makes a vital contribution to theorizing and making explicit the incidental learning processes arising from and contributing to engagement in a range of social struggles. Foley emphasizes the importance of "developing an understanding of learning in popular struggle" (p.140). His attention to documenting, making explicit, and valuing incidental forms of learning and knowledge production in social action is in keeping with others who understand that critical consciousness, rigorous research, and theory can and do emerge from engagement in action and organizing contexts, rather than as ideas developed elsewhere by movement elites and dropped down from "above" to "the people" (Smith, 1999; Shragge, 2003; Carroll, 2004; Bevington & Dixon, 2005; Kelley, 2002; Kinsman, 2006; Newman, 2006). In doing so, Foley cautions that although learning through involvement in social struggles can indeed transform power relations, it can also be contradictory and ambiguous.

Critical alternatives arise from struggle, active engagement, reflection and action. There remains much work to be done in thinking through what kinds of social relations, contexts and circumstances help people move from learning only to adapt to learning that supports resistance, and which can generate theoretical insights and more complex understandings about the world. For Foley (1999) this involves theorizing experience, standing back from it, and reordering it, using categories like power, conflict, structure, values and choice. Novelli (2010) highlights the dialectics of strategic learning through struggle and contestation which includes incidental, formal, informal, and non-formal education. This implies an engagement in "strategic analysis, which in turn leads to strategic action, and then to intended and unintended consequences of action, and to further reflection/analysis and action" (p.124). Foley suggests that we need to make case studies of learning in struggle which make explanatory connections "between learning and education on the one hand, and analysis of political economy, micro-politics, ideology and discourse (or 'discursive practices') on the other (p.9). He highlights the importance of embracing a broad conception of education and learning, the relationship between struggle and learning, and an analytical framework which connects learning to its context.

I turn now to discuss two examples of activist learning, knowledge production, research and theorizing in social action contexts to further illustrate the significance of these sites and their contributions to intellectual work. Firstly, I reflect upon questions of knowledge production, research and theorizing in the context of 'global justice' struggles against trade and investment liberalization in networks of NGOs, trade unions and social movements opposing the Asia Pacific Economic Cooperation (APEC) forum during the 1990s. Secondly, I discuss aspects of the learning and knowledge production in contemporary immigrant and migrant workers' struggles. Finally, I share some critiques of NGOization which have emerged from within activist milieus engaged in struggles against global capitalism in recent decades.

RESEARCH, KNOWLEDGE PRODUCTION AND ACTIVISM

As noted earlier, social movements and activist milieux can be important sites of research which takes place outside of formal and/or professionalized research settings such as universities. Effective research can help move activist practice beyond reacting only to the immediate, and inform longer-term strategy and vision. This is not to claim that all 'activist research' is inherently progressive or rigorous - anymore than all university research can claim to be rigorous and immaculately constructed. Nor is it argued that academic and activist research necessarily exist in finite, separate worlds, although sometimes this might seem to be the case.

Much activist research of the kind that I have engaged in involves an ongoing process of research in which information has to serve a purpose, is ongoing, and not usually channeled towards the production of one particular research output. Taking the time to "get the research right" is crucial–whether in the case of adequately researching details of a meeting venue in order to mount an effective protest action, or in the more formal sense of research on a corporation, policy or practice, which, if poorly researched, can be easily, and publicly discredited by a far better-resourced protagonist and media outlets. This in turn can have serious effects on efforts to build a campaign through reaching and mobilizing a broader base of people. A central aspect of effective activist research is the relationship of trust and engagement built up with social struggles and movements. Articulating or explicating activist research methodologies from our own practices (and those of colleagues) is an interesting, and perhaps challenging task which falls outside of the scope of this article. But the notion that there is some kind of natural separation between what some have called the 'brain' and the 'brawn' of movement is to be challenged since intellectual work, knowledge production, and forms of investigation/research which take place within activism are often inextricably linked to action in many mobilizations, although sometimes overlooked or unrecognized (see Choudry and Kuyek, forthcoming, 2012). Kinsman (2006) warns: "Sometimes when we talk about research and activism in the academic world we replicate distinctions around notions of consciousness and activity that are detrimental to our objectives. We can fall back on research as being an analysis, or a particular form of consciousness, and activism as about doing things "out there", which leads to a divorce between consciousness and practice" (p.153). In turn, we should also be wary of replicating such dynamics in activist milieux.

Political activist ethnography, which builds on Dorothy Smith's (1987) work on institutional ethnography, offers useful tools for activist research and knowledge production. George Smith (2006) suggests that for activist researchers, there is a wealth of research material and signposts derived from moments of confrontation to explore the way that power in our world is socially organized. He contends that being interrogated by insiders to a ruling regime, like a crown attorney for example, brings a researcher into direct contact with the conceptual relevancies and organizing principles of such regimes.

Moments of confrontation with ruling regimes were crucial to uncovering aspects of their social organization in global justice activism and research which I have been part of, before entering the university as a student, and, more recently, as faculty. During the 1990s, I was an organizer, educator and researcher for two small Aotearoa/New Zealand-based activist groups, GATT Watchdog and the Aotearoa/New Zealand APEC Monitoring Group which focused on building opposition to free trade and investment agreements, at domestic and regional (Asia-Pacific) levels. A major focus was the Asia Pacific Economic Cooperation (APEC) process that included 21 governments in the region, with a goal to advance trade and investment liberalization. APEC's highest profile event was a Leaders' summit, which rotated among APEC member countries each year, and had become a target for mobilizations against neoliberal globalization. An important goal for anti-APEC activism has been to delegitimize the APEC forum and to expose APEC governments' claims of 'civil society' involvement and consultation as a sham. Analysis of official texts was a key aspect of practice that informed strategy for the opposition to the hosting of APEC 1999 in Aotearoa/New Zealand. In 1998, well in advance of the start of New Zealand's chairing of APEC the following year, I obtained a New Zealand Cabinet Strategy Committee paper "APEC 1999–Engagement With NGOs" (New Zealand Government, 1998) for GATT Watchdog under New Zealand's Official Information Act (Access to Information Act). From analyzing this document, it became evident that government intentions were to co-opt NGOs and harness them to promote APEC domestically, and also to project to international audiences an image of a democratic government which valued differing opinions. Deletions in the document clearly refer to managing the risks (militant opposition to APEC), since there are several references to risk management and preparedness for "a protest element", but gave no specific details to what this entailed, corresponding to sections that have been withheld. What remains in the document is instructive. On the positive side, the Government has a real opportunity to develop a wider sense of ownership and participation. Ensuring constructive participation by NGOs in the APEC process will be a critical part of the overall strategy of communicating the what, why and how of APEC to the New Zealand community. It would serve to demonstrate to the international community New Zealand's ability, as a participatory democracy, to accommodate debate and dissent among a variety of NGOs… On the other hand, as the experience of CHOGM and the MAI indicated, there is significant risk of disruption and protest at APEC events. In particular we are likely to see a protest element around the Leaders' Meeting in Auckland in September (p.3).

The document also advised that "New Zealand's chairing of APEC should reflect the values of an open and participatory democracy where NGOs have an opportunity freely to express their views" (p.5). "We propose a dual strategy of constructive engagement: [paragraph deleted]" and then:

The target audience in this strategy is not just NGOs per se, but also the wider group of "middle" New Zealand who will want to see NGO voices given a fair hearing. [Deletion] This will require engaging effectively with responsive groups and helping to meet, as far as possible, their own objectives of being seen to influence outcomes…the requirement for cost-effectiveness suggests there will be limits to the extent of outreach that may be possible. It will be important to avoid getting bogged down in long, resource-intensive consultations (p.6).

The strategy "involves building broad support for APEC and actively managing the risk of disruption" (my italics) (p.7). The New Zealand government's NGO engagement strategy paper was a clear example of a document which operates in the state's interest in drawing up a plan to contain dissent and manage the government's image, rather than being a background paper to inform a dialogue among equals. By its use of the term "responsive groups", the government assumed the right to determine who was in and who was out in New Zealand 'civil society'. It also clearly sought to divide and rule NGOs (and other groups) into supposedly constructive and disruptive elements.

For GATT Watchdog and Aotearoa/New Zealand APEC Monitoring Group activists, our reading of the document was accomplished because of our own confrontation with the government over APEC, experience of being targeted by New Zealand state security forces for lawful dissent against APEC in 1996, involvement in previous years' anti-APEC mobilizations in several countries, and interactions with police at demonstrations and increased surveillance during 1999. Having these experiences and analysis was important, but collecting, analyzing and disseminating these documents was essential to building an effective strategy to counter the government's promotion of APEC to NGO networks and community organizations. Drawing from these documents, a key part of our anti-APEC strategy of 1999 was to explicitly and publicly denounce the New Zealand Government's APEC Taskforce communications strategy, and to politicize attempts to co-opt or silence critics through 'dialogue' in a similar fashion to that revealed in Canadian official documents relating to the Vancouver APEC summit.

This included a picket of the first dialogue on APEC 1999 with NGOs outside the office of the Ministry of Foreign Affairs and Trade in Wellington in January 1999, and a rejection of approaches made by the official APEC NGO Liaison officer (hired by the New Zealand Government's APEC Taskforce) to discuss APEC matters. Through media work and dissemination through NGO and community group mailings and meetings, we publicly revealed the government strategy of containment and propaganda through limited dialogue and state surveillance and harassment of the more radical critics. Our strategy involved politicizing the disjuncture between stated intentions for dialogue, the calculated actual rationale expressed by the official documents obtained under the Official Information Act, and past actual experience of state practice of criminalization of lawful dissenters who were critical of free trade and investment. After we circulated the Cabinet papers to a wide range of NGOs and trade unions, the government's plan to co-opt NGOs and harness them to do their work of selling APEC to "middle" New Zealand failed dismally, with few attending their NGO consultation sessions. The operation of the Official Information Act, and broader questions of transparency, state power and claims of democracy became politicized in this research activism work when various government ministries either refused to divulge or release information, or insisted on imposing expensive processing fees before even considering a request. In turn, we publicized this through mainstream and independent media, finding some journalists sympathetic on this issue for their own reasons of frustration over obstacles to accessing official information, and willing to write critical articles on the matter.

LEARNING AND KNOWLEDGE PRODUCTION IN IM/MIGRANT WORKERS' STRUGGLES

I turn now to focus on aspects of the politics of learning and knowledge production in migrant and immigrant workers' struggles both in Canada and in international networks. DeFilippis, Fisher and Shragge (2010) argue that for community organizations to be part of a broader longer-term movement for social change, social analysis and political education are vital. They argue that "[b]oth contribute to understanding that the specific gains made and the struggles organizations undertake are part of something larger, but so is the broader political economy that structures organizational choices" (p.177).

Montreal's Immigrant Workers' Centre (IWC) was set up in 2000 as a community-based workers' organization in the diverse, working-class neighbourhood of Côte-des-Neiges by some Filipino-Canadian union and former union organizers, and other activist and academic allies.[3] The IWC engages in individual rights counseling and casework, as well as popular education and political campaigns that reflect the general issues facing immigrant and temporary foreign workers–dismissal, problems with employers, and sometimes inadequate representation by their unions. Often these arise from individual cases and form the basis for campaigns and demands which are expressed collectively. Labour education is a priority, targeting organizations in the community and increasing workers' skills and analysis. Workshops on themes such as the history of the labour movement, the Labour Standards Act and collective organizing processes have been presented in many organizations that work with immigrants as well as at the IWC itself. For example, the "Skills for Change" program teaches basic computer literacy, while incorporating workplace analysis and information on labour rights and supporting individuals in becoming more active in defending those rights in their workplaces. The IWC strives to develop leadership among immigrant workers in order to take action on their own behalf. Support for self-organizing, direct action, coalition-building and campaigning are used to win gains for workers and to build broader awareness of and support for systemic change in relation to their working conditions and, often, immigration status. As IWC organizer Mostafa Henaway (forthcoming 2012) puts it, the Centre:

tries to build from an organizing model that incorporates radical traditions, going back to basics, focusing on outreach, collective organizing, casework, and education. At times, there are many challenges faced in balancing all of these facets in the organization; but each facet

3 Immigrant Workers Centre Website: http://iwc-cti.ca

has proven to be critically important to the political work of the centre, such as weekly outreach outside Metro [subway] stations, building relationships with both communities and individual immigrant workers, or attempts to collectivize the casework and individual issues faced by workers, and to respond in a politicized way. The foundation of this organizing has come from these principal organizing methods, in addition to a flexibility in tactics and strategy, due to ever-changing economic conditions in Montreal, and globally.

Significantly, organizations such as the Immigrant Workers Centre, and the workers' struggles that they support can be key sites of informal and non-formal learning and knowledge production for labour justice struggles. This process occurs through workers' struggles and contestation of their conditions and rights and is important in winning gains for workers. A recent study on immigrant workers' struggles in Quebec, which conducted extensive interviews (Choudry et al. 2009, p. 112) notes:

Individuals that did eventually take action always did so with the support of others, who provided information and other resources to help them in a dispute with an employer. These others can be unions, community organizations or co-workers or friends with whom they have informal relationships. 'Street smarts' and small victories are shared between people: this in turn encourages others to take action. Such learning most often grows out of pre-existing relations with other individuals, peers or friends. However, organizations play a key role.

This study found that learning to question or to resist exists in tension with learning to cope, adapt or 'get by'–as indeed it does in workplace industrial relations since the emergence of capitalism. Sometimes, as Rodriguez (2010) notes, such knowledge forms contest not only the power (and knowledge) produced by governments, but also that of professionalized non-governmental organizations (NGOs) which purport to speak on behalf of migrant workers. But building alliances with trade unions, through education and supporting internal debates occurring within organized labour to encourage unions to more meaningfully represent the needs and concerns of immigrant and migrant workers is an important aspect of these local and global struggles for justice. As Mathew (2005) and others note, migrant and immigrant workers can and do bring their own histories of struggle and organizing strategies from their countries of origin to the new countries in which they labour.

For those of us located in universities and engaged in research on im/migrant workers this work requires some careful reflection and political commitment. Commenting on the role of a growing number of NGOs and think-tanks which purport to represent migrant workers' interests at national and international levels, yet exclude workers themselves, Rodriguez (2010) argues that it is vital to pay attention to the knowledge production of those excluded from official venues and who cannot participate in the circuits, virtual and otherwise, frequented by others in the 'global justice movement'. She says (p. 67),

In order to be able to document the kinds of struggles engaged in by migrant worker activists…requires some level of political investment on our part as scholars, for it is in spaces outside of the seats of power, like the space of the street, where migrants can come together not only to narrate their experiences, but also to articulate radical alternatives to the contemporary global order.

We must also be aware of the politics of which campaigns, organizations and movements are documented, and which are not. For, as Rahila Gupta (2004, p. 3) of Southall Black Sisters, a long-established organization supporting Asian and African-Caribbean women against violence in Britain notes, it is not easy for activists "to sit down and record their work, but in this age of information overload you need to record in order almost to prove that you exist." Indeed, for engaged academics working on immigration and labour issues, and for organizers on the frontlines of struggles for social justice, the analyses and knowledge produced in the course of such struggles can be seen as not only important intellectual contributions, but as rich conceptual resources for understanding and challenging the continued exploitation and commodification of migrant workers and immigrants, locally and internationally.

The politics of activist research are inevitably impacted by challenges related to mobilizing and maintaining support, continuity and accountability among (and between) activist researchers and broader social struggles. Funding and institutional recognition of movement research is not necessarily proportionate to the utility of such work, especially if it is disconnected from the task of building and supporting movements, but rather oriented towards outputs intended to influence decision-makers in government, private sectors or international organizations. Indeed, some NGO research is driven by project-centric cycles and/or compartmentalized logics that are disconnected from social struggles, and more reflective of tensions around funding priorities (Petras and Veltmeyer, 2001; Bazan *et al.*, 2008). In the above examples, small activist groups which operated on a shoestring budget were able to uncover, analyze and disseminate their research through popular education and relationships with other organizations.

NGOS, NGOIZATION AND THE 'GLOBAL JUSTICE' MOVEMENT

The past decades have seen the ascendancy of non-governmental organizations (NGOs) and the widespread valorization of the notion of "civil society" at global and local levels. Fowler (2000) sees a number of factors which account for the growth of NGOs involved in Third World development, and their increased relationships with governments and the private sector. He sees the rightwards shift in Northern politics during the Reagan-Thatcher era as key to "the start of the rise in official finance to, and number of NGOs that continues today" (p. 2). This was due to the move away from government to the market as the engine of growth and progress, and "meant more responsibility to citizens and their organizations" (ibid). Although funds used to flow primarily from Northern governments or financial institutions to Southern governments, NGOs have increasingly become channels for, and direct recipients of this 'development assistance' (Hancock, 1989; Biel, 2000; Petras and Veltmeyer, 2001; Wallace, 2003; Hewson, 2005). There has been an enormous amount of celebratory and triumphalist writing about "civil society", and both development and advocacy NGOs as being inherently "good" - forces for progressive change. Such claims often fail to consider who is included in and excluded from "civil society", and pay inadequate attention to the power and role of the state, private sector and international institutions in relation to NGO/community organization milieus which, many argue, are complicit with, and dependent upon the state. Even before the fiscal austerity and public sector cuts of the Reagan-Thatcher era, United Nations conferences, increasing intergovernmental forums, agreements, treaties and negotiations had been accompanied by a parallel process of international NGO meetings, campaigns and other activity. Besides the institutionalization of NGO involvement in the various arms of the United Nations, the policies and statements of intergovernmental organizations such as the World Bank (2008) and the Asian Development Bank (Asian Development Bank, 1998) and their representatives have also set parameters for which kinds of NGOs will be validated by dialogue or other forms of engagement.

Alongside this, for many years, a number of critiques of NGOs and "NGOization" have been advanced by feminist, Marxist, critical race and other critical scholars. These include Jad's (2004) work on the NGOization, cooptation and undermining of the women's movement and other parts of Palestinian "civil society", Kamat's (2002, 2004) work on the impacts of NGOization and the growth of NGOs on political space and development in India and internationally, and INCITE! Women of Color

Against Violence's (2007) recent analyses of the "non-profit industrial complex" in the Americas. For Petras and Veltmeyer, (2005), and others, the professionalization of community-based NGOs and their depoliticization works well for neoliberal regimes, keeping "the existing power structure (vis-à-vis the distribution of society's resources) intact while promoting a degree (and a local form) of change and development" (p.20). Indeed, neoliberal states have often downloaded, privatized and individualized responsibility for social welfare and 'development' via NGOs and community organizations. In turn, if we trace the lineage of existing scholarly critiques of NGOs and institutionalization/demobilization, such analyses of NGOization often owe a debt to collective forms of critical knowledge production, learning and debates emerging from within social movements and activist networks committed to progressive social change. Often these tensions and critiques are raised and even worked out in practice before being subjected to academic inquiry.

There is a relationship between the NGOization of social change and its impact on knowledge production, and the disciplining of dissent at national and global levels. Elsewhere (Choudry, 2009, 2010a, 2010b, Choudry and Shragge, 2011), I interrogate how, within supposedly 'alternative' global justice networks, a relatively small NGO elite attempts to claim positional superiority for forms of professionalized knowledge and advocacy that attempt to sideline, filter, or erase more critical positions opposed to capitalism and colonialism. While emphasizing the importance of context-specific approaches to understanding NGOs and social movements, I contend that the dominant tendency of NGOs is to compartmentalize the world into 'issues,' and 'projects', and the practice of an "ideology of pragmatism" (Choudry, 2010b, p.20) which entails an unwillingness to name or confront capitalism. A form of colonial amnesia seems particularly entrenched in many social justice networks in settler colonial-states like Aotearoa/New Zealand, Canada and Australia. A liberal "white economic progressive nationalist" (Choudry, 2010b, p.27) nostalgia underpins the framing of alternatives to neoliberalism, entailing the erasure or writing out of Canada's own ongoing colonial injustices and struggles by Indigenous Peoples for self-determination, and rendering invisible the historical and present-day experiences and struggles of racialized communities. These positions, which replicate, rather than challenge dominant national practices, serve to undermine and contain more critical forms of knowledge production and action in relation to confronting global capitalism. But these processes are also being challenged by ideas and mobilization strategies arising from past and present anti-imperialist and anti-colonial struggles.

In sum, even within movement networks purportedly committed to 'global justice', one finds hierarchies and dynamics around power and knowledge similar to that found in the academy. Frequently, for example, questions of immigration, indigenous sovereignty, racism and colonialism are viewed as separate, unrelated issues by NGOs and activists critical of neoliberal globalization in the North, while they are often seen as intimately connected by movements in the South (Sivanandan, 1982; Petras and Veltmeyer, 2001; Mathew, 2005). Many NGOs in the North and South replicate dominant approaches to hierarchies of knowledge by favouring academic, professionalized forms over learning developed in social struggles.

CONCLUSION: A CALL FOR REENGAGEMENT OF ACADEMICS

There is a danger that the conventional processes of production of academic scholarship, and assumptions or claims that such activity constitutes the apex of intellectual rigour and inquiry, can in fact overlook the complexities and dynamics of activism, and the intellectual contributions of activist practice (Bevington & Dixon, 2005; Frampton et al., 2006). I do not imply that these various epistemologies of knowledge (academic and activist) and processes of knowledge production and learning (formal, non-formal, and informal) exist in completely separate universes. Yet it seems important to consider how critically engaged scholars located in universities can avoid replicating the tendency to ignore or misconstrue forms of social action and the knowledge produced therein, because they do not fit neatly within a pre-established theoretical framework? Academic work on activism and social movements requires some level of political investment on our part as scholars. It also requires an acknowledgement of the intellectual debts that many of us have to knowledge and theory arising from conversations, debates, discussions, dilemmas in the everyday worlds of organizing for social change, reconnecting with ideas and action and the importance of context/dynamics of institutionalization. If we are to play a role in creating a future in a world marked by devastating economic and ecological crises, militarized violence, war and occupation, in which Canada is complicit, we need to urgently direct some thought and energy towards building social movements. We now face a period of global economic and political crisis–to be addressed by austerity measures which download the social costs onto the poor and marginalized (McNally, 2011). We need movements to create counterpower and radical alternatives to the prevailing world order which is steeped in colonialism, imperialism and war, by building upon, and in dialogue with the intellectual/conceptual resources produced in the course of social movement activism. Perhaps one of the most important challenges in the early part of the 21st century for those of us who are privileged to work in universities and are committed to social justice, is to connect, reconnect, renew and ground our scholarly work with/in continuing struggles here in Canada, and around the world. And to make our work count. For, as Marx (1968) noted nearly two hundred years ago, "The philosophers have only interpreted the world, in various ways; the point is to change it". In *Theses on Feuerbach (ibid)*, he further reminds us: "All social life is essentially practical. All mysteries which lead theory to mysticism find their rational solution in human practice and in the comprehension of this practice."

REFERENCES:

Ahmad, A. (2000). *Lineages of the present: Ideology and politics in contemporary South Asia*. London: Verso.

Allman, P (2001). *Critical education against global capitalism: Karl Marx and revolutionary critical education*. Westport, CT.: Bergin and Garvey.

Asian Development Bank. (1998, April). *Cooperation between the Asian Development Bank and nongovernment organizations*. Manila: Asian Development Bank. Retrieved January 20, 2008, from http://adb.org/Documents/Policies/Cooperation_with_NGOs/default.asp?p=polici es

Austin, D. (2009). Education and liberation. *McGill Journal of Education*, 44(1), 107-117.

Bannerji, H. (2011). *Demography and democracy: Essays on nationalism, gender and ideology*. Toronto: Canadian Scholars' Press.

Bayat, A. (1997). *Street politics: Poor people's movement's in Iran*. New York: Columbia University Press.

Bayat, A. (2010). *Life as politics: How ordinary people change the Middle East*. Stanford, CA: Stanford University Press.

Bazan, C., Cuellar, N., Gómez, I., Illsley, C., Monterroso, I., Pardo, J., Rocha, J.L., Torres, P., Bebbington, A J.. (2008). Producing knowledge, generating alternatives? Challenges to research oriented NGOs in Central America and Mexico. In Bebbington, A. J., Hickey, S., and Mitlin, D.C. (eds.). *Can NGOs make a difference? The challenge of development alternatives* (pp. 174-195). London and New York: Zed Books.

Bevington, D., and Dixon, C. (2005). "Movement-relevant theory: Rethinking social movement scholarship and activism," *Social Movement Studies* 4(3), 185-208.

Biel, R. (2000). *The New Imperialism: Crisis and Contradictions in North/South Relations.* London and New York: Zed Books.

Buck-Morss, S. (2009). *Hegel, Haiti and universal history*. Pittsburgh: University of Pittsburgh Press.

Carroll, W.K. (ed.). (2004). *Critical strategies for social research.* Toronto: Canadian Scholars' Press.

Choudry, A, and Kapoor, D. (eds). (2010) *Learning from the ground up: Global perspectives on social movements and knowledge production.* New York: Palgrave Macmillan.

Choudry, A. (2009). Challenging colonial amnesia in social justice activism. In Kapoor, D (ed). *Education, decolonization and development: Perspectives from Asia, Africa and the Americas* (pp. 95-110). Rotterdam: Sense.

Choudry, A. (2010a). What's left? Canada's 'global justice' movement and colonial amnesia. *Race and Class,* 52(1), 97-102.

Choudry, A. (2010b). Global justice? Contesting NGOization: Knowledge politics and containment in antiglobalization networks. In Choudry, A, and Kapoor, D. (eds). (2010) *Learning from the ground up: Global perspectives on social movements and knowledge production* (pp.17-34). New York: Palgrave Macmillan.

Choudry, A. and Kuyek, D. (2012, forthcoming). Activist research: Mapping power relations, informing struggles. In Choudry, A., Hanley, J., and Shragge, E. (eds.). *Organize! Building from the local for global justice.* Oakland: CA.:PM Press.

Choudry, A. and Shragge, E. (2011). Disciplining Dissent: NGOs and community organizations. *Globalizations,* 8:4, 503-517.

Choudry, A., Hanley, J., Jordan, S., Shragge, E., and Stiegman, M. (2009). *Fight Back. Workplace justice for immigrants.* Blacks Point, N.S.: Fernwood.

DeFilippis, J., Fisher, R., and Shragge, E. (2010). Contesting community: The limits and potential of local organizing. New Brunswick, NJ.:Rutgers University Press.

Dunayevskaya, R. (1958). *Marxism and freedom: From 1776 until today.* New York: Bookman Associates.

Eschle, C. (2001). Globalizing civil society? Social movements and the challenge of global politics from below. In Hamel, P., Lustiger-Thaler, H., Nederveen Pieterse, J., and Roseneil, S. (eds.). *Globalization and social movements* (pp. 61-85). Basingstoke: Palgrave.

Fanon, F. (1968). Concerning violence. In *The wretched of the earth* (pp. 35-106). New York: Grove Press.

Foley, G. (1999). *Learning in social action: A contribution to understanding informal education* London and New York: Zed Books.

Fowler, A. F. (2000). Introduction — Beyond partnership: Getting real about NGO relationships in the aid system. In Fowler, A. F. (ed.). Questioning partnership: The reality of aid and NGO relations — special issue of *Institute of Development Studies Bulletin, 31* (3), 1–13.

Gupta, R. (2004). Some recurring themes: Southall Black Sisters 1979–2003 and still going strong. In *From homebreakers to jailbreakers: Southall black sisters*, ed. R. Gupta, pp. 1–27. London: Zed Books.

Hancock, G. (1989). *Lords of Poverty*. London: Macmillan.

Henaway, M. (2012, forthcoming). Immigrant worker organizing in a time of crisis: Adapting to the new realities of class and resistance. In Choudry, A., Hanley, J., and Shragge, E. (eds.). *Organize! Building from the local for global justice.* Oakland: CA.: PM Press.

Hewson, P. (2005). 'It's the politics, stupid'. How neoliberal politicians, NGOs and rock stars hijacked the global justice movement at Gleneagles…and how we let them. In Harvie, D., Milburn, K., Trott, B, and Watts, D. *Shut them down! The G8, Gleneagles 2005 and the movement of movements.* (pp. 135-149). Leeds: Dissent! and New York: Autonomedia.

Holst, J. D. (2002). *Social movements, civil society, and radical adult education.* Westport, CT.: Bergin and Garvey.

INCITE! Women of Color Against Violence. (eds.). (2007). *The revolution will not be funded: Beyond the non-profit industrial complex* Boston, MA.: South End Press.

Jad, I. (2004), The NGO-isation of Arab Women's Movements. IDS Bulletin, 35: 34–42.

James, C.L.R. (1963). *The Black Jacobins: Toussaint L'Ouverture and the San Domingo revolution.* New York: *Vintage.*

Kamat, S. (2002). Development Hegemony: NGOs and the State in India. Oxford: Oxford University Press.

Kamat, S. (2004). The privatization of public interest: Theorizing NGO discourse in a neoliberal era. *Review of International Political Economy, 11* (1) (February), 155-176.

Kelley, R. D. G. (2002). *Freedom dreams: The black radical imagination.* Boston: Beacon Press.

Kinsman, G. (2006). "Mapping social relations of struggle: Activism, ethnography, social organization" in *Sociology for changing the world: Social movements/social research,* ed. Frampton, C., G. Kinsman, A.K. Thompson, and K Tilleczek. Black Point, N.S.: Fernwood.

Lynd. S. (2010). *From here to there: The Staughton Lynd reader*. Oakland. CA.:PM Press.

Marx, K. (1968). Theses on Feuerbach. In *Karl Marx and Frederich Engels: Selected Works*. New York: International. Accessed online at: http://www.marxists.org/archive/marx/works/1845/theses/theses.htm

Marx, K. (1984). *The Civil War in France: The Paris Commune*. New York: International Publishers.

McNally, D. (2011). Global slump: The economics and politics of crisis and resistance. Oakland, CA.: PM Press.

New Zealand Government, Cabinet Office. (1998, 24 August). "APEC 1999. Engagement with NGOs", STR (98)203.

Newman, M. (2006). Teaching defiance: Stories and strategies for activist educators. San Francisco, CA.: Jossey-Bass.

Novelli, M. (2010). Learning to win: Exploring knowledge and strategy development in anti-privatization struggles in Colombia. In Choudry, A, and Kapoor, D. (eds.). *Learning from the ground up: Global perspectives on social movements and knowledge production* (pp. 121-137). New York: Palgrave Macmillan.

Petras, J. and Veltmeyer, H. (2005). *Social movements and state power: Argentina, Brazil, Bolivia, Ecuador*. London: Pluto Press.

Petras, J., and Veltmeyer, H. (2001). Globalization unmasked: Imperialism in the 21st century. New Delhi: Madhyam.

Rodriguez, R.M. (2010). On the question of expertise: A critical reflection on "civil society" processes. In Choudry, A, and Kapoor, D. (eds.). *Learning from the ground up: Global perspectives on social movements and knowledge production* (pp. 53-68). New York: Palgrave Macmillan.

Sears, A. (2005). *A good book, in theory: A guide to theoretical thinking*. Toronto: Broadview Press.

Shragge, E. (2003). Activism and social change: Lessons for community and local organizing. Toronto: University of Toronto Press.

Smith, D.E. (1987). *The everyday world as problematic: A feminist sociology*. Toronto: University of Toronto Press.

Smith, G. W. (2006). Political activist as ethnographer. In *Sociology for changing the world: Social movements/social research*, ed. G. Kinsman, A. K. Thompson, & K. Tilleczek, pp. 44–70. Black Point, NS: Fernwood.

Smith, L.T. (1999). *Decolonising methodologies: Research and Indigenous Peoples*. London: Zed Books.

Tavares, P. (1992). Hegel et Haiti, ou le silence de Hegel sur Saint-Domingue", *Chemins Critiques* 2 (May 1992): 113-31.

Wallace, T. (2003). NGO Dilemmas: Trojan horses for global neoliberalism? In Panitch, L., and Leys, C. (eds.). *Socialist Register 2004: The New Imperial Challenge* (pp. 202-219). London: Merlin.

World Bank. (2008, January). World Bank civil society engagement newsletter. Retrieved 4 February 2008, from http://web.worldbank.org/WBSITE/EXTERNAL/TOPICS/CSO/0,,contentMDK:216 14446~pagePK:220503~piPK:220476~theSitePK:228717,00.html on.

Socialism as a Life-Coherent Society

Jeff Noonan[1]

All varieties of socialism share this trait in common: they are systematic alternatives to capitalism. But why should a systematic alternative to capitalism be necessary? Has it not proven to be the most productive economic system in history? Has it not created social conditions in which the powers of human imagination, creativity, and scientific understanding have grown to wider scope than in any previous society? Has it not enabled human beings to extend their life span and live healthier and more active lives than ever before? Has it not proven extraordinarily plastic, able to solve unforeseen problems in ways that its opponents continue to predict that it cannot, thus proving itself superior to any proposed alternative? These are difficult questions that anyone who claims that an alternative is necessary must take seriously.

There is little use in denying that one part of honest answers to the foregoing questions is "yes." No system has proven as productive, has enabled the development of imagination, creativity, and science to as wide a compass, cured more diseases, or proven as adaptable and protean as capitalism. However, since capitalism is not on trial here, but under analysis, more than yes or no answers are permitted. When more complex answers to the questions are proffered, the grounds supporting the need for a systematic alternative which builds upon the real achievements of capitalism become clear.

Notwithstanding those real achievements, an alternative is ultimately necessary because the social processes through which capitalism reproduces and develops itself are ecologically unsustainable and socially, politically, and culturally contradictory. At

the root of capitalism's unsustainable and contradictory nature is its ruling money-value system. The money-value system reduces the good

---

1 Jeff Noonan is Professor and Head of the Department of Philosophy at the University of Windsor. He is the author of *Critical Humanism and the Politics of Difference, Democratic Society and Human Needs,* and *Materialist Ethics and Life-Value* (2012, forthcoming). He can be reached at: jnoonan@uwindsor.ca

across all dimensions of human life-activity to increasing the money-value available for appropriation by private market agents, rendering the system blind to any harms that it imposes on natural life-support and social life-development systems which are not measurable in money-value terms. Beneath the apparent freedom of interest and activity enabled by capitalism lies a structure of social dependence upon possession of money-value for the satisfaction of life's requirements.

Peering into this structure of dependence discloses the secret of capitalist unsustainability and contradiction: it systematically confuses life-value with money-value. Life-value is that which is instrumentally or intrinsically good for living things. All life-requirement satisfiers, i.e., those resources, institutions, relationships, and practices that enable life to survive, reproduce, and develop, have instrumental life-value (McMurtry, 1998, 164). The experiences and activities which living things are able to have and realise because life-requirements are satisfied are, in general, intrinsically life-valuable, the substance of the good life. Capitalism does indeed produce instrumental life-value and enable the expression of intrinsic life-value, but in systematically life-incoherent ways. Rather than "consistently enabling ecological and human life together," as a life-coherent society would, capitalism systematically degrades and depletes natural life-support systems at an accelerating pace, deprives those without the money to pay of the means of satisfying their natural and socio-cultural life-requirements, selects for expression and enjoyment only those experiences and activities which are money-valuable, and subjects even those experiences and activities to competitive zero sum games which ensures that the good of some people's lives is sacrificed for the sake of the good of other people's lives (McMurtry, 2011, 4). A socialist alternative to capitalism is necessary because capitalism generates life-crises in the natural and socio-cultural dimensions of life-support and life-development. The warrant and value of this alternative is determined by the extent to which socialism proves capable of solving capitalist life-crises in life-coherent ways. As will become clear, conceiving socialism as a life-coherent society requires important revisions to prevailing interpretations of its traditional justificatory values.

CAPITALIST LIFE-INCOHERENCE AND TRADITIONAL SOCIALIST VALUES

There is a large and growing body of socialist literature that focuses on the long-term unsustainability of capitalist society. The main conclusion of this literature is that capitalism is materially irrational because the expansion of money-value it demands contracts the natural system of life-support upon which its existence as a social system depends. As

Meszaros argues, "The system is and must remain expansion oriented and driven by accumulation. Naturally, what is at issue in this regard is not a process designed for ensuring the satisfaction of human need. Rather, it is the expansion of capital as an end in itself, serving the preservation of a system which could not survive without consistently asserting its power as an extended mode of reproduction" (Meszaros, 2008, 65). This system-need to expand money-capital is the driver of capitalist life-incoherence. The good of the system, ever expanding production of money-capital, undermines, over the long term, the natural life-support system upon which the system itself depends. As Kovel argues, "the [capitalist] imperative to expand continually erodes the edges of ecologies along an ever expanding perimeter, overwhelming or displacing recuperative efforts, and accelerating a cascade of destabilization" (Kovel, 2007, p. 51, see also Meszaros, 2008, p. 99-100, Kovel and Lowy, 2011). It is no good to rejoin to worries about long-term consequences that in the long term we are all dead, as Keynes said, so that only short and medium term thinking in economics makes sense (Keynes, 1924, p. 88). The rejoinder commits a fallacy of composition. It is true that every human individual exists for a fixed period of time, but it does not follow that the species faces the same limits. The species can reproduce itself indefinitely into the future. To the extent that economics focuses on the life of individuals as moments of the open-ended life of the species, long term, life-coherent thinking is required.

However, the problem of life-incoherence has not always been recognised in the history of socialist thought. As Lebowitz has recently noted, the history of socialism is riven by a tension between productvist and humanist interpretations. "Rather than ... focus upon the full development of human potential, ... the dominant conception of socialism in the twentieth century tended to stress the development of the productive forces ... An important part of the socialist vision was lost—human beings at the centre" (Lebowitz, 2010, 21). This tension was not invented by twentieth century socialists. It can be found in Marx himself who understood the necessity of socialism as arising not from the long-term life-incoherence of capitalist productivity, but from the systematic blockage that capitalist relations of production imposed upon the ability of the productive forces to expand (Marx, 1970, 21, Marx and Engels, 1975, 54-58). While it is true, as John Bellamy Foster has demonstrated, that Marx did not ignore the natural foundations of human life but in fact understood labour as humanity's metabolism with nature and criticised capitalism for imposing a "metabolic rift" between human beings and their natural life-support system, it remains true that Marx understood an essential element of socialism to be the unlocking of productive potential suppressed by capitalism (Bellamy Foster, 2000, p. 141-177). While the historical context in which Marx wrote explains his belief that productive force expansion and socialism were essentially connected, in our changed circumstances the opposite relationship is demanded: socialism as a life-coherent society must end the hypertrophied growth of productive forces.

If today the viability of the socialist project depends upon rejecting the traditional belief that socialism will be a society of unbounded productivity in favour of the suppressed alternative, socialism as a society with human needs and human capacities at the centre, we must ask in what human needs consist and to what extent and in what directions it is good to develop human capacities. If we start, as materialists must, from the natural basis of human life, then human needs originate in those non-optional physical-organic life-requirements without which biological life is impossible. So much is clear from Marx in The German Ideology (Marx, 1975, p 37). But when we venture beyond the physical-organic bases of life the history of socialist thought loses sight of the essential connection between needs and the range of objective requirements of human life. Despite Marx's understanding of real wealth as lying in human needs and capacities, he nowhere provides a criterion to distinguish between social needs which are not directly organic and consumer demands, and in some cases directly conflates needs and consumer demands. The most egregious example of this failure to rigorously distinguish real needs (objective natural and social life-requirements) from consumer demands occurs in Wage Labour and Capital, where Marx argues that a house which meets a person's material need for shelter is enjoyed as such, so long as no one builds a bigger house next door. As soon as that happens, the owner of the smaller house now feels that his modest dwelling shows that "he has only very slight or no demands to make" (Marx, 1973, p. 163). Yet, this belief that one's happiness as a human being depends upon ever higher levels of consumption, as opposed to the sufficient satisfaction of one's real life-requirements, is just the psychology of consumer desire exploited by capitalist advertisers. As I have argued in more detail elsewhere, Marx's failure to define needs as real life-requirements blinds him to the life-destructive implications of the equation of happiness with rising levels of consumption (Noonan, 2006, p. 121-130).

For the most part this elision has not been challenged by subsequent Marxists. Neither Agnes Heller nor Ian Fraser, who have provided the most detailed studies of Marx's conception of human needs, exposed this conflation of needs and consumer demands (Heller, 1976; Fraser, 1998). Alan Gilbert, who grounds his Marxist theory of moral realism in human needs, likewise provides no explicit criterion by which objective human life-requirements can be rigorously distinguished from stimulated consumer demands (Gilbert, 1982; Gilbert, 1986). In the midst of ecological crisis today, this conceptual lacuna can no longer be accepted, as the failure to limit needs to what is universally required by human life to survive and socially develop impedes the formulation of a life-coherent conception of socialism.

Sympathetic critics of my position might point to the work of Marcuse or, more recently, the work of eco-socialists like Joel Kovel as having already filled in this lacuna. It is true that Marcuse's conception of "true" and "false" needs in *One Dimensional Man* implies that the differentia specifica of true needs is that they are objective life-requirements, but he does not state this criterion explicitly and he provides no systematic account of the limits of our needs (Marcuse, 1964, p. 4-5). This failure to distinguish needs as life-requirements from consumer demands persists in the thought even of those socialists who have gone the furthest towards making the implicit life-coherence of the socialist alternative explicit. Thus Kovel contrasts the capitalist prioritisation of exchange value to the socialist alternative of prioritization of use-value, without noting the obvious, that there are life-destructive use-values that socialism ought not waste resources producing (Kovel, 2007, p. 39). Kovel does, it is true, argue that a socialist economy ought to produce only those use-values that satisfy human needs, but provides no criterion by which to distinguish need and consumer demand, and at one point conflates needs with advertising-induced addictions. "As capitalism penetrates life-worlds, it alters them in ways that foster its accumulation, chiefly by introducing a sense of dissatisfaction or lack...In this way, children develop such a craving for caffeine-laced sugar-loaded, or artificially sweetened soft drinks that it may be said that they positively need them" (Kovel, 2007, p. 53). If one defines needs as life-requirements, then it can never be the case that our addictions are needs. Life-requirements are not simply demands for use-values that we lack, they are our actual, positive connection to the natural field of life-support and the social field of life-development. As such they are our essential guide to the fundamentally practical question of what a life-coherent socialism must produce. If we allow that consumer addictions are needs, then we use need in a purely descriptive sense, which then undermines the normative force of the difference between a life-requirement and consumer-demand.

An analogous problem applies to the human potential or human capacities that socialism is supposed to better enable. Lebowitz' s most recent defence of socialism contends that "real wealth is the development of human capacities, the development of human potential."(Lebowitz, 2010, p. 43). Stated in this unqualified way this position has no answer to the objection that capitalism has developed human potential and capacities better than any alternative, because it again lacks a criterion by which to distinguish life-valuable and life-disvaluable capacities and potentials. Surely the capacities of human beings to instrumentally exploit nature have been developed under capitalism, and the potential to invent destructive weapons has been realized to an exquisite degree. Are these the potentials and the capacities that Lebowitz thinks socialism ought to better develop? Clearly not. But when we ask "why not? we do not find the conceptual grounds for a principled answer, even though that answer is vital to explaining and defending the socialist alternative that Lebowitiz is attempting to construct. The conceptual basis of that principled answer lies in the idea of life-value, to a more nuanced explanation of which I now turn.

SOCIALISM, LIFE-VALUE, AND LIFE-COHERENCE

I noted in the introduction that life-values are either instrumental or intrinsic. Instrumental life-values are defined by the range of life-requirements that a given organism must satisfy if it is to survive, develop, and express its vital capacities. Human beings share with all other life-forms physical-organic requirements of survival, but our much richer cognitive, imaginative, and practical-creative capacities entail socio-cultural and temporal requirements for which we know of no real analogues in the rest of nature. The free expression and enjoyment of our capacities for social self-consciousness and intentional agency require definite forms of loving and caring interpersonal relationships, education, cultural spaces and institutions in which creative self and collective expression can be developed and enjoyed, political institutions in which collective rules of social life can be decided, opportunities for meaningful creation and contribution through productive work, and time experienced as an open matrix of possibilities for action. Thus human beings share three sets of life-requirements corresponding to the three dimensions of human life:

physical-organic requirements of biological life, socio-cultural requirements of human life as a socially self-conscious agent, and temporal requirements of free human life.

In all three cases we can apply a test to distinguish between resources, practices, relationships, and institutional structures which have instrumental life-value, and are therefore objective life-requirements, or needs, and consumer demands and preferences which may be desired, but are not life-requirements, and are therefore either of no life-value or negative life-value (life-destructive). In order to distinguish between life-requirements and consumer demands we must ask: if anyone were deprived of the given resource, relationship, practice, or institutional structure, would they suffer harm to any of their human capacities to experience the world through the senses, to feel the range of human emotions, to think and imagine, or act and create in life-valuable ways (McMurtry, 2008, p. 164)? If deprivation causes objective harm in the form of loss of life or vital capacity, such as would ensue if one were deprived of all shelter in a cold climate, then the object, relationship, practice or institutional structure in question is a requirement of organic-social human life. If only subjective feelings of relative deprivation ensue, as in the case of Marx's man jealous of his neighbour's house, then no life-requirement is involved, but only a consumer demand with no or negative life-value. Let me give one example from each class of life-requirements to clarify my meaning.

All of our sentient, cognitive, and imaginative capacities depend upon the functioning of our brains. Without adequate protein, brain function is degraded, and thus so too the capacities to sense, think, and imagine. There is an objective relationship between protein intake and brain function such that objective harm in the form of degradation of the various capacities of the brain necessarily follows deprivation. It does not follow that there is only one way to satisfy this life-requirement for protein; the life requirement is not for any particular form of food but for any food that will satisfy the brain's requirement for protein. Analogous forms of harm are caused by the deprivation of socio-cultural life-requirements, although here the harm is not to the organic systems themselves but to the human forms of experience, thought, and activity they enable. Adequately functioning eyes and brains can perfectly well sense the world, but it does not follow that they will see all that there is to experience. Unless the person to whom the eyes and brain belong receives some degree of education and cultivation, it is quite possible for the person not to see the natural and humanly created beauty of the world. As Marx says, "the care burdened man in need has no sense for the finest play."(Marx, 1975a, p. 302). The human form of capacity expression emerges out of the biological organization of the human body, but is not reducible to it. Well-functioning biological machines may be sociopathically indifferent to the others' pain which they observe. Healthy people may be illiterate, or live in social circumstances that prevent them from participating in political life, or be forced into mindless drudgery as their life's work. In cases such as these there is no impairment of biological functioning but there certainly is harm to the human form of expression of our sentient, cognitive, imaginative, and creative capacities. I admit that verbal scepticism about socio-cultural life-requirements

s possible, but that it would only prove practically convincing were the sceptic willing to deprive him or herself permanently of that which he or she claims is not a real life-requirement: loving and caring concern between people, education, political participation, intrinsically and instrumentally life-valuable and democratically governed work, and the experience of all natural and humanly created beauty. Deprivation of the third class of life-requirement, the requirement of mortal beings for the experience of time as free, also causes objective harm, this time to our ability to express our life-capacities freely. By the expression "the experience of time as free" I do not mean the availability of "empty time," time in which no external force compels us to do one thing rather than another (Noonan, 2009, p. 377-393). Some degree of empty time is a material condition of the experience of time as free, but the latter is not reducible to empty time. Rather, it is essentially an experience of time as an open matrix of possibilities for life-valuable activity, in contrast to unfree time, the experience of time as an inescapable, externally imposed routine. As the human form of capacity expression develops out of our biological organism, so too their free realization grows out of their human form. Freedom requires in addition to the satisfaction of biological and socio-cultural life-requirements some degree of free time in which the person can contemplate different possibilities for capacity expression and development and decide between them. There is thus a difference between a life rich in content of human capacity expression and a life in which this content is developed freely. Someone trapped in the "rat race" of capitalism may express complex and challenging capacities in a particularly human way at work and yet feel oppressed rather than free. If money-value pressures cause these capacities to be expressed in routinized ways, then the capacities are not freely developed but coerced by the structure of work in which the person is trapped.

Since human beings have only a finite life-span, they are harmed to the extent that their life-time is structured as a closed routine rather than an open matrix of possibilities for life-valuable activity. Again, sceptical rejoinders are possible, but presuppose exactly what they deny. No one without the time to freely mull over the structure and implications of philosophical arguments makes sceptical rejoinders. Hence I conclude that these three-dimensions of human life-requirement are objectively real, the material foundation of any humanly possible good life, and that anyone is harmed to the extent that they are deprived of one or more of them.

Capitalism is systematically harmful to people because: it degrades the natural field of life-support upon which our biological organism depends and makes the satisfaction of natural, socio-cultural, and temporal life-requirements contingent on their serving the master capitalist goal of money-value accumulation. In thus making life-requirement satisfaction contingent on the ability to pay, capitalism treats life-requirements as instruments for the expansion of money-value rather than instruments of the creation of intrinsic life-value. It thus reduces social institutions to structures of exploitation rather than life-requirement satisfaction and free life-capacity realization. Finally, capitalism reifies time such that it is experienced as an oppressive structure in which human activity is systematically routinized in the service of external powers. If socialism is the solution for these harms then it must solve these problems in a life-coherent manner. What would such a solution entail?

As I noted in the introductory comments, life-coherence requires enabling ecological and human life together. It might seem that the simultaneous satisfaction of these twin demands is impossible, that the good life for humans requires more and more things, such that human life can only be enabled if ecological life is damaged. In fact, the accumulation of things beyond life-requirements does not make life any better, because life is essentially creative activity, and most consumer goods are passivity-inducing, which is why shopping for them tends to be more enjoyable than possessing them (Kasser, 2002, p. 85-86). Thin a social activity it may be, but shopping is nevertheless a social activity. Once the new gadget has been brought home, boredom with it soon ensues. The life-requirements set out above are the natural, social, and temporal conditions for the widest possible life-coherent expression of human capacities. Since their satisfaction can be achieved without much of what advertisers tell us are necessities but which in reality have no committed life-function in any dimension of being humanly alive, socialist production can enable human and ecological life together by progressively reducing the energy and resources devoted to the production of life-disvaluable commodities. As it is the wealthy societies of the Global North that waste the most energy and resources in the consumption of commodities which contribute nothing to life-maintenance, development, or enjoyment, the shift in priorities of production would, while reducing the overall ecological impact of human economies, make more resources available for life-development of the Global South, and still enable more active and enjoyable lives in the global North. In this way, socialism as a life-coherent society can enable human and ecological life together by limiting the output of production to that which is required by our organism and to fund the institutions, relationships and free time required to freely cultivate our capacities.

To put this point another way, minimizing the energy and resources it takes to produce instrumental life-value is the condition for the maximization of intrinsic life-value over the open-ended future of the human species. Intrinsic life-value, recall, is the enjoyed, life-coherent expression of freely realized life-capacities. Capitalism is life incoherent in relation to the expression and enjoyment of human capacities because its ruling value system does not valorise the universal and comprehensive satisfaction of life-requirements. Thus the lives of most people are dependent upon finding paid work, which in turn is not organized so as to enable the comprehensive expression and enjoyment of the full-range of life-capacities, but to maximise profits for the firm which purchases the labour-power through which the capacities are expressed. Life-capacities may be developed, but not as intrinsic life-values, but as exploitable inputs to the production of money-value. Even where human capacities are developed in rich and complex ways, the ends they serve are often life-destructive. And even where the ends they serve are not life-destructive, the distribution of positions is not according to talent and aptitude, but limited by the demands of profitability, which means that people who are willing and able to contribute their talents and aptitudes to life-valuable social tasks cannot find work.

Traditionally, socialism has encapsulated its solution to these structural impediments to the free expression and enjoyment of capacities in slogans like "from

each according to their abilities, to each according their needs" (Marx, 1978, p. 531). But just as in the case of needs, which have not been consistently and coherently defined in terms of the three classes of life-requirements, so too has the question of the limits of life-valuable capacity development been left unaddressed. Instead of systematic interrogation of these limits we too often find socialism identified with the transcendence of all limits. Lebowitz quotes Marx with approval for his claim that socialism will develop "all human powers as such as ends in themselves," without noting the obvious problem, all too clear from the history of capitalist industry, that the set of all human powers includes life-destructive powers. Clearly Marx and Lebowitz do not mean to affirm the power to destroy, but by not tying down the human powers whose development they affirm to the required life-coherence limitation, they open themselves to objections of this sort. Such critiques are not only abstract philosophical objections but also political, as in environmentalist critiques of socialism as ecologically destructive or radical feminist critiques of Marxism as still rooted in masculinist psychologies of violence and conquest.(Benton, 1989, p. 51-86; Wittig, 1997, p. 224-225).

To obviate these objections and to build political links to those who lodge them it must be made clear the ways in which the principle of life-coherence would govern the development of human capacities in a future socialist society. Just as it is not the case that every use-value has instrumental life-value, so too not every expression of human capacities has intrinsic life-value. Absolute intrinsic life-value attaches only to the raw capacities to sense, feel, think, imagine, and act. Definite constellations of these raw capacities in concrete expressions are subject to evaluation according to the principle of life-coherence. This principle rules out forms of capacity expression which: (1) permanently degrade the natural life-support system or destroy non-human life for no higher, long-term life-serving purpose; and (2) depend necessarily on the exploitation of others' life-requirements, such that the exploited other is prevented from expressing and enjoying his or her life-capacities as a necessary consequence of the structure of exploitation within which he or she lives.

The normal expression of life-capacities under capitalism violates both of these limitations. The extent of their development is limited not by the principle of life-coherence but by the degree to which the development of any given capacity is money-valuable. Even where eco-destruction is avoided, the development and expression of life-capacities cannot escape the structures of exploitative work and oppressive socio-cultural institutions and ideologies that dominate life in activity in capitalist society. The life-coherent solution to these systematic problems is to create the social conditions in which human capacities are expressed and enjoyed only in those forms that enable ecological and human life together. If that which is intrinsically valuable in its effects destroys the natural and social life-support and life-development systems upon which its very existence depends, then this conception of intrinsic value must be materially irrational. If socialism is to solve the problems of capitalism and secure the comprehensive conditions for everyone to enjoy their lives through making valuable contributions to the natural and social worlds, it must take care to specify clearly the limits that life-support systems and the shared life-interests of other people impose on individual goals and projects. Analogous limits must govern the forms of political struggle through which socialism can be progressively built. To an explanation and defence of a life-coherent political practice I now turn in conclusion.

LIFE-COHERENCE AND POLITICAL PRACTICE

As Lebowitz rightly argues, new societies do not "drop from the sky" or emerge "pristine and complete from the conceptions of intellectuals," but rather "emerge within and in opposition to the existing society" (Lebowitz, 2006, p. 62). His point, as I interpret it, is that the task of building socialism is not like constructing a new building from blueprints, but like an on-going project of renovating an existing building piece by piece until a different building sits on the same foundations. As he argues in relation to the emergence in Venezuela of new neighbourhood-based democratic councils and workers' co-management of enterprises, "the emergence of both these new elements is a process—a process of learning and a process of development."(Lebowitz, 2006, p. 112). They are elements of a socialist alternative developing within an existing capitalist society. Building socialism is thus not a process that awaits a revolutionary break with capitalism but is itself that break which emerges within and in tension and struggle with the prevailing capitalist institutions. Some socialists might vociferously object to the implications of the metaphor by noting that it claims that a new society can be built upon on the same foundations as the old. The objection can be met by pointing out that all societies have the same material foundations: the natural life-support system and human labour as "metabolic interchange" with it. Nevertheless, it is true that the metaphor is meant to emphasise more than is usual the continuities that link present capitalist society to a future socialist society. Socialists have paid most attention, for obvious reasons, to questions about how best to bring about fundamental social transformation: can it be achieved through reforms, or is revolution necessary? If revolution is necessary, what does revolution mean? Can it be the spontaneous product of workers' self-activity, or does it require a vanguard party? What ought the relationship be between workers and the party, or between workers as a class and other oppressed groups whose members belong to different classes? These questions define in large part the political history of different socialist movements, and I will have something to say, in general, about them at the end. To begin, however, I want to say something about what would remain continuous between socialist and capitalist society, not for the sake of novelty, but because I think that the principle of life-coherence sheds light on this under-examined issue in a way that has important practical implications for rebuilding a democratic socialist movement.

Capitalism is able to reproduce itself in the short and medium term despite the manifold economic, political, social, and environmental crises it regularly generates because people believe themselves to be ultimately dependent upon access to its labour and commodity markets for their survival and development. Although the ultimate foundations of human life are not markets and commodities, but natural resources and human labour, this belief is not completely mistaken. It is supported by the fact that in capitalist social reality money is required to exchange for the commodities that one's life and development requires. So long as the belief persists that capitalist labour and commodity markets are the ultimate foundations of life and development it will appear to all who hold this belief that any attack on the existing society is an attack on the very foundations of life and life-development.

By this claim I do not mean that people never fight back unless they believe that a completely different world is possible, but rather that they fight back in self-limiting ways because they cannot see any real possibility for successfully building a fundamentally different society. To take a recent case as illustration of the meaning of my claim, in June 2011 postal workers went on strike against Canada Post. Fearing back to work legislation, they decided to engage in rotating strikes rather than an all-out nation-wide strike. In response, Canada Post locked them out and the Conservative government then passed back to work legislation. Yet, the strategy, though it ultimately proved self-undermining, is understandable, not simply as conservatism on the part of the union leadership, but as rooted in genuine fear of the consequences of all-out challenges to capitalist power in an era where a systematic alternative seems remote. As Albo, Gindin, and Panitch argue, capitalism has consistently "compelled workers to become more dependent on the market as individuals so as to limit their ability to contest the social relations of the capitalist market as a class" (Albo, Gindin, and Pantich, 2010, p. 90). From the standpoint of anyone enmeshed in the daily struggle to make money in order to survive, talk of total social transformation does not sound utopian, but suicidal. Hence oppositional politics, especially in wealthy societies, remains limited to promises of piecemeal reform that do not upset "the markets" for fear of compromising money-value growth upon which life and life-development appear to depend. Systemic causes are never addressed, and society lurches from one crisis to the next.

This fear cannot be overcome by talk of "smashing" and "destroying" capitalism that sometimes tempt socialists because people for the most part do not believe that it can be smashed or destroyed. In order to build movements broad-based and powerful enough to solve the causes of life-crises, socialists might do better to emphasise the natural and institutional continuity between capitalism and socialism. By 'natural and institutional continuity' I refer to the natural system of life-support that underlies any human society and supplies all the physical-organic requirements of life, and existing social institutions, relationships, and practices in so far as they actually fulfill their life-coherent function: enabling the development of human capacities through the satisfaction of life-requirements. The point of emphasising natural and institutional continuity is not to attenuate the essential opposition between capitalism and socialism, but rather to bring to light the longer and deeper history of collective labour and struggle through which social institutions have been built up from their natural bases and progressively turned from support of the particular interests of ruling classes towards universal provision of life-requirements across the three dimensions of human life. If we ground the struggle for socialism in those aspects of existing institutions which actually serve the shared life-interest, stressing always the role that struggle has played historically in extending this life-service, then the task of building socialism no longer appears as a suicidal destruction of existing means of life-support, but an organic development beyond the achieved plateaus of life-requirement satisfaction found in actually existing civil commons institutions and practices.

The civil commons is McMurtry's term for all non-commodified social goods which enable human life to freely develop (McMurtry, 2002, p. 117). These institutions and practices range from languages and love for children through to free education, health care, and the democratic principle that all who are subject to institutions ought to play an active role in their governance. The universality of life-requirement provision that defines the civil commons contrast with privacy of monetary benefit that defines the system-value that governs institutions today. All social institutions are marked by this contradiction. People love their children, but often express this love by buying them things which they in no sense require and which contribute to inculcating the habitual equation of enjoyment with the purchase of commodities. Publically funded health care in Canada is a civil commons institution, but it is continually eroded at the margins by the commodified medical industry. Education is a public civil commons good, but at the post-secondary level it is becoming increasingly commodified and bent to the purposes of private industry. Existing political institutions are formally democratic, but determined by the master purpose of protecting the existing structure of power and ruling value system, and thus not coherently anchored in protection and satisfaction of the shared life-interest.

My contention is that socialism indeed does not drop from the sky but finds its organic basis in the achieved level of civil commons development. Motivating people in the struggle for socialism is thus not a task, which even socialists sometimes present it as being, of winning people to an alien ideology, but disclosing how socialist values are already embodied in the civil commons function of existing institutions which people already support, and whose erosion they lament, if not always actively resist. The politically relevant contradiction, the one that socialists ought to focus people's attention on, is between the goodness of the civil commons function of these institutions, and the ways in which this actually existing goodness is negated to the extent that private money-value interests seize control. Let me illustrate my claim through the paradigmatic example of Canadian public health care.

The principle if not the complete practice of public medicine in Canada is "to each according to her or his need." People might debate the cogency of this principle in the abstract, but as concretely applied to medical care, the majority of Canadians consistently defend it. More importantly, by any metric one cares to choose: cost effectiveness, health outcomes, or equity of access it is demonstrably superior to commodified medicine (Armstrong, Armstrong, Bourgeault, Choniere, Lexchin, Mykhalovsky, Peters, and White, 2004, p. 13-38). Thus public medical care is a real life, if partial and imperfect, realization of the socialist principle of distribution. When it is attacked, people mobilise to defend it. What they defend it from is the core distributive principle of capitalism: to each according to his or her ability to pay, regardless of his or her own or others' need. Yet, proponents of public medical care rarely equate it with the demonstrably superior outcomes of the socialist principle of distribution that underlies it. "Socialism" is most often only mentioned by opponents who castigate it as such. Defenders typically bend over backwards trying to distance their defence of public medical care from socialism, and Marxists too often treat it as nothing more than a "reform" within capitalism. But this response misses a crucial opportunity to link socialism with a practice that enjoys majority support and actually works.

Of course it is true that a means of health care delivery is not a whole society. My point is not to claim that advanced capitalism is implicitly socialist. Nor I am not arguing that the path towards socialism can be advanced by what Erik Olin Wright calls "symbiotic" forms of social transformation (Wright, 2010, p. 337-365). Symbiotic forms of

social transformation are processes of social change which achieve real reform for workers and other subordinate groups while at the same time solve certain problems for capitalists. Universal suffrage is an example: it solved the problem of containing radical opposition to capitalism while also enabling workers to gain and use political power to advance certain other economic goals. Although real reform is possible through such strategies, fundamental social change is not. Eventually the logic of the existing system is going to put a stop to the evolving counter-logic of the alternative.

My point is thus not that radical change can be achieved by progressive reforms extended over an open ended time frame, but rather that past social struggles have created civil commons institutions which demonstrably function according to socialist principles. This point can become the centre of political education for mass mobilization– another world is possible because elements of it are actual, and have been made so through successful struggles. The fact that these institutions work better than market alternatives provides an organic basis for socialist politics. By "organic" I mean actually existing and functioning in the present as means of life-requirement satisfaction. Organic is to be contrasted with "theoretical," i.e., abstract arguments that claim to prove that a systematic socialist alternative to capitalism is possible, but whose plausibility depends entirely upon the internal logical cogency of argument. In other words, the term is meant to stress that the struggle for socialism occurs along an historical continuum of building up civil commons institutions whose real value is the universal enabling of life-coherent capacities through comprehensive satisfaction of life-requirements. By arguing from the achieved level of civil commons development, and demonstrating how this development demands collective as opposed to private appropriation of social wealth, socialists can refute the capitalist critique of socialism by embracing it. All that socialists need as an effective rejoinder is to say: yes it is socialist, and look, it actually works. Conceiving of socialism as an organic development out struggles oriented by the universal goal of comprehensive satisfaction of life requirements takes us beyond sterile debates about reform or revolution. The real problem is not constructing an abstract proof that capitalism is or is not reformable, but securing public control over life-sustaining and life-developing resources and institutions, and using them in life-coherent ways. The practicability of this task is proven by the existing level of civil commons development. The task of building socialism is thus a task of extending existing civil commons practices into the core economic and political systems of capitalist society. To conclude I will examine whether or not there are any existing practices which can serve as an organic basis from which to build struggles capable of transforming these core systems.

It is a well-known objection to capitalist democracy that it is at best incomplete because it does not extend into economic institutions (see for example Meiksins Wood, 1995). One of the great achievements in the history of socialist struggle is the development of workers' councils, novel political institutions through which the coercive economic power exercised by money-value and management as its servant over workers can be overcome. In the experience of the contemporary working class in North America and Europe there appear to be no analogues of workers councils. Hence the demand for workers councils would sound exactly like a demand "dropping from the sky" and be unlikely to mobilise significant numbers of people.

While there are no existing analogues of institutions like workers' councils in contemporary Western capitalism, there is a civil commons institution which embodies the principle of workplace democracy. That institution is the trade union understood as a forum in which workers debate together about how best to structure their conditions of work. Like other civil commons institutions under capitalism unions are imperfect expressions of the democratic principle of workers control of production because unions presuppose management as a bargaining opponent and the money-value system as the object of bargaining. Nevertheless, unions are an organic basis for socialist arguments in favour of the more comprehensive democratization of work life because, when they are functioning well, they draw workers out of self-enclosed concern for doing their job and getting paid into political debates about how work life ought to be governed and what its universal social significance is. Without minimizing any of the challenges facing unions or the limitations of their current mode of operation, it remains true to say, as Hilary Wainwright recently has, that "unions are, in many countries, the largest, the best resourced, most stable, most institutional, and in some respects to most rooted ... movements in civil society...Unions can facilitate the organization of knowledge, practical actions, expert research, and popular expression of the mass of people to defend social needs and the means of meeting them" (Wainwright, 2011, p. 3). Consciously turned in the direction of contesting the authority of management at work and the rule of money-value over life-requirement satisfaction, unions could function as the organic foundation for deeper struggles for the democratization, i.e., the rule of the common life-interest within, economic life generally.

But is not the principle of the rule of the common life-interest the deepest justification of existing democratic institutions? The very first value affirmed by the American Declaration of Independence, for example, is "life." Yet we know through observation that it is not the value of life that actually rules, but the power of money. Nevertheless, existing democratic institutions cannot openly reject the principle that they are designed to allow people to govern themselves in the shared life-interest, for to break openly with it would be to compromise the deepest legitimating value of liberal-democratic capitalism: freedom.

Thus the political institutions of existing liberal-democratic capitalism also provide an organic basis for the comprehensive life-coherent democratic institutions that socialism would require. Marx himself argued that the working class must win the battle of democracy (Marx and Engles, 1986, p. 53; see also Nimtz, 2000). Today I believe that struggles need to be organized around gaining political control of existing political institutions and using them for life-valuable ends. The age of revolutionary vanguardism and the "Noah complex" (the belief that nothing new can be built until the old world has been washed away) has passed (Collier, 2009, p. 98). While certainly far from perfect, the examples of Venezuela and Bolivia provide evidence that existing parliamentary institutions need not be instruments of class power, but can be transformed from institutions of class rule to institutions of genuine life-coherent democracy. The history of revolutionary vanguardism proves that the violent conquest of the existing ruling class does not at all entail success in building a life-coherent society. The construction of a life-coherent alternative does not so much depend upon single-minded devotion to the cause—always a mindset that carries with it profound dangers—as it does learning to distinguish in every case between the life-value of a given institution and the system-value that prevents the full expression of that life-value. Radical political practice today depends not so much on the invention of new institutions as the fuller realization of the life-value of the existing institution. In the case of existing political institutions the life-value is that their legitimacy enables ruling parties to use state power to implement their agenda.

If this agenda is a comprehensive program of life-coherent social transformation, then its democratic legitimacy cannot be coherently contested by opponents. If its democratic legitimacy cannot be contested, then the only way in which it can be attacked is for opponents to drop all pretence to democracy and violently assert their particular interests against the universal life-interest. In doing so they deprive themselves of the legitimacy

REFERENCES:

Albo, Greg, Gindin, sam, and Panitch, Leo. (2010). *In and Out of Crisis*. Oakland, CA: PM Press.

Armstrong, Pat, Armstrong, Hugh, Bourgeault, Ivy Lynn, Choniere, Jacqueline, Lexchin, Joel, Mykhalovsky, Eric, Peters, Suzanne, and White, Jerry. (2004). AMarket Principle, Business Practices, and Health Care: Comparing the U.S. and Canadian Experiences,@ *International Journal of Canadian Studies*, No. 28, (Fall, 2004), 13-38.

Bellamy Foster, John. (2000). *Marx's Ecology*. New York: Monthly Review Press.

Benton, Ted. (1989). "Marxism and Natural Limits," New Left Review, no. 178, (Nov.- Dec. 1989, 51-86.

Collier, Andrew. (2009). "Marx and Conservatism," *Karl Marx and Contemporary Philosophy*, Andrew Chitty and Martin McIvor, eds. London: Palgrave MacMillan.

Fraser, Ian. (1998). *Hegel and Marx: The Concept of Need*. Edinburgh: University of Edinburgh Press.

Gilbert, Alan. (1982). "An Ambiguity in Marx and Engel's Account of Justice and Equality," *American Political Science Review*. Vol. 76, No. 2 (June, 1982). 328-346.

Gilbert, Alan. (1986). "Moral Realism, Individuality, and Justice in War," *Political Theory*. Vol. 14, No. 1 (February 1986). 105-135.

Heller, Agnes. (1976). *The Theory of Need in Marx*. New York: St. Martin's Press.

Kasser, Tim. (2002). *The High Price of Materialism*. Cambridge MA: MIT Press.

Keynes, John Maynard. (1924). *ATract on Monetary Reform*. New York: Harcourt Brace.

Kovel, Joel. (2007). *The Enemy of Nature*. New York: Zed Books.

Kovel, Joel, and Lowy, Michael Lowy. (2011). *An Ecosocialist Manifesto* (http://www.ecosocialistnetwork.org/Docs/EcoManifesto.htm (accessed, February 28th, 2011).

Lebowitz, Michael. (2006). *Build it Now*. New York: Monthly Review Press.

Lebowitz, Michael. (2010). *The Socialist Alternative: Real Human Development*. New York: Monthly Review Press.

Marcuse, Herbert. (1964). *One Dimensional Man*. Boston: Beacon Press.

Marx, Karl. (1970). *A Contribution to the Critique of Political Economy*. Moscow: Progress Publishers.

Marx, Karl. (1973). "Wage Labour and Capital," *Marx and Engels, Selected Works, Volume 1*. Moscow: Progress Publishers.

Marx, Karl, and Engels, Friedrich. (1975). *The German Ideology*. Moscow: Progress Publishers.

Marx, Karl. (1975a). "Economic and Philosophical Manuscripts of 1844," Karl Marx and

Friedrich Engels, *Collected Works, Volume 3*. New York: International Publishers.

Marx, Karl. (1978). "Critique of the Gotha Program," *The Marx-Engels Reader*. Robert

C. Tucker, ed. New York: W.W. Norton, 525-541.

Marx, Karl, and Engels, Friedrich. (1986). *The Communist Manifesto*. Moscow: Progress Publishers.

Meiksins Wood, Ellen. (1995). *Democracy Against Capitalism*. New York: Cambridge University Press.

McMurtry, John. (1998). *Unequal Freedoms*. Toronto: Garamond)..

McMurtry, John. (2002). *Value Wars*. London: Pluto Press.

McMurtry, John. (2011). "Human Rights v. Corporate Rights: Understanding Life-Value, The Civil Commons, and Social Justice." *Studies in Social Justice*, Vol.5, No. 1 (Summer, 2011). 1-38.

Meszaros, Istvan. (2008). *The Challenge and Burden of Historical Time*. New York: Monthly Review Press.

Nimtz, August H. (2000). *Marx and Engles: Their Contribution to the Democratic Breakthrough*. Albany NY: State University of New York Press.

Noonan, Jeff. (2006). *Democratic Society and Human Needs*. Montreal: McGill-Queen's University Press.

Noonan, Jeff. (2009). "Free Time as a Condition of a Free Human Life," *Contemporary Political Theory*, Vol. 8, No. 4, 377-393.

Wainwright, Hilary. (2011). "A New Trade Unionism in the Making?" *The Bullet*. No. 488. www.socialistproject.ca/bullet/488.php (Accessed April 8th, 2011).

Wittig, Monique. (1997). "One is not Born Woman," *Feminisms*. Susan Kemp and Judith Squires, eds. Oxford: Oxford University Press, 220-226.

Wright, Erik Olin. (2010). *Envisaging Real Utopias*. London: Verso.

Commentary:

Profit Pathology and Disposable Planet

Michael Parenti *is an award-winning author and lecturer. His recent books include* God and His Demons, Contrary Notions: The Michael Parenti Reader, *and* The Face of Imperialism. *For more information, please visit his website: www.michaelparenti.org*

Some years ago in New England, a group of environmentalists asked a corporate executive how his company (a paper mill) could justify dumping its raw industrial effluent into a nearby river. The river—which had taken Mother Nature centuries to create–was used for drinking water, fishing, boating, and swimming. In just a few years, the paper mill had turned it into a highly toxic open sewer.

The executive shrugged and said that river dumping was the most cost-effective way of removing the mill's wastes. If the company had to absorb the additional expense of having to clean up after itself, it might not be able to maintain its competitive edge and would then have to go out of business or move to a cheaper labor market, resulting in a loss of jobs for the local economy.

FREE MARKET ÜBER ALLES

It was a familiar argument: the company had no choice. It was compelled to act that way in a competitive market. The mill was not in the business of protecting the environment but in the business of making a profit, the highest possible profit at the highest possible rate of return. *Profit* is the name of the game, as business leaders make clear when pressed on the point. The overriding purpose of business is capital accumulation.

To justify its single-minded profiteering, Corporate America promotes the classic laissez-faire theory which claims that the *free market*--a congestion of unregulated and unbridled enterprises all selfishly pursuing their own ends--is governed by a benign "invisible hand" that miraculously produces optimal outputs for everybody.

The free marketeers have a deep all-abiding faith in laissez-faire for it is a faith that serves them well. It means no government oversight, no being held accountable for the environmental disasters they perpetrate. Like greedy spoiled brats, they repeatedly get bailed out by the government (some free market!) so that they can continue to take irresponsible risks, plunder the land, poison the seas, sicken whole communities, lay waste to entire regions, and pocket obscene profits.

This corporate system of capital accumulation treats the Earth's life-sustaining resources (arable land, groundwater, wetlands, foliage, forests, fisheries, ocean beds, bays, rivers, air quality) as disposable ingredients presumed to be of limitless supply, to be consumed or toxified at will. As British Petroleum demonstrated so well in the Gulf-of-Mexico catastrophe, considerations of cost weigh much more heavily than considerations of safety. As one Congressional inquiry concluded: "Time after time, it appears that BP made decisions that increased the risk of a blowout to save the company time or expense" (Associated Press, 2011).

Indeed, the function of the transnational corporation is not to promote a healthy ecology but to extract as much marketable value out of the natural world as possible even if it means treating the environment like a septic tank. An ever-expanding corporate capitalism and a fragile finite ecology are on a calamitous collision course, so much so that the support systems of the entire ecosphere--the Earth's thin skin of fresh air, water, and topsoil--are at risk.

It is not true that the ruling politico-economic interests are in a state of denial about all this. Far worse than denial, they have shown outright antagonism toward those who think our planet is more important than their profits. So they defame environmentalists as "eco-terrorists," "EPA gestapo," "Earth day alarmists," "tree huggers," and purveyors of "Green hysteria."

In an enormous departure from free-market ideology, most of the diseconomies of big business are foisted upon the general populace, including the costs of cleaning up toxic wastes, the cost of monitoring production, the cost of disposing of industrial effluence (which composes 40 to 60 percent of the loads treated by taxpayer-supported municipal sewer plants), the cost of developing new water sources (while industry and agribusiness consume 80 percent of the nation's daily water supply), and the costs of attending to the sickness and disease caused by all the toxicity created. With many of these diseconomies regularly passed on to the government, the private sector then boasts of its superior cost-efficiency over the public sector.

THE SUPERRICH ARE DIFFERENT FROM US

Isn't ecological disaster a threat to the health and survival of corporate plutocrats just as it is to us ordinary citizens? We can understand why the corporate rich might want to destroy public housing, public education, Social Security, Medicare, and Medicaid. Such cutbacks would bring us closer to a free market society devoid of the publicly-funded "socialistic" human services that the ideological reactionaries detest. And such cuts would not deprive the superrich and their families of anything. The superrich have more than sufficient private wealth to procure whatever services and protections they need for themselves.

But the environment is a different story, is it not? Don't wealthy reactionaries and their corporate lobbyists inhabit the same polluted planet as everyone else, eat the same chemicalized food, and breathe the same toxified air? In fact, they do not live exactly as everyone else. They experience a different class reality, often residing in places where the air is markedly better than in low and middle income areas. They have access to food that is organically raised and specially transported and prepared.

The nation's toxic dumps and freeways usually are not situated in or near their swanky neighborhoods. In fact, the superrich do not live in neighborhoods as such. They usually reside on landed estates with plenty of wooded areas, streams, meadows, and only a few well-monitored access roads. Pesticide sprays are not poured over their trees and gardens. Clear cutting does not desolate their ranches, estates, family forests, lakes, and prime vacation spots.

Still, should they not fear the threat of an ecological apocalypse brought on by global warming? Do they want to see life on Earth, including their own lives, destroyed? In the long run they indeed will be sealing their own doom along with everyone else's. However, like us all, they live not in the long run but in the here and now. What is now at stake for them is something more proximate and more urgent than global ecology; it is global profits. The fate of the biosphere seems like a remote abstraction compared to the fate of one's immediate–and enormous–investments.

With their eye on the bottom line, big business leaders know that every dollar a company spends on oddball things like environmental protection is one less dollar in earnings. Moving away from fossil fuels and toward solar, wind, and tidal energy could help avert ecological disaster, but six of the world's ten top industrial corporations are involved primarily in the production of oil, gasoline, and motor vehicles. Fossil fuel pollution brings billions of dollars in returns. Ecologically sustainable forms of production threaten to compromise such profits, the big producers are convinced.

Immediate gain for oneself is a far more compelling consideration than a future loss shared by the general public. Every time you drive your car, you are putting your immediate need to get somewhere ahead of the collective need to avoid poisoning the air we all breathe. So, with the big players, the social cost of turning a forest into a wasteland weighs little against the immense and immediate profit that comes from harvesting the timber and walking away with a neat bundle of cash. And it can always be rationalized away: there are lots of other forests for people to visit, they don't need this one; society needs the timber; lumberjacks need the jobs, and so on.

THE FUTURE IS NOW

Some of the very same scientists and environmentalists who see the ecological crisis as urgent rather annoyingly warn us of a catastrophic climate crisis by "the end of this century." But that's some ninety years away when all of us and most of our kids will be dead--which makes global warming a much less urgent issue.

There are other scientists who manage to be even more irritating by warning us of an impending ecological crisis then putting it even further into the future: "We'll have to stop thinking in terms of eons and start thinking in terms of centuries," one scientific sage was quoted in the *New York Times* in 2006. This is supposed to put us on alert? If a global catastrophe is a century or several centuries away, who is going to make the terribly difficult and costly decisions today whose effects will be felt far in the future?

Often we are told to think of our dear *grandchildren* who will be fully victimized by it all (an appeal usually made in a beseeching tone). But most of the young people I address on college campuses have a hard time imagining the world that their nonexistent grandchildren will be experiencing thirty or forty years hence.

Such appeals should be put to rest. We do not have centuries or generations or even many decades before disaster is upon us. Ecological crisis is not some *distant* urgency. Most of us alive today probably will not have the luxury of saying "*Après moi, le déluge*" because we will still be around to experience the catastrophe ourselves. We know this to be true because the ecological crisis is already acting upon us with an accelerated and compounded effect that may soon prove irreversible.

THE PROFITEERING MADNESS

Sad to say, the environment cannot defend itself. It is up to us to protect it—or what's left of it. But all the superrich want is to keep transforming living nature into commodities and commodities into dead capital. Impending ecological disasters are of no great moment to the corporate plunderers. Of living nature they have no measure.

Wealth becomes addictive. Fortune whets the appetite for still more fortune. There is no end to the amount of money one might wish to accumulate, driven onward by the *auri sacra fames,* the cursed hunger for gold. So the money addicts grab more and more for themselves, more than can be spent in a thousand lifetimes of limitless indulgence, driven by what begins to resemble an obsessional pathology, a monomania that blots out every other human consideration.

They are more wedded to their wealth than to the Earth upon which they live, more concerned about the fate of their fortunes than the fate of humanity, so possessed by their pursuit of profit as to not see the disaster looming ahead. There was a *New Yorker* cartoon showing a corporate executive standing at a lectern addressing a business meeting with these words: "And so, while the end-of-the-world scenario will be rife with unimaginable horrors, we believe that the pre-end period will be filled with unprecedented opportunities for profit."

Not such a joke. Years ago I remarked that those who denied the existence of global warming would not change their opinion until the North Pole itself started melting. (I never expected it to actually start dissolving in my lifetime.) Today we are facing an Arctic meltdown that carries horrendous implications for the oceanic gulf streams, coastal water levels, the planet's entire temperate zone, and world agricultural output.

So how are the captains of industry and finance responding? As we might expect: like monomaniacal profiteers. They hear the music: ca-ching, ca-ching. First, the Arctic melting will open a direct northwest passage between the two great oceans, a dream older than Lewis and Clark. This will make for shorter and more accessible and inexpensive global trade routes. No more having to plod through the Panama Canal or around Cape Horn. Lower transportation costs mean more trade and higher profits.

Second, they joyfully note that the melting is opening up vast new oil reserves to drilling. They will be able to drill-baby-drill for more of the same fossil fuel that is causing the very calamity descending upon us. More meltdown means more oil and more profits; such is the mantra of the free marketeers who think the world belongs only to them.

Imagine now that we are all inside one big bus hurtling down a road that is headed for a fatal plunge into a deep ravine. What are our profit addicts doing? They are hustling up and down the aisle, selling us crash cushions and seat belts at exorbitant prices. They planned ahead for this sales opportunity.

We have to get up from our seats, quickly place them under adult supervision, rush the front of the bus, yank the driver away, grab hold of the wheel, slow the bus down, and turn it around. Not easy but maybe still possible. With me it's a recurrent dream.

An Interview with Pat Armstrong

Canadian Health Care: Privatization and Gendered Labour

Priscillia Lefebvre is a collaborative Ph.D. student at the Department of Sociology and Anthropology/Institute of Political Economy, Carleton University (Ottawa, Canada). Pat Armstrong is Professor of Sociology and Women's Studies at York University (Toronto, Canada). She held a CHSRF/CIHR Chair in Health Services and Nursing Research, focused on gender and chaired the group Women and Health Care Reform for more than a decade. She has published on a wide range of issues related to gender, health care and work. Pat was interviewed by Priscillia Lefebvre over August 2011.

Priscillia Lefebvre (PL): A large focus on your research seems to be the ways in which gender and labour intersect from the vantage point of health care delivery. What have been the main influences that have affected the trajectory of your research in terms of a feminist rooted political economy approach? Why is this approach so important in understanding the contradictions that exist regarding the role of women within health care?

Pat Armstrong (PA): It is difficult to identify the main influences on my thinking and research. Growing up in a family where community involvement was not only encouraged but required meant seeking engagement at university. Also, the red Tory approach in our household did not fit so comfortably with the Marx I read as a student in the 1960s or with the growing feminist movement I participated in. As Juliet Mitchell[1] explained, Marx was not good about women and did not provide a detailed blueprint for analysis, but he did offer a way to make systems transparent and to think about progressive change.

In my reading of Marx, work and the political economy are where the analysis should start because they are so powerful in shaping our lives; however, both productive and reproductive work have to be understood in historically specific ways and in ways that comprehend contradictions as well as interrelations. Indeed, contradictions can provide a basis for creating alternatives. Starting with power and economic forces did not imply ignoring ideas, discourses and cultural practices, but it did put those ideas, often blamed for women's subordination, into a context that allowed us to see the power embedded in them and in their reproduction. Furthermore, starting with the political economy did not mean ignoring gender and other basis for inequities. Rather, as we are argued in the 1970s and 1980s, gender had to be theorized at the highest level of abstraction if we are to think through the implications for change in our lives. This relates, in turn, to another influence, which was involvement in student and other politics.

My feminist political economy approach develops in such practices, as well as through engagement with other academics. Canadian Studies at Carleton University in the early 1970s provided fertile ground for the further development of my ideas about political economy with a clearly Canadian twist and so has my continuing policy work. As I became increasingly interested in feminist issues, I abandoned a thesis on the class origins of student activists and focused instead on women's paid and unpaid work. The result was *The Double Ghetto; Canadian Women and their Segregated Work,*[2] a joint project with my partner Hugh Armstrong, as is much of my research. When our daughter broke her leg and ended up in the hospital for weeks, we realized that health care covered all aspects of women's work. Paid and unpaid work overlapped in obvious and gendered ways, as the staff told me, but not Hugh, where I could get our daughter juice and empty the bed pan. There were unionized and non-union workers, full, part-time and casual jobs, work defined as highly skilled and jobs defined as unskilled, occupations dominated by women classified as managerial, clerical, professional, and service, with many women from racialized and/ or immigrant groups. What it took us longer to realize - but what we should have realized as political economists - was that health care provides a unique context and required us to learn about a wider range of forces, policies and practices in care.

Women are not only the majority of workers, but also the majority of patients and of those who take others for care, creating complicated and often contradictory gender relations. Equally important from our perspective, health care in Canada offers a clear example of how universal programmes can create social solidarity by demonstrating the impact of collective action. What a political economy approach allows us to do is think through the ways work, gender and other inequities intersect, to explore the ways economic and political forces shape not only services and employment, but also ideas, and to bring together the complexity of work relations within this specific historical context. This approach also helps us see the contradictions in, for example, nurses fighting to distance themselves from links with women's caring.[3]

PL: In a previous article published in a 1983 special edition of Alternate Routes[1], you outline the problematic nature of quantitative data analysis as gender-blind. Since then, you have been involved in several working groups, including the National Coordinating Group on Health Care Reform and Women (now Women and Health care Reform), dedicated to researching health care reform policies and their impact on women both as health care providers and recipients. In your experience, what have been the greatest research challenges in gathering information on gender and sex differences within health care in Canada? In your opinion, what needs to be explored further?

PA: In my view, many of the challenges remain the same. There are still problems with the way data are collected and categorized, with the failure to collect some kinds of data and a further problem with the way the data are analyzed and with what gets accepted as good science. In too many cases, quantitative data are still seen as providing the truth and the whole truth, while qualitative data are too often treated as suspect. Especially in health care, there is a hierarchy of evidence in terms of what kinds of data are accepted as legitimate and worthy of attention with the meta-analysis of double-blind randomized clinical trials taken as the gold standard because they are assumed to remove all bias. Yet numbers, and categories, continue to reflect values.

One example from our recent research is the definition of industry.[4] In the past, Statistics Canada defined industry as 'where people work.' Thus, everyone who worked in hospital would be counted as working in the health care industry. Now industry is defined as 'who you work for,' removing from health care all those whose jobs have been contracted out, most of whom are women and many of whom are from racialized groups. A second example comes from data on work-related violence.[5] Our interviews with women employed in long-term residential care indicate that many women fail to report violence, in part because they will be blamed, in part because they won't be believed, and in part because it takes too much time. The result is underestimates of violence in the numbers.

1 *Beyond numbers: Problems with Quantitative Data,* by Pat Armstrong and Hugh Armstrong in *Alternate Routes: A Critical Review,* Vol. 6. Ottawa, Ontario: Carleton University, 1983. Pages: 1-40.

At the same time, research is still published that failed to collect data by sex, and even more frequently, without analyzing the data by sex or gender. Most frequently, the approach to data collection and analysis makes it impossible to do a gender analysis. Women and Health Care Reform has illustrated the problem by looking at wait times for hip and knee surgery, demonstrating that we need to look at the entire patient journey to see the ways gender influences how long women wait and even whether or not women get the surgery they need.[6] A mere comparison of the number of women who get surgery compared to the number of men tells us little about equity. As Women and Health Care Reform struggled to figure out how to ensure gender could be included as a criterion in meta-analysis such as Cochrane reviews, we came to realize that in their attempt to ensure scientific validity such reviews sought to eliminate context. As a result, they eliminated gender and racialization because both are about social relations in context.

In addition, new problems have arisen since we wrote that article. At the time Statistics Canada data were free and now much of it must be paid for. In the past, we could analyze the data in the way we saw fit. Now for access to much of the original data, you apply for access and then you have to go through a data analysis centre where the analysis must be vetted. Of course, the government has attacked the long-form Census in general and a critical question for feminist in particular, the one that asked about unpaid work. Does gender have an impact, and in what ways, needs to always be part of the question, whatever the research, but this lesson has still not been learned by far too many researchers and policy makers. So, what needs to be explored further is a huge question. In short, we have some more data by sex, but too little analysis by gender and too much faith in numbers.

PL: Much of your work focuses on the privatization of health care and its detrimental effects in terms of access to treatment and quality of care. In *Exposing Privatization*[2] (p. 163), you outline the introduction of privatization measures to health care beginning with the majority Conservative government in Ontario in the mid-90s. Given the current Tory majority at the federal level and provincial inroads to privatization in Ontario, do you see this as a particularly critical time in defending health care as a public good, rather than a competitive market com-

2 Bernier, Kay Wilson, Karen R. Grant, and Ann Pederson. Toronto, Ontario: University of Toronto Press, 2001. $24.76 CDN, paper. ISBN-13: 978-1551930374. Pages: 1-310.

modity? What are your thoughts regarding Stephen Harper's recent statement that, although the federal Conservatives have no plans to go private, he cannot control the kinds of alternative delivery models used at the provincial level?

PA: The best defence of public health care is popular support and we need to mobilize that support more than ever because we are facing a huge threat. The biggest threat now, in my view, is not costs but further privatization in all its forms. Those pushing for privatization know that medicare is Canada's best loved social programme and so have privatized by stealth, always promising public payment. They have claimed there is a crisis and that health care cannot be sustained; that it must be radically transformed in order to save it. Fear is a powerful force, especially when your health is at stake. Our biggest problem in defending public care is complexity and the difficulty of getting people to understand why it is wrong to have for-profit delivery, even if the money comes from the public purse rather than from private payment, and why health care is as sustainable as we want it to be. I think the Federal government will be very crafty while promoting deep privatization. It will negotiate individually with provinces and territories, allowing them to go their own way and blame the consequences on them. Of course, the Prime Minister can stop that. Monique Begin did when she was Minister of Health and Welfare. But Prime Minister Harper will not intervene, so we need to put pressure at the local level and keep educating people about the perils of profits in care. If we do not stop this erosion soon, it will be too late.

PL: In your opinion, how harmful are agreements such as the Canada-European Union Comprehensive Economic and Trade Agreement (EU-CETA) to Canadian health care and how are women affected in particular?

PA: In many ways, these new agreements have much the same impact as earlier ones and have particularly negative consequences for women as a group and for particular groups of women.[7] The agreements are written to promote profit and limit governments' capacity to shape their own economies and public policies. It is much harder to influence policies if governments are prohibited from acting in the public's interests and are instead forced to act in the interests of global profits. Because more women than men depend on the state for services, financial support, jobs and protections against things like violence at work, agreements that limit or prevent governments from regulating, protecting, and providing have a particularly negative impact on them. The result is likely to be greater inequities among women, as well as greater inequity between women and men.

PL: Labour disputes, in particular organized labour, have received much political attention recently. For example, in an unprecedented move, postal workers were recently legislated back to work on a lockout. Do you consider the recent use of back to work legislation in both the private and public sectors as threatening to the collective bargaining rights of unions? Also, how do you think these latest negotiations will affect the collective organization and labour struggles of health service workers (for example, nurses and home care workers)?

PA: The attacks on labour are no surprise and it should be clear that attacks on unions in the public sector are attacks on women who make up the majority of unionized workers there. One factor that kept families going during the most recent economic crisis was women's employment in the public sector in general.[8] We are building up to massive cuts in the health sector, where four out of five workers are women and where one in five women works. Those who keep their jobs are likely to see them get worse as privatization is pushed further. Cutbacks in public pensions and benefits will also hurt these women, as well as their families. At the same time however, women employed in health care enjoy tremendous public support. If the unions in the public sector can come together and resist, we may see real limits on attacks from the government. Few doubt these women work hard, few think they are overpaid or pandered to by their employers, so it is much harder to sell the line about being pampered employees or to promote the politics of envy with them, as has been done with other unionized workers.

PL: Finally, in *Critical to Care*[3] (p. 53), you argue that much of the labour performed by women in health services is essential in terms of providing care, yet remains peripheral in terms of social and economic status. Your research indicates that due to this gendered division of labour in health care women are the primary health care providers in Canada, yet women hold very little decision making power when it comes to policy. Also, not only is it highly gendered, it is highly racialized. In your opinion, to what extent has the introduction of state level initiatives, such as the Foreign Live-In Caregiver Program,

---

3 *Critical to Care: The Invisible Women in Health Services,* by Pat Armstrong, Hugh Armstrong, and Krista Scott-Dixon. Toronto, Ontario: University of Toronto Press, 2008. $20.76 CDN, paper. ISBN-13: 978-0802096081. Pages: 1-176.

perpetuated these inequities? Also, even if such initiatives did not exist, how far do you think 'within system' efforts, such as changes to policy, will go in resolving these inequities? Is a shift beyond the present political system also needed?

PA: These are complicated questions and difficult to answer in part because I think there are contradictory policies and practices. Universal health care has undoubtedly helped women, both as care providers and as those with care needs. Women's employment conditions are better in the public sector and they have more power there, in large measure because unions have been strong, but also because there are pressures within and outside government to respond to calls for human rights and to set an example as a model employer.[9] Initiatives such as Pay and Employment Equity have helped make employment in the public sector more equitable than in the private sector. Of course, these gains are precisely why there is pressure on governments to abandon these policies and to attack unions; attacks supported by many within governments.

This is not to claim that health care has been equally accessible or that employment practices in the public sector have resulted in equity but we can demonstrate that women do better in the public sector than they do in the for-profit one. At the same time, the way health care has been organized and policies developed have in many ways reinforced not only women's responsibilities for care, but also the inequities among women. This is happening increasingly with current reforms. Nor is it to argue that we should try to return to some 'good old days.' Those days were not all good and, in any case, they are gone. We are dealing with a new reality and 'old' means of undermining the gains we made. Nevertheless, I think that we should struggle for government policies that promote equity. Universal public daycare combined with more public homecare, for example, could help make the Foreign Live-in Caregiver Programme irrelevant. If workers in these services were unionized and supported by strong anti-racist programmes, it would help address some inequities.

However, it is not sufficient, in my view, to rely on governments alone. We need strategies that address conditions of work and care within the voluntary and for-profit sectors as well, even while we work for public care. We also need strategies to change the power inequities within households. I agree, then, with the implications of your question that we need to shift beyond the system and that we need to connect multiple policies in and outside the state, but I think that it is still important to work to change public policies.

NOTES

1 *Women's Estate* by Juliet Mitchell. Harmondsworth: Penguin, 1971 and "Marxism and Women's Liberation" by Juliet Mitchell. *Social Praxis* 1(1):23-33.

2 *The Double Ghetto: Canadian Women and Their Segregated Work* by Pat Armstrong and Hugh Armstrong. Toronto: McClelland and Stewart, 1978.

3 "Contradictions at Work: Struggles for Control in Canadian health care" by Pat Armstrong and Hugh Armstrong in *Morbid Symptoms Health Under Capitalism,* edited by Leo Panitch and Colin Leys. 2009. Pontypool: Merlin Press, Pages 145-183

4 "Doubtful Data: Why Paradigms Matter in Counting the Health-Care Labor Force" by Pat Armstrong, Hugh Armstrong and Kate Laxer in. *Work in Tumultuous Times: Critical Perspectives*, edited byVivian Shalla and Wallace Clement. Montreal and Kingston: McGill-Queen's University Press, 2007 "Precarious Work, Privatization, and the health care Industry: The Case of Ancillary Workers" . Pat Armstrong and Kate Laxer in *Precarious Employment. Understanding Labour Market Insecurity in Canada* edited by Leah Vosko. Montreal: McGill-Queen's University Press, 2006.

5 *Critical to Care: The Invisible Women in Health Services,* by Pat Armstrong, Hugh Armstrong, and Krista Scott-Dixon. Toronto, Ontario: University of Toronto Press, 2008. $20.76 CDN, paper. ISBN-13: 978-0802096081. Pages: 1-176.

6 "Waiting to Wait: Improving Wait Times Evidence through Gender-Based Analysis by Beth Jackson, Ann Pederson and Madeline Boscoe in *Women's Health. Intersections of Policy, Research, and Practice*. Edited by Pat Arsmtrong and Jennifer Deadman. Toronto: Women's Press, 2009. Pages 35-52.

7 "Trade Agreements, Home Care and Women's Health." By Olena Hankivsky, Marina Morrow, Pat Armstrong, Lindsay, Galvin and Holly Grinvalds. Ottawa: Status of Women in Canada, 2004.

8 "Women Forced to Work Longer, harder, For Less Pay by Pat Armstrong in *Speaking Truth to Power* edited by Trish Hennessey and Ed Finn. Ottawa: CCPA, 2010. Pages 7-14.

9 Precarious Work, Privatization, and the health care Industry: The Case of Ancillary Workers" . Pat Armstrong and Kate Laxer in *Precarious Employment. Understanding Labour Market Insecurity in Canada* edited by Leah Vosko. Montreal: McGill-Queen's University Press, 2006.

An Interview with Sut Jhally

Articulation, Cultural Studies, and Education

Justin Paulson is an Assistant Professor of Sociology at Carleton University (Ottawa, Canada), where he teaches political economy and social theory. He recently co-edited Capitalism and Confrontation: Critical Perspectives. ***Sut Jhally** is Professor of Communication at the University of Massachusetts (Massachusetts, U.S.A) and founder and Executive Director of the Media Education Foundation. He is the author of numerous books, articles, and films on advertising, media, and culture. For more information, please visit his website: www.sutjhally.com. Justin spoke with Sut Jhally on September 8, 2011.*

Justin Paulson (JP): As you know, *Alternate Routes* was recently relaunched after several years of dormancy, and we are quite pleased to have the opportunity to hear from you again. You were not only one of the first contributors to *AR* (vol. 3, 1979), but I understand that the journal also carried your first publication as a scholar?

Sut Jhally (SJ): Yes, that's why *Alternate Routes* has always held a very fond place in my heart. I was a Master's student in Sociology at the University of Victoria, and this was the very first thing that I had published. I remember having to provide a copy-ready piece to the journal, and because this was before the age of computers, a secretary had to type up my paper. The process was just very different than today, and reflects how the practices of intellectual life have changed over the last 30 years–from a time when almost every thing was written by hand, and then someone typed it, to a situation now where writing by hand is almost non-existent, and everyone types straight into a computer. And I think that is a very significant change. I remember talking to Stuart Hall about this a few years ago, and he believed that writing on a computer had actually negatively affected the quality of his prose. His reasoning was that using a typewriter makes major corrections difficult, so you really had to think carefully about sentence construction, etc., before committing it to paper. Whereas with computers, you just write down your first conceptualization, knowing you can always change it later on. The problem is, once un-thoughtful stuff is in some (if only virtual) form, that becomes the starting point for both theorizing and writing.

JP: Let's talk about that early piece for a minute. In "Marxism and Underdevelopment: the Modes of Production Debate," you reviewed the debates of the 1970s on what constitute the modes of production and how societies transition to capitalism. On the face of it, your work since then took you in a very different direction: you are well-known today as a leading media critic and an expert in cultural studies. But I'm wondering how, or if, this early publication nevertheless helped to shape your future direction as a scholar. Do you ever find yourself taking up such theoretical debates in your more recent work, or in your teaching?

SJ: Although I didn't really follow up on the specific content of that piece–I haven't written about underdevelopment or international relations since that time, in fact–I think the broader problematic that they were located in has never gone away. There is a very key theoretical term–"articulation"– that has been important to me, and to the debates in cultural studies in general, that is infused throughout the article. So when I teach these issues today, for example in a graduate class I teach on the cultural studies theorist, Stuart Hall, I refer back to the Frank-Laclau debate as the first time that I really came across the term articulation, and the modes of production debate as really one of the first places that it was used to theorize relations between things that seem separate but are connected in some way, a way to talk about sameness and difference.

JP: I'm reminded of Hall's working paper from the mid-70s on Marx's 1857 introduction to the *Grundrisse*, which touched on similar issues. Were you influenced by that as well?

SJ: Absolutely. What I find interesting right now is that the modes of production debate that focused around articulation led Laclau then to move from thinking about modes of production within a social formation, to thinking about the relationship between different levels of the social formation (between culture and politics and economics, etc.) and he really became, along with Chantal Mouffe, one of the leading theorists in how to conceptualize that question. But the first place he dealt with this was not in the realm of politics, culture or social movements, which is where he ended up, but in the articulation between much larger structures. Hall also has a 1980 piece "Race, articulation and societies structured in dominance" where articulation is employed in an analysis of modes of production, colonialism and neo-colonialism. So I always refer back to this kind of forgotten genesis of articulation, that it actually really emerged in another place and then went from the modes of production debate to becoming a central conceptual piece within western Marxism to talk about social movements and culture, politics, the state, etc. So, going back to your original question, although I haven't really bumped into the same themes in content, conceptually I think I have retained that interest in how to conceptualize connection.

JP: I wonder if we ought to go full circle and bring the concept of articulation back into conversation with political economy.

SJ: Actually, that is my trajectory into these issues, because my first cut into media studies per se, in the realm of communication specifically (rather than through sociology, for example), came though the work of Dallas Smythe, who was a Canadian communication theorist teaching at Simon Fraser. He argued that Marxism had a "blind spot" when it came to communication in that it regarded the media as principally an ideological institution, whereas it's really an economic institution. So he wanted to re-think within the Marxist tradition how media should be properly conceptualized. Because at that time, and we're talking in the late 1970s, within political economy the media were still largely regarded as ideological institutions that were functional to the state, that were functional to the reproductive process of capitalism. What Dallas argued was that instead, we should think about them first as economic institutions that produce surplus in and of themselves, but then also look at the role they play in the circulation and distribution of commodities. And in this understanding advertising was absolutely fundamental. So that was really the first time I started to think about advertising.

And it was the same problematic of part-whole understandings, of how to understand what seems to be secondary and peripheral in terms of its place within the entire system. Looking back, actually at around the same time I got interested in the debates that were taking place in cultural studies, through the Working Papers series of the Birmingham Centre, about how women's domestic work, housework, should be understood in economic terms. Was housework part of wage labor? Was it separate from wage labor? Did it produce value? Essentially it was asking those same questions, which is 'what's the relationship between this activity, which seems to be not an economic activity or a key economic activity, and what people thought was real economic activity in the workplace?' Again, the same set of questions as the modes of production debate. Are housework and wage labor the same? Are they different? What's the connection between them? What's the articulation between them? That was really interesting to me, and then from that I started to think about advertising within the context of all this material I was reading about the relationships between things that seem different but are connected. That was what the modes of production debate was really about. So as I said, the content of it certainly didn't stick but the general kind of conceptual questions that were raised have remained with me since then, and partly I think they remain with me because they were always central to cultural studies.

JP: Could you talk a little bit about the concept of critique that you worked with? The 1979 essay operated within a particular framework, yet also subjected that framework to significant criticism. In one sense this is the true meaning of critique, but it also strikes me as somewhat distinct from our academic publishing environment today, in which young scholars are too often content to simply denounce those who preceded them and move on–even if it means throwing the baby out with the bathwater. It's less common to see students arguing that a particular framework is basically correct, and yet needs to be critiqued and improved for X or Y reasons. Have you noticed a change in the nature of critique over the thirty years you've been engaged in scholarship?

SJ: I'm not too sure I've seen it change a great deal because I think there have always been those different kinds of approaches to criticism, those different dimensions to it. What I do think exists is good critique and bad critique, and that has always been around. For me critique has to be productive, a kind of sympathetic critique, otherwise its just criticism. I don't think you should be sympathetic to everything, I think there are some things that are just wrong and you need to say that they're wrong. But in my view theory doesn't proceed with giant steps. Theory proceeds in small steps, and it proceeds on the shoulders of people who have gone before. I think that's exactly how Marx operated. He started his work with existing economic thinkers because that was the most developed work at that time. He didn't say this was all wrong, he didn't say classical economics was all wrong–he started there because he thought that was the most sophisticated understanding of where things were, but it didn't get everything. And he proceeded to critique it in a pretty fundamental way. He called his work after all "a critique of political economy". Everything operates on the basis of what has gone before.

I guess I take my intellectual lead here again from Stuart Hall, who I think has always had this kind of very generous way of reading theory–which is, you can evaluate literatures, you can evaluate people's work, but if you want to move it on, let's take the best of what's there without rejecting everything. So, I think that's the notion that I would urge young scholars to engage in. When I think back to when I was first a grad student, I think the piece that you refer to may be the first time where I was perhaps becoming more thoughtful and really trying to dig out what was useful in people's work. It was only when I realized how much I didn't know, how much we didn't know, that's when I think I started to develop a more mature view of intellectual work and research. Not starting off with what you know you want to find out, but by really not knowing what it is you're going to find out, really not knowing where you're going to end up. If you know where you're going to end up when you start doing research, I wouldn't really call that research, I'd call that something else.

So for me, open-mindedness, a kind of sympathetic view of what's gone before is a key aspect of advancing knowledge. I am not saying that everything that's gone on before is great, but taking the most productive aspects and moving theory on, one step at a time. I think that Marx operates that way and I think that Stuart Hall operates that way–in this very, very sympathetic and productive way where you keep on theorizing, you don't stop at any time and it's a constant process of evaluating what's there and moving on slowly.

JP: I liked the way you framed that. I think you once noted that your interest in the question of determination is not based in political dogmatism, it's simply in the nature of being a social scientist. And similarly you've argued that the function of universities is to train people to change the world in some way–not necessarily to offer them a pre-written script for how to do that, or to tell them what kind of world to change it into–but universities shouldn't merely reproduce knowledge about the world nor merely train people for jobs. And this conviction has led you to become a public intellectual. But as a public intellectual based in the university, do you find much resistance to these principles? Is the university changing in its ability to train students to think critically, and try to change the world in some way? Is it becoming less receptive for criticism and praxis, and more about career training?

SJ: I think it depends on which university, and which sector of higher education you look at. There's no doubt that the American university is changing. Public universities are becoming less public in that there is just less public money that goes into education now. And as that has dried up, what's taken its place is corporate money, and so I think you're seeing a kind of corporatization and a militarization of the university in terms of its funding that you never saw before. For example, at the university where I am there are essentially two campuses: there's the sciences which have all the external research money (either corporate or federal) and then there's the social sciences and humanities, and we're very much the poor neighbours of the rich people who live up the hill. Our function is essentially to teach people, and the function of the north side of the university is to bring in the money and do the research.

And as public money is drying up, the nature of teaching is changing as well in that there are just less tenure track people and positions, with a lot of them being converted to adjunct positions, or to limited term positions. So there's just a lack of stability on the employment side. I think tenure is fundamental to the intellectual life of a university in that it gives you the chance to experiment, it gives you the chance to take a risk, it gives you the opportunity to say things that might be unpopular in the classroom. And that aspect of academic life is changing, at least in the U.S. I don't think that tenure is being taken away in some major way; it's just being slowly eroded because there's fewer of those kinds of positions. So the people who are teaching students these days, especially in the social sciences and humanities, don't have the stability and the protection that they perhaps once would have had. And I think that is influencing both research and teaching.

At the same time I think students are also changing in the sense that a post-secondary education is seen by many students as a necessity, and as training for a job. So there is a push for professional training, the push for something that's practical, that will provide a more or less immediate return on the very large personal investment many students make in their education. There has of course always been an element of this, but I think the emphasis is increasing, and it's really putting the notion of a "liberal education" under pressure, and changing the context within which we operate in the classroom. So I think we just have be much more aware of what we are doing in our pedagogy.

Teaching for me is a key component of being an intellectual (as important as research and writing). Actually, it is a key component of being a public intellectual, because the public is not just out there beyond the ivory tower–the classroom is also a public space populated by people who do not read our disciplinary journals. These publications have an important role in our professional lives, but our scholarly articles are written for a particular audience of our colleagues that require a quite specialized, technical and sometime jargonistic language.

So in that sense I think teaching is a vital practice for people who aspire to have some kind of "public" presence, who regard the function of knowledge as being broader than just job qualification. I think there is a sense that if you want to have this kind of more engaged public presence, you have to think beyond the walls of the academy. But there is a great opportunity within the academy to talk to people who you wouldn't be otherwise able to reach, and to be able to get them to ask questions in a new way.

Now one of the questions you asked me was about the nature of critique, and how you engage that. I don't think my job, especially in the classroom, is to tell people *what* to do–that's *their* job to figure out, and will be driven by their own ethical and moral sense about their lives. That's not a function that universities should engage in, to tell what people what kinds of political action they should take. I think our job is to get people to see the world as clearly as possible, and that in itself is a radical act. To see the world as clearly as possible in all its complexity and with the implications of why the world operates like it does, and then to say, look, the world isn't just created, it doesn't fall from heaven fully formed, it's created by people, it's created by interests, it's created by human activity, and you can either be a bystander to that, or you can participate actively in the creation of the world in which you want to live. But if you're a bystander, don't tell me you're not political, bystanders are also political, bystanders are essentially going along with the world the way it is. That is also a political statement.

So what is the function of knowledge? It's to destroy the illusion that people are somehow separate from the world. I want to destroy the illusion that people do not have a responsibility to the world. In my classes, when students leave I want them to think about what their moral responsibility is. My student evaluations at the end of the semester are quite interesting sometimes. One person wrote, "I guess it's good to know this stuff, but I just wish I didn't." Because ignorance is, literally, bliss. I think that should be the key intellectual function of universities, to destroy ignorance, and to give people real information and understandings about the world in which they live, and to empower them to be able to take a stance in and to the world. I'll say to my students, "Look, I'm not telling you what to do, you want to go and work in business, in corporations, then that's fine, but be aware of what you're doing, that you're making a moral decision, an ethical decision, that you are going to participate in this system which we just spent a semester looking at. That the values of that system are now *your* values, you are not just going along blindly, you are now part of that." That's what I want to do, to empower people in terms of their own responsibilities and on the basis that they really understand the world as clearly as possible. Beyond that I don't think that's there's much we can, or even should do.

But having said that, I think there's a reason why a lot of students come out of universities with a different political viewpoint than when they went in. Because the post-secondary sector, at least in the United States, is the last place in the culture where there is any kind of intellectual diversity left. The political culture is now totally bought up, it's totally colonized, and there is no way that you can have any kind of real meaningful debate about fundamental things within the political sphere. That was one the most brilliant things that corporations figured out–we'll take over not only the Republican Party, that's our traditional party, but we'll take over the Democratic Party as well, and in that way take over the whole of politics. That is how corporate interests become the national interest.

The political sphere is gone, the media sphere is gone, the public sphere is gone, the state is gone. The universities and colleges are the last place left, and that's why they're now coming under attack from the right wing, why they're coming under attack from corporations–it's an attempt to shut down the last bastion of seeming diversity. But it's no accident that when young people are exposed to diversity, when they're given opposing view points, it's not surprising to me that they often think that those left wing progressive ideas actually make sense. That's what always gives me hope, that the right is scared stiff of real debate, the right is scared stiff of real knowledge because they know the vast majority of people, if you presented things to them in a fair way, that the game of hegemony will be over. So they have to shut down that debate through monopoly. For those of us who are in the university, I think we are engaged in one of the last efforts of resistance to this corporate takeover.

JP: And this was one of the insights of cultural studies, was it not? That most people aren't simply stupid or beset with 'false consciousness', but that if given the opportunity to think critically, without proselytization by the Party, that they will look somewhat askance at what's going on in the world.

SJ: The question I would want to pose is "Why do the majority of people vote solemnly every four years against their economic interests?" I don't think that's because they're stupid, I think that's because there are more aspects of people's identities than just their economic identities. And the right has figured this out, and especially in the United States, has really made quite explicit appeals to racial identity. And I think that's one of the things that Marxists couldn't quite figure out, that there are other things in people's experiences were just as powerful, perhaps more powerful, than class. For them it was as people got poorer and poorer, the more radical they would become, the more the proletarian consciousness will rise.

What that ignored was some of the key findings of cultural studies, that there is never a straightforward relationship between reality and peoples' perception of that reality. That the perception of reality always goes through a cultural and symbolic filter, and if you can control that cultural and symbolic filter you can appeal to people on some other level, and tell a story about why they're poor, and how the people to blame for why they're poor aren't capitalists but those filthy immigrants who have come and taken our jobs. This is what Althusser called an "imaginary relationship of individuals to their real conditions of existence." It is important to stress that it wasn't a "false" relationship, but an imaginary one that audiences have to actively engage with, and there is no guarantee as to its success.

However, I think sometimes cultural studies went too far on the active audience stuff, the idea that people are really active and you can't control them. Well, I think people are active, as human beings we are always active in the creation of meaning because there is never such a thing as natural meaning. Meaning is always up for grabs, so the idea of an active audience is fundamentally built into the nature of us as human beings. But that doesn't mean that active audiences can't be controlled. The "imaginary relation" that we are encouraged to experience the world through can be a very powerful filter of control that talks to you, again in Althusser's terms it "interpellates" you in powerful ways, and leads you down a particular direction.

In that way you can actively make meaning (actually I don't know any other way you make meaning if not actively) but someone else can direct it because the conditions of interpretation are not of your own making. And that is why the institutions of public relations and advertising form such a large part of the work of control of modern society.

Unfortunately, cultural studies lurched for a time into a direction where that broader social, economic and cultural context of interpretation kind of disappeared, and what we got were lots of fan studies about pleasure, about why people were doing certain kinds of things, making certain kinds of meanings divorced from this broader structure. And I think that's still the case.

So I encourage graduate students to go back to the kinds of concerns that animated cultural studies in the original phase. For example the book *Policing the Crisis,* which I think is one of the seminal pieces that emerged out of cultural studies with a central focus on questions of articulation and of conjuncture, is in my mind an exemplary methodological and theoretical text. It starts off with the phenomena in the mid 1970s of British (English actually) judges starting to hand down these ridiculously lengthy jail sentences, twenty years, for what were very common crimes that used to be punished by a few years. And Stuart Hall and his colleagues at the Birmingham Centre for Contemporary Cultural Studies started to ask, 'What is going on here? Why are black youth being treated in this way?' And starting from these small incidents they teased out, theoretically and empirically, what was going on in society as a whole, that this was part of a new conjuncture, a new economic-political conjuncture that was responding to the changing imperial role of Britain in global terms. Hall argues that we are still in the hegemonic project that was birthed at that time: Thatcherism was the first part, Blair was the second , and now the Conservative-Liberal Coalition is the third.

JP: You've seen the reaction to the riots–someone was jailed three years for stealing a loaf of bread?

SJ: And four years for simply posting on Facebook! Again, we are in that moment where these sentences tell you something else about what's going on. That was the brilliance of *Policing the Crisis*. They started off somewhere small and they ended up with a crisis of the whole society. That is the best kind of sociological work, empirically grounded and theoretically important. I think the best work has to be empirically grounded. We need theory, yes, but theory by itself is not enough. For me (and I might be unusual in this) theory only helps make sense of the world, helps make sense of something we could call reality. And for that you need to have other ways of linking theory up with the world: *evidence*.

In my own work, and in my teaching, its always about evidence. I start off telling my students that they shouldn't believe me, that I am just spinning them a story about the world and how it works. So how do we decide what is useful for explaining the world? How do we decide between different "theories"? Well, that requires intellectual work. That requires research. That requires proof. I think that's what C. Wright Mills called 'the sociological imagination'. You need the sociological imagination. Otherwise, you're just in religion, you're just in faith–"I think this is correct this because I believe it."

This is really relevant within the United States right now because there are actually questions about how best to understand the world: by a kind of rational, scientific view of the world, or a view of the world that just refuses that and is based on faith. It's really a very, very worrying sign right now that the next President of the United States, if he's one of the Republican frontrunners, may not believe in science, won't believe in evolution, doesn't believe the science around climate change.

JP: I don't think the last one did, either.

SJ: Well, the view on Bush was that he was just a front, and that the people running behind him were much more rational. But there wasn't this anti-scientific view that is really now so powerful within the mainstream of the Republican Party. And again, I don't think that's just an accident. It's being created and spun through public relations and through ideological work. The fact that 40 percent of the population in the United States doesn't believe that climate change is connected to human activity isn't just because Americans are stupid. It's because there has been an immense amount of ideological work that has gone into constructing that as an opinion.

JP: So thinking about teaching again, do you see the role of teaching in part to inoculate students against this kind of, what shall we call it, faith-based storytelling?

SJ: I think it actually is much more to do with an old-fashioned sense of what "liberal education" is, what learning is, and figuring out exactly how the world works in some kind of rational way. It is a commitment to a rational view of the world, it is a commitment to the Enlightenment view of the world that for a long time we didn't even question. What's happening right now is that that view of the world is being questioned from both the right (who see the truth in faith) and the postmodernists who don't see truth anywhere. At the very moment when we need scientific clarity to deal with the collapse of our physical and financial environment is the very moment when a commitment to that view of the world is eroding.

JP: Speaking of collapse, you argued in "Advertising and the End of the World" that advertising would be responsible for destroying the world as we knew it in about ten years. It's now more than a decade later, and the world seems to sputter on in some recognizable form.

SJ: What I think I said was that the environmental catastrophe would hit some 70 or 80 years down the road, but to avert it, we have to take action now, so that we have very little time left to deal with it. Actually, given where we are in terms of climate change and the collapse of the oceans and fishing, 70 years may have optimistic! And while it is impossible to predict with any certainty *when* things will happen, I don't think there is any doubt that they *will* happen. The actual crisis when we won't be able to continue might be a long time coming, and will certainly happen after I am dead and my ashes scattered in the ocean. And yet to stop that crisis occurring *then*, we have to take action *now*. Which is why I always use the metaphor (which I got from my doctoral advisor Bill Leiss) of the oil tanker, which because of its size and momentum has to start turning well before their seems to be any visible danger, heading towards the shore,. And that's where we are right now. We have to make that change right now, even though the effects of it may not be felt for quite a while.

I think that's what some people call the "sunny day syndrome". Things seem to be fine, the sun is shining, the weather isn't *that* extreme, you turn on your tap and water comes out of it, and right now we're saying, "Where's the crisis?" And so you've got to have this long-term view of the world. Which is very difficult to do. I mean, from an evolutionary perspective, we have never had to think about our actions that far into the future. Most of the time through human history we've been, "Okay, how do we survive until tomorrow? How do we get enough food now, and perhaps last us through the winter?" And so we're actually, in one sense, going against eons of evolution, in terms of having to think that far into the future. And I think that's the function of knowledge, and we have to evolve, or at least develop, a new way of thinking about ourselves.

I think actually everything I said in "Advertising and the End of the World" is quite accurate. The crises have just gotten worse and worse, our environmental crisis, our ecological crisis, just the resource crisis around oil. I mean when I first wrote "Advertising at the Edge of the Apocalypse" peak oil wasn't really a thing at that time. Now we know we are in trouble around resources. We know that our oceans are in trouble, through acidification. We're over-fishing and fish are being made extinct by the day. Our financial systems are collapsing.

And I don't think there's any guarantee that the collapse of capitalism will led to socialism. As Marx said, "the future could be either socialism or barbarism." And I think there's very strong evidence, and especially if this kind of the anti-scientific, faith-based view of the world is going to continue–I'm not sure it's going to predominate, but it's going to stop the political system from functioning properly–that our future may be barbarism.

Again in the article and film, I talked about how the cultural and intellectual ground on which we operate will determine how far into the future we can see and what we regard as important issues. To the extent that advertising remains the ground, it remains the environment within which we think about these things, all these questions, these long-term questions, they're beyond the horizon, they're beyond our capability to think about. And it's partly also that advertising and marketing, to the extent that they are so fundamental to promoting expanding consumption, are pushing the environmental and resource collapse even faster.

Actually in the film I pointed to the depletion of the ozone layer as an indication of the coming catastrophe. But I think we can actually point to that as a way of showing what a possible solution may be, because the depletion of the ozone layer has partly been dealt with by taking collective action. By nations coming together and deciding to take collective action, and that's exactly what we need.

I think we're at a time in the world where urgent action is needed. And one piece of advice I give to graduate students in particular is to concentrate your intellectual work on something that's important, research something that's connected to the world out there. Don't just do research on things that you find interesting in and of themselves. Your work is part of this movement that needs to change how we look at things, and we all play small parts in that. What role are you going to play? For example, within communication, are you going to study (and I don't mean to insult people) the ironic dimensions of The Simpsons and the contradictions of postmodern ideology, or are you going to look at really something much more fundamental? Are you going to look at, for example, how the Simpsons and irony are used to paralyze people from actually taking action? Because they think they are taking action by watching the Simpsons, by laughing along at the irony.

JP: Before we wrap up, I'd like to ask you a bit about how you view your work with the Media Education Foundation. With the rise of so much social media, is there a continued role for documentary films, the kinds of things that the Media Education Foundation produces? Is that going to have to change at some point, or will there still be a role for 'old-fashioned' films in the classroom?

SJ: Well I hope there's a role for it, because that's how the Media Education Foundation is going to survive, and I think there will be a role for it, but you have to watch things as they progress. Classroom technology is changing, and it's much easier now for people to be directly connected to the web when they are teaching. It's easier for students to be connected too, and it's one of the most maddening things teachers face these days–students who are on their cell phones and on laptops checking their Facebook pages when they're in class. But instructors also have access to this, and I think that will change things. You can go straight to a YouTube clip to show something. And I think that's a positive move forward. There's more access to immediate knowledge, there are more possibilities for people to use things that are going to engage students.

But I think we will continue to do serious documentaries, because at some point, you can't just communicate through three-minute clips. At some point you need sustained intellectual attention to something to really understand it. And that's actually one of the things I worry about most, is what is happening to our ability to engage in this sustained intellectual effort. Can young people who have grown up in an internet age where everything is short, read a book of theory? Can they read a book of research? Do they have the ability to focus for how long it takes to read a book? Can they sit in a lecture for an hour and a quarter, without being disrupted by having to check their email or Twitter account? I know I sound like an old grump, and it is not because I am a reflexive Luddite. But environment and context is everything in my book, and intellectual work requires sustained focus on one thing. But at the same time, I am not going to fight some defensive battle around this. If the new context requires shorter, snappier pieces, then that's the language and form we will have to use.

JP: Would the shorter pieces be teasers for longer documentary films?

SJ: I don't think so. I'm not sure if you've seen this animated piece that was produced in conjunction with a David Harvey lecture called "The Crisis of Capitalism." It is really quite wonderful and a great way to communicate complex ideas. You look at YouTube, and the Harvey lecture got a million and a half hits! And so I'm actually really interested in that as a model, experimenting with those kinds of techniques and those kinds of animation strategies to get people to think about—in two or three minute pieces–something like the healthcare system in the U.S. in a new way. Can you get them to think about welfare in a new way? Can you get them to think about immigration? I don't know that it's going to transform how people are thinking, but these are small ideas that will be seeds, I hope, to something else.

You know I don't really consider myself a film maker per se, even though that's what I do these days. I've always considered myself an educator, and educators have to go wherever the action is. You have to go where the attention is. If the attention now is through Facebook and social media sites and YouTube etc. then I think we have to have a strategy for getting into that space. So I'm thinking, okay, how does MEF really evolve beyond just making films for the classroom, which I want to keep doing, but also making things that will engage people where they are.

And again, I think that's the same question for progressive intellectuals about engaging in a public discourse, and the question of how you translate the work that you do into a form whereby a lay person, or a non specialist, could understand it. How do you translate high theoretical work into a form of exposition that can be comprehended by a smart and eager non-specialist? I think a lot of academics actually are very very bad at that, they haven't really thought about how you speak to the public.

There's a lot of critique about the monopolization of the media and culture by the right and there is no doubt that those are vital questions. But I often wonder, if we had access to the mass of the people, what would we say that would engage them and move them to take action? Would we be able to get them to pay attention, to engage with, interact with our ideas and our values?

And I'm not too sure we would, because I don't think we as academics have really thought about it a great deal. You go to an academic conference and you see the papers people present–a lot of them are unlistenable. I mean people literally read papers and sometimes say "Oh I've got a 20 page paper I'll just read until I run out of time!" They talk in really heavy theoretical ways, and you look around the room and most people are dozing off because they have no idea what people are talking about. For me, that's just being lazy.

I have to say that one of the things I do is to take every opportunity to speak really seriously. I always ask, "who's my audience", and then how do you communicate with that audience. If I'm talking to a group of heavy Marxist theorists I'll have one way of speaking, but if I'm talking to a group of 18 year old students who are interested in coming to the university you have to talk in a different way. If you talk to communication students who already are interested in these issues, and you've had them in a class before, you talk to them in a different way. That requires thought, it requires really thinking through, it actually requires having the viewpoint of an advertiser.

Advertisers are always interested in communication, they're never interested in just exposure, they're interested in communicating an idea. I wish more intellectuals were interested in the idea of communication, and of how you translate your work into a form where someone can actually understand it and can actually engage in it. They may not agree with it–that's the nature of politics, there is no guarantee in politics–but engaging people is the goal.

Stuart Hall argues that progressive intellectuals, organic intellectuals in Gramsci's language, have two responsibilities. The first is to understand the world better than anyone else. There's no room for dogma in understanding the world. You have to understand it the best way you can. That may require specialist language, that may require high theory, that may require jargon. That's the work of knowledge *production*. And then second, you have to think about how you translate that into a form where someone else can understand it? And although Hall articulated this for me in a formal way, I think I already understood it instinctively right back at the beginning of my career when I was working on that *Alternate Routes* article, because I was reading Marx's *Grundrisse*, his notebooks. And the *Grundrisse* is literally unreadable and it's unreadable because this is Marx's mind in operation, he is trying to work things out.

JP: There's a reason he didn't publish the notebooks.

SJ: Yes, absolutely. They are works in progress, where he was developing his analysis. Some people have actually called them the *mode of analysis*. By contrast *Capital* is the *mode of exposition* and it is beautifully written. It is a rhetorical *tour de force*. Marx spent a long time writing *Capital* (especially Volume One) in a way that workers would be able to understand. And those are two different moments. I wish more intellectuals understood that the work of analysis is *not* the work of exposition, and that exposition takes time and effort. You have to really think about translation.

Again, I think that's one of things that I did very early on, partly because I took teaching seriously. For me, teaching wasn't just part of what I had to do, it was this opportunity to get in front of people who otherwise wouldn't be exposed to these ideas. So once you've got that chance, how do you go about it? For me, the teaching, the research, the politics, is all very closely connected. That's why I always say, the most important part of Media Education Foundation is the "education" part: it's Media *Education* Foundation. What we're trying to do is to take the best work that's been done in the academy, and in line with what Hall argues, in line with Marx's intellectual practice, to take the ivory tower of the intellectual mind into different places, to take it into hallways, into classrooms. Take it into church basements, to community centres, take it into other places where people actually gather and where this vital debate has to take place.

An Interview with Michael Perelman

The Invisible Handcuffs of Capitalism: How Market Tyranny Stifles The Economy By Stunting Workers

by Michael Perelman. New York, New York: Monthly Review Press, 2011. $19.95 U.S., paper. ISBN-13: 978-1-58367-229-7. Pages: 1-360.

Carlo Fanelli** is a Ph.D. Candidate at the Department of Sociology & Anthropology, Carleton University, with interests in critical political economy, labour studies, Canadian public policy, social movements, urban sociology and education. Carlo serves as editor of* Alternate Routes: A Journal of Critical Social Research, *and recently co-edited Capitalism & Confrontation: Critical Perspectives.* ***Michael Perelman *teaches economics at California State University, Chico. He has published 19 books, including,* The Confiscation of American Prosperity, Railroading Economics, Manufacturing Discontent, The Perverse Economy, and The Invention of Capitalism. *Michael spoke to Carlo Fanelli about his most recent book over June 2011.*

Carlo Fanelli (CF): Your early work pays a great deal of attention to the classical political economists (e.g. Ricardo, Smith, J.B. Say, J.S. Mill, Marx, etc.), with later writings engaging with economic luminaries such as Alfred Marshal and John Maynard Keynes. Could you briefly discuss how this research has influenced your thinking about economics? And in what ways has this motivated your present explorations?

Michael Perelman (MP): The disconnect between what purports to be objective analysis and the underlying power relationships fascinates me. Like Moliere's bourgeois gentlemen, who was unaware that he was speaking prose, economists have developed a culture in which they communicate without any recognition of how much they have internalized the distorted perspective of a capitalist system. What is more surprising is how thoroughly the economists were able to propagate their flawed worldview throughout much of society. The economic worldview loses sight of essential elements of the world economists to analyze. Once their simplistic world of economics spins out control, economists' instinct is to explain away their deficiencies rather than finally coming to grips with the real world. In that sense,

I feel that a critical study of economists and their economics becomes useful as a means of self-defense against the tyranny of markets.

CF: A central theme running throughout much of your work has been to denaturalize capitalism–that is, as one of your previous book titles indicates, show how capitalism was "invented" and is not, as is commonly assumed, the natural culmination of age-old historical practices. Rather your studies show how, as Marx put it, capitalism was 'written in the annals of mankind in letters of blood and fire.' In this book you critique Adam Smith's notion of fair, harmonious and efficient markets, and instead, argue that wage-labour depended on violence and coercion to accept the discipline of the workplace. How does this compare with previous forms of social organization? Could you illustrate this with some examples?

MP: To be fair, capitalism was not invented in some Eureka moment. Already in pre-historical times, people traded, but, of course, trade is a necessary, but not sufficient condition for capitalism. Early on, people began to take up trades, moving the world closer to a capitalist economy. Next, people would face hard times or need money for weddings or funerals. Unable to pay their debts, they might find themselves forced into wage labor. However, wage labor at this stage of development represented a relatively small portion of the population. A mixture of wage labor and slavery existed in Greece and Rome, hence the word proletariat. Once the great empires fell, feudal lords acquired far more power. Serfdom increased at the expense wage labor. Eventually, as modern technology took hold, power shifted again in the direction of traders, often under the shadow of the newly emerging European empires.

The landed gentry either lost power or joined in the commercial revolution, which morphed into the industrial revolution. At this point, forcing people to work to make commodities for foreign trade became a high priority. Marx described this process as primitive accumulation, where he wrote about the blood and fire. I followed up his work in my book, The Invention of Capitalism, where I described some of the harsh measures used to drive people off the land, where they could provide for their own needs, leaving them with the necessity of having to work for wages. The laws against hunting were particularly interesting. The legend of Robin Hood represented the feudal measures to protect the aristocrats' hunting preserves. By the early 17th century, these laws had fallen into disuse. At the end of the century, as the shoots of modern capitalism were being laid down, the law was suddenly enforced again. Hunting became a capital offense. During the next century, Australia became populated with by leaders of these game laws. At the same time, clumps of aristocratic hunters were allowed to ride across farmers' land, in order to chase down foxes.

In their published books, the political economists at the time ignored the injustices associated with the enforcement of the feudal game laws, as well as the enormous economic damage done by the hunters. Instead, they described the economy as the result of voluntary transactions between willing buyers and sellers. Away from the public eye, these same economists applauded the displacement of rural masses, which was providing new bodies for the emerging proletariat. In this sense, capitalism was invented as I described in The Invention of Capitalism. Capitalism was invented in another sense. The early economists described the emergence of capitalism as a voluntary system that benefited everybody. This falsification of history, which was central to their analysis, was a very creative invention.

CF: Your most recent book, as you state (p.9), takes aim at capitalism in terms of its own basic rationale: the creation of an efficient method of organizing production. You argue that the failure by economists and employers alike to adequately take work, workers and working conditions into account has led to actions that have stifled the economy. This inattention, however, has not been accidental. Can you describe the consequences of this largely ignored dimension of market inefficiency?

MP: Good question. In *The Invisible Handcuffs,* I tried to show how economists tried to frame capitalism as a system of voluntary transactions, as I mentioned in my previous answer. One can understand how the economists could have gotten away with this evasion of reality in a world when literacy was limited and communications, expensive. In a modern world, to be able to get away with such nonsense is an audacious act of genius. Economic theory also abstracts from virtually anything having to do with time. For example, business is assumed to invest efficiently when it purchases durable equipment. How is that possible when business has no knowledge about future demand conditions, technology, or competition? Considerations of such matters would make mathematical models impossible. How is it possible to efficiently value the existing stock of resource, such as petroleum, when nobody knows precisely how much petroleum there is, or whether alternative sources of energy will appear, or whether creating even more carbon dioxide would be too dangerous to contemplate?

What economics does do very well is to create an effective ideological system that pretends to prove that whatever business wants to do is good. Within this framework of voluntary transactions, workers agree to a wage bargain in which they give up their leisure time in return for wages, which more than compensate for their lost leisure. No thought is given to the context in which the transaction is made. From this perspective, the conditions of workers who accept the lethal consequences of accepting a job at the Fukushima nuclear plant are no different a high priced athlete playing an enjoyable game. Also missing from this picture is anything having to do with work, workers, and working conditions. The only relevant action is the wage bargain. Just as an individual consumer tries to buy commodities at the cheapest possible price, employers want to buy their workers for as little as they can. Unions become framed as a monopoly that interferes with the transactions. At the same time, this transaction-based perspective, neither employers nor society have any reason to nurture the skills or the creativity of the working class. Why not break the unions and defund education. Not surprisingly, productivity suffers.

Traumatized workers, as Alan Greenspan called them, may often be docile, but their fear of job loss is likely to interfere with efficient performance. But since all that counts is buying work at the cheapest possible price, even though the ultimate effect of that arrangement is detrimental to productivity, as well as society at large. In the book, I do describe the hostile treatment meted out to economists who stray from this perspective. In part, this attitude reflects the defensive behavior of academics who want to defend the purity of their supposed science, but, I suspect, that there may also be an intuition that to move beyond the transaction perspective ultimately leads to Marx. Part of what is involved is the unproductive effort used to maintain of power relations. Once a worker is reduced to a means of production and managers can believe that they are selected because of their superior abilities.

This perspective is obviously detrimental to workers' creativity. In one of my favorite cases, when computerization was first being introduced into manufacturing, a paper mill opened up its computer system to the whole workforce. The workers who manned the factory took advantage of this access to information and quickly ramped up productivity and efficiency. Recognizing the growing threat to their authority, management quickly shut off their access. Imagine a team sport–basketball or soccer–in which no one could do anything without prior authorization from their coach. Any deviations would be punished. Not only would the players' restriction hurt their play, but the players' development would also suffer.

CF: You make the case in *The Invention of Capitalism* (p. 10) that economics is an ideology masquerading as a science buttressed by mathematical models. Scientific pretentions aside, the economics profession in your view supports the interests of the rich and powerful at the expense of the vast majority of the working class. Contra mainstream economics, you show how the interests of employers and employees are fundamentally at odds. Instead, you contend that what might be called "invisible handcuffs" blind workers from realizing how capitalism both constrains their potential and degrades their quality of life. Can you briefly describe what you mean by this? In what ways has the economics profession, particularly their role in academe, played in reinforcing capitalism? How do neoclassical presuppositions, such as natural assumptions concerning human behavior, differ from your own starting points?

MP: Let me take issue with your premise. You suggest that economics supports the (perceived) interest of the rich. I inserted the parenthesis to suggest that economists are not doing the rich a real favor. I am convinced that a more egalitarian society would improve the general quality of life, not just of the working class. By all measures, the quality of life increases with equality. Ignoring that point, in the United States the economics profession, fearing to suggest anything that will upset the rich and powerful, has practiced severe self-censorship for more than a century. Other countries are not as extreme in this respect, but diversity is relatively rare in the study of economics around the world.

A leftist– let alone a Marxist–can hope to get a job in literary criticism or even sociology, but the chances in an economics department is less than slim. There are a few liberal arts college, some Jesuit institutions, and a handful of state universities that are less rigid, but nonetheless relatively few of them. There was a brief opening in the 60s, but that has long passed. Besides, the rigor (mortis?) of economists' training is extremely demanding in terms of mastering mathematics and statistics. Even if a student is already advanced enough to breeze through that work, he or she will have to find a sympathetic professor to oversee anything outside of the mainstream. If that effort is successful, the vast majority of departments would not consider that person as a potential colleague.

I am fascinated by human potential—what unlikely people are able to accomplish despite the odds. I believe that everybody has the capacity to be the worlds best at something; that the role of society (not just family, or education) should be to help people discover what that something is. To the extent that this kind of discovery becomes widespread, societies will prosper. Hierarchical systems prevent that kind of discovery and need to be eliminated as soon as possible.

CF: You argue (p.29) that the promise of job creation drives the rhetoric of almost all economic policies. How has this influenced policymakers and what have been the consequences? What role have large corporations played? And how have changes in the organization of work, workers and working conditions affected the quality of employment?

MP: The rhetoric of job creation smacks of blackmail. Give us everything you want or we will make unemployment worse. But if you look at the last decade, business got virtually everything it requested, but without much job creation. What is worse, the largest corporations were most effective in reducing jobs. Besides, real hourly wages peaked back in 1973. The corporations run around from state to state, offering to create new jobs in return for tax breaks and other incentives. Sometimes the jobs never materialize; other times they do, but disappear soon after.

CF: With the focus on workplace (especially union) concessions and attacks against the public provision of social services a current flashpoint of political contestation, how does economics serve to obscure relations of class and the compulsions of the market?

MP: Abstract economics does not play much of a role, either in the discussion of job creation or in the concessions and cutbacks that are rolling across the country. The basic justification is that business, by its very nature, will create all of the preconditions for prosperity as long as nothing impedes "the magic of the marketplace." Adults should not believe in magic. As long as opportunities exist to cut back on wages and benefits by moving work abroad to where people work for pennies an hour, expectation of a tsunami of good, high-paying jobs is ridiculous–even more so when companies get tax breaks to take advantage of such labor arbitrage.

CF: Finally, where do we go from here? How may economists and the economic profession, within and external to academe, be challenged in progressive ways? What role does political education and mobilization play? How might academics, activists and trade unionists begin to break the chains of the "invisible handcuffs" ?

MP: Now you are getting to the toughest question. Even Marx never described the specifics of his ideal society. Although he frequently recommended tactics to address particular situations, he never laid out a long-term strategy. In a sense, he had no choice. He was trying to assemble disparate political factions who could never agree on anything. Some of his German followers then adopted the attitude that they should just wait for the crisis to open the door to a new society. Now, after more than a century, that quietist strategy should be thoroughly discredited. The first step is the easiest. Develop the thoroughgoing critique of the status quo. Unfortunately, radicals have been quicker to snipe at each other's analysis than to collaborate on something to appeal to the larger population. In short, the easiest part is still difficult. Next, we must be able to communicate an alternative. Merely to suggest the abstract idea of socialism is vulnerable to the charge of proposing to duplicate all the abuses, real or imagined, of any society that purports to be socialist. Now, in the midst of a sadistic round of austerity, proposing an alternative should be easier than ever, but I haven't seen much progress in that regard. The next step becomes even more difficult. People need to be able to organize in a way that not only appeals to the masses, but it makes them feel empowered. Although I have not offered any concrete program, I think it might be useful in considering any action to think about how it might contribute to, or detract from the simple steps that I suggested.

An Interview with Noam Chomsky

Democracy and the Public University

***Rebecca Schein** is Assistant Professor and Acting Coordinator of the Human Rights stream at the Institute of Interdisciplinary Studies, Carleton University (Ottawa, Canada). Her teaching and research interests include: nationalism and cosmopolitanism; citizenship and civic pedagogies; social movements; social and economic rights; science studies. Research projects include: a critical cultural study of the U.S. Peace Corps and American cosmopolitanism; an examination of "risk management", data ownership, and contemporary ideals of competent citizenship.* **Noam Chomsky** *is a political theorist and activist, and Institute Professor Emeritus of linguistics at the Massachusetts Institute of Technology (Massachusetts, U.S.A). In addition to his work in linguistics, Chomsky has written widely on U.S. foreign and domestic policy, power and ideology, as well as the corporate media. Having authored more than 100 books, his most recent include:* Profit Over People, Rogue States, The Essential Chomsky, *and* Power and Terror. *Noam Chomsky was interviewed by Rebecca Schein at Carleton University on April 8, 2011.*[1]

Rebecca Schein (RS): The title of this discussion was "Democracy and the Public university" and I thought I would start with a really big question which is what do we mean when we talk about a public university? What is it that makes a public university?

Noam Chomsky (NC): Well there's a technical definition. This depends on who is in charge of the administration, the finances and so on. It's either the government or the private institution. If it's the government it's a public university, if it's a private institution it's a private university. Actually that's just technical–the boundaries are extremely flexible. Take my own university, MIT. Technically it's a private university, but it's overwhelmingly subsidized by the government. In fact when I got there in 1955 and up through the early 1970s probably ninety percent of the academic program was paid by the Pentagon.

The political science department was openly funded by the CIA until the early 60s, when it got kind of embarrassing. After that some other technique was used and since then the funding has shifted for interesting reasons having to do with the nature of the economy. So

1 Interview transcribed by Kate Gentle. A recording of this interview is available at: http://www1.carleton.ca/iis/news/noam-chomsky/

technically, MIT is private but from another point of view it's public. The administration is private and the trustees are not specifically responsible to state authorities. On the other hand, if you go down the street to the University of Massachusetts it's entirely public and also gets some funding from the Federal Government. Harvard has the biggest private endowment in the world. It's a private University but again there is plenty of government funded work going on.

RS: Most of us are probably not imagining a time of Pentagon funding or its equivalent when we talk about the need to defend or restore the public-ness of our universities, nor would most of us be likely to see Pentagon funding as supportive of a democratic mission for universities. What is the relationship between democracy and a university's public-ness?

NC: You just can't draw mechanical conclusions about how research will be carried out from the source of the funding. A lot of my friends on the Left think that if you are Pentagon funded you must be working for the military. Its exactly the opposite. When you were Pentagon funded they didn't care what you did. If you wanted to overthrow the government in your spare time that's ok. In 1968, when MIT was completely Pentagon funded, I was in a lab that was one-hundred percent funded by the three armed services. That lab was also the centre of anti-war resistance in the country. Several of us, including me, were on the verge of long jail sentences. That was all under Pentagon funding and there was no interference. For twenty-five years I was teaching undergraduate courses in social and political issues and social change. They were open to the community and usually met in the evening. I was doing them in my own time but the University didn't shut them down. A lot of the students who came out were involved in the activism of the 60s. Some of the former students are doing things right now. As I say, it was the centre of anti-war resistance but there was no interference. There was a little harassment of the courses from the FBI but not from the Pentagon.

Interestingly, it was the increase in corporate funding through the later period that led to greater secrecy. In 1969, there was a period of a lot of student activism [at MIT]. There were protests about military labs, which were administered by MIT, and it was reaching a crisis which nobody wanted. So everybody did what you do when there's a crisis–you establish a commission to look into it. I was on the commission which looked into institute financing. It turned out that about half the institute budget was administering the military labs, and the other half was the academic budget. The military labs did classified secret military work, but that was kind of a joke too. Technically it was secret, but the academic side was open. Again a kind of porous distinction. Of the academic budget in 1969 maybe ninety percent was Pentagon funded. There was no war work except for the Political Science department. The Political Science department was involved in pacification programs in Vietnam, and naturally this was under the rubric of a peace research institute. They had secret seminars and things like that, which you're not supposed to have, but outside the Political Science department there was no dedicated war work.

The Pentagon was not funding war work–they were funding the high tech economy.

The Pentagon was a technique. They were deluding tax payers into providing funds for the future benefit of private corporations. The Pentagon funded advances in computing, the development of the internet, lasers–in fact the whole IT revolution that enabled the high tech economy. The funding for innovation and initiative comes in many ways through the state sector, and for business that's great. They wait around and eventually reap the profits of publicly resourced innovation. The tax payers pay them on the assumption that we're saving ourselves from the Russians or something like that. That's basically the system.

Through the 50's and the 60's the cutting edge of the economy was electronics-based, and the Pentagon was a good cover for that sort of research. Now the cutting edge of the economy is more biology based. So we see funding shift to other government institutes like the National Institutes of Health. The shift in the sources of government money largely reflects the direction of the economy is headed, just as it did in the 1950's and 60's around MIT and other research Universities. This happens all over the country. MIT is extreme but it is all over Stanford, North Carolina and so on. Around the research Universities you get small start ups. Those are faculty members who are using the government funded research and development to start up small businesses.

Back then they were electronics-based, and if they were successful they'd be bought up by Raytheon and I-Tech and other big high tech companies. Now if you go around the campus the start-ups are genetic engineering, biotechnology, pharmaceuticals, and the big buildings around are Novartis and all these guys who want to milk the research development that is going on under government auspices in the University. That's the basis for a lot of the economy. This goes a long way back but it really took off after the Second World War–partly because of changes in the nature of science and technology. In the 1950's, when I was there, MIT was actually an engineering school: you went there if you wanted to build things. Now if you want to build a bridge or an electric circuit you go to Wentworth Institute or some other place. MIT is a science University–you study basic science and basic math and you take pretty much the same courses whether you're in aeronautical engineering or electrical engineering. The technology changes fast, so if the students learns the technology of today, they won't be able to get a job twenty years from now. Technology will be different. If they learn fundamental science they can grow with it. So everything changed. The same is true in the biological-based areas such as pharmaceuticals.

At the same time, we see an increase in corporate funding in universities, and that has to do not with changes in science and technology, but with changes in the way the economy is structured. There is more of an effort to build a business model for everything, and corporate funding is part of that picture. Corporate funding has an effect. For one thing it tends to drive research towards short term applied work. When the Pentagon or NIH is funding something, they're thinking about the long term health of the economy. When Merck is funding something, they want something for themselves, not their competitors, and they want it tomorrow. So you end up getting more short term applied research.

You also get secrecy for the first time. There was no secrecy under the Pentagon. They wanted to be as open as possible because it just impedes communication between scientists and engineers. In fact there was no security in the buildings. You could walk in twenty-four hours a day. A corporation may not be able to enforce secrecy, but it can make it clear that you're not going to get your contract renewed if something gets out.

So there's a coarsening effect, which you'd expect when a business model is imposed on research.

RS: So is it reasonable to think that *public* universities, specifically, have a democratic function? Can you spell out the relationship between publicness and democracy?

NC: Well you know, MIT was a private university which means you have to pay tuition to get in. The tuition is not exorbitant, but it's tuition. A public university is supposed to be free. Its supposed to be for the public. That used to be the case. The University of Pennsylvania is an ivy league college, and when I went it was one hundred dollars. You could easily get a scholarship, which I did. Working students could get a scholarship. Now it's probably $20, 000, $30,000 and the public universities have changed radically since the 1970's. I don't know about here in Canada. I'm talking about the United States. Let me give you a personal example.

A couple of months ago I happened to be giving talks in Mexico City at the National University. It's a big university–it has a couple of hundred thousand students, pretty high quality, good facilities, smart students, good faculty, low salaries by our standards but quite an efficient, good university. A perfectly respectable university. It's free. Ten years ago the government tried to slightly raise tuition. There was a national student strike and the government backed off. In fact one of the main administration buildings on campus, I discovered, is still occupied by students from that strike and it has become kind of a movement centre, a community activities centre. The administration doesn't like it. A lot of the students don't like it, but they're not calling in the police to throw them out. In Mexico City there is a public university that is not only free but open admissions, so it's open to everyone. They have compensatory courses because a lot of the students don't have the right background. I was there, met students, talked to faculty. It was pretty impressive. Mexico is a very poor country, and I went from there to California, which is maybe the richest place in the world. In California they are consciously destroying the best public education system in the world.

The California public education system was pretty amazing. The universities were great universities. There's lower tiers like state colleges, lower colleges, other universities, all quite high level, and they used to be free. Tuitions have gone sky high. In fact its very likely that Berkeley and UCLA, the two stars in the system, will be privatized. They're almost private universities now if you look at the tuition and the endowments,. The rest of the system will be lowered in quality–more vocationally oriented and less funding. That's one of the richest places in the world. In fact this year for the first time I think less than half of the cost of the university is provided by public funding. Mostly it's tuition. That's true in many states in the United States now.

These are all steps towards privatizing society and creating a kind of two-tiered society– these are big processes, happening not just in universities. None of this is economically driven. You can see that by comparing Mexico to the United States. Mexico is a very poor country. The United states is the richest country in history. So it's not economic. These are social decisions both in Mexico and in the United States. What's a public university supposed to be? Like Mexico. It should be free, there should be an option for open admissions, and resources should go into it to making sure it works. It is not impossible.

RS: Rising tuition fees, increasing reliance on student fees for operating budgets, endowments–to what extent do you see all these trends as part of a general divestment from the public sphere?

NC: Its partly general, but I think some of this is oriented specifically toward the universities. This hasn't really been studied so I'm just telling you what I think. All of this stuff began in the 70's. There were a lot of changes in the economy in the 70's, but one crucial thing changed with regard to the universities. The late 60's was a period of a lot of activism and it terrified the business world and it also terrified liberal intellectuals across the spectrum. They were terrified. "The students are out of control, there's too much democracy, what are we going to do?" There's some very interesting reactions that you can read. There are two main ones at the opposite ends of the spectrum and they're worth looking up. One of them is a book and the other you can find on the internet.

At the right end of the spectrum, we have the Powell Memo. Lewis Powell, was a corporate lawyer who became a Justice of the Supreme Court, and he wrote a memorandum to the education committee of the Chamber of Commerce in 1971. His memorandum was essentially reflected the paranoia of the business world. The business world is basically totalitarian. They're used to running everything, and if anything gets out of control the world is falling apart. That's a typical aspect of the totalitarian mentality. It shows up in foreign policy and all over the place. So his perspective was that the whole university system, as well as the media, television, and even the government, had been taken over by raging Marxist lunatics.

All of this is so surreal if you know anything about the facts. You'd laugh if you didn't understand that this is a natural perception of the totalitarian mentality. You can't allow anything to get out of control, and its true, things were partially out of control. So Herbert Marcuse was teaching some students in Harvard that Ralph Nader was popular, and to the business world that meant that all the world was falling apart. So Powell wrote to the Chamber of Commerce, the main business lobby, saying we've got to do something to "restore the balance". Do something to make sure that in the universities, in television, in the media, there's at least some small voice that says the United States is not Nazi Germany and maybe something in American history is not just extermination and massacre. Powell says to the business world, look, we're the trustees of the universities, we're the ones who make the decisions, we provide the tax funds, and we own the media. We ought to mobilize instead of letting Ralph Nader and Herbert Marcuse steal the whole world away from us. We ought to mobilize and use our power to "restore the balance".

Powell's suggestions were followed by the business world in all kinds of ways, and I think one of them is raising tuitions. Its at that time that tuition starts to go up. That's a disciplinary technique. Kids in the 60's assumed, "I can take off for a couple of years and become a political activist and work for women's rights or civil rights, then I can come back and pick up my career." That's a dangerous situation–it frees people to think and that's a terrible idea.

So what you want to do is trap them. Maybe some guy thinks that he wants to be a public interest lawyer. If you make sure he comes out of law school $100,000 in debt, he's going to go into a corporate law firm because he just has no choice. Once he's in there he'll internalize the culture and he'll be safe. It's the same across the board. Raising tuition is a disciplinary technique.

So we have the Powell Memo on the right. On the other end of the spectrum, which is in a way even more interesting, there's an important book called *The Crisis of Democracy*. It comes out in 1974 and it's the first publication of the Trilateral Commission. (The Trilateral Commission brought together liberal Internationalists in the three major state capitalist societies–North America, Western Europe, Japan. To get the tenor of it that's what the Carter administration was drawn from.)

Well what's *The crisis of Democracy*? The crisis of democracy is that there's too much democracy. Segments of the population that are usually passive and apathetic and obedient are entering the public arena and pressing their demands–women, youth, the elderly, workers and farmers. The population, in other words, or what they call the special interests. And that's too much pressure on the state. They can't deal with all the special interests. They have to be beaten back to establish what they called more moderation in democracy.

With regard to the schools it was quite interesting. They said that the institutions that are responsible for the indoctrination of the young are not doing their job. Schools, universities, churches–they're not indoctrinating the young properly." (This is the liberals that I'm talking about!) "We've got to do something to make sure they indoctrinate the young properly." Then comes various suggestions. They even wanted to control the media, because they're too adversarial and free. Well the two ends of the political spectrum are almost identical and that tells you something. My strong suspicion is that the attacks on public universities, including things like tuition, quite possibly came out of this whole sort of mentality.

It was related to things happening in the economy. This is the period in the 1970s when the postwar economy was being dismantled–we see moves towards financialization and the off shoring of production. A lot of things happened. This was one of them. They tried to re-impose discipline so we wouldn't have problems from these students, who aren't indoctrinated properly. I think there was a confluence of all these things and it's led to the period of increasing repression which we're living under in the schools and everywhere else.

There is a cultural dimension to the transition happening in thte economy–the fear of student independence and the fear of freedom. Freedom is a scary thing so you want to make sure people are properly indoctrinated and controlled. You have a lot of debt and not a lot of choices, you're insecure–you can't take chances. In fact if you listen to Alan Greenspan's testimony to Congress every year, he's crowing about the wonderful economy he's administering, and he says straight out its best feature is what he calls "growing worker insecurity." That's the best feature of the economy and that makes sense on his assumptions.

Growing worker insecurity means that working people are afraid to ask for a raise in wages, decent working conditions, for secure jobs and so on. They'll just grab on to anything they can, and that's great. It makes the economy more healthy by standard economic principles. So yes, growing worker insecurity is a great thing and it's the same with students. If they're insecure they're not going to go out onto the streets and demand things, and think about things. My feeling is that all of this is tied together very closely.

RS: So if students are disciplined by things like rising student debt and rising student fees, you could also argue that the people who are in charge of indoctrinating those students are also disciplined by this casualization of the labour force.

NC: That's right because you have to discipline both students and teachers. When the Trilateral Commission goes after the institutions responsible for the indoctrination for the young, they're saying it's the teachers, the ministers, church figures, the people in charge are out of control. They're out of control so they have to be disciplined. And its called casualization of the labour force, or cut backs, threats to tenure, and so on. That is disciplining the faculty. Academic freedom always had two aspects. The freedom to teach and the freedom to learn and you've got to cut them both back if you want to really control people.

RS: I think that you have said that you are uneasy about the notion of a politically engaged university, but that you also think that universities have a responsibility to foster political engagement. Could you say more about that?

NC: Well take MIT. I didn't think myself that MIT ought to become involved in the anti-war movement. It's not their job. Nor did I think they should become involved in the war. If they're going to develop technology for the military they ought to also be developing technology for guerilla resistance. But in fact they should be doing neither.

However, the university should be an open arena for people to get involved, and as I said, MIT was at the centre of academic anti-war resistance. I think it was 1968 that the whole university was closed down for a couple of weeks. A small number of students, including Mike Albert (who now runs Z-Net), Steve Shallow, and a few others decided to organize a sanctuary for deserters. That was the kind of thing going on then, mostly in churches. A kid decides he wants to desert, so you organize a sort of sanctuary and people stay with him until the FBI comes and takes him.

I should say I was against it. I thought this was just going to crash but their intuition was much better. The deserter was a very interesting young guy from the marines. He knew what he was doing–he had had a lot of briefing, thought about it, knew the consequences, and he wanted to do it. They had a press conference in a room in the student centre and about five people showed up. In about three days the whole institute was closed down. There were thousands of students in the student centre twenty-four hours a day doing everything that students do–everything from smoking pot to having seminars.

It was quite exciting. There were two weeks of really active engagement on campus and the institute was virtually closed. A lot of things came out of that experience. One thing that came out of it was the commission I was talking about earlier. Another was that the institute itself officially devoted a full day just to consider the uses of technology in society. This is the main technological institute in the world and the question had never come up. So it was March 4th 1969. The day was set aside for meetings, discussions, rallies, all sorts of things on the uses of technology in society. One thing that came out of that day was the Union of Concerned Scientists, which is still around and very active. The whole culture of the place changed, and it's never going back to what it was. It's not as active as it was back in 68 but it's just a changed place.

This is the kind of thing the university ought to be open to. It's right for the university to concern itself with the uses of technology in society; it should be open to letting these issues be discussed and debated. The discussion that happened at MIT had a very good impact broadly over all kinds of subjects.

One of the biggest issues in Toronto is the School of Public Affairs that is being endowed by Peter Munk, who is the head of Barrick Gold, a big gold mining company. What should be done? Mining is an absolute international scandal, extremely destructive. It's environmentally destructive, it's destructive of communities all over the place and Canada has the worst record in the world for this. Gold mining is absolutely the worst. So I think that what Monk and the Global Affairs Institute ought to do is investigate mining–gold mining in particular. And don't just investigate, but offer a voice for people who have no voice. You go down in the summer to visit remote and endangered communities in Colombia and they're trying to protect themselves from mining. They have no voice. Nobody's going to hear them but people here do have a voice and they can support them. That's a perfectly fine research and teaching engagement for a university, and out of it can come pretty good actions. I think you see things like that all over the place. You're not trapped by funders. They may want to carry out indoctrination of the young but it doesn't mean they have to succeed.

Commentary

Imaginaries and Realities, Utopia and Dystopia

Garry Potter *is Associate Professor of Sociology at Wilfred Laurier University (Waterloo, Ontario, Canada). He is author of* The Bet: Truth in Science, Literature and Everyday Knowledges, The Philosophy of Social Science: New Perspectives, *and co-edited (with Jose Lopez)* After Postmodernism. *More recently he wrote and published Dystopia: What is to be done? and made a documentary film of the same title. The film can be viewed for free and downloaded for educational purposes from the website www.DystopiaFilm.com.*

INTRODUCTION: CONTRADICTIONS OF HOPE AND DESPAIR

The dystopia thesis is an analysis of humanity's most serious problems of the present and a prediction of them being exacerbated and added to in the near future. I have presented this thesis in some detail in my 2010 book *Dystopia: What is to be done?* I also made a documentary film of the same name that is available for free viewing (http://www.DystopiaFilm.com). What I intend to do here, is to give a summarised flavour of the overall argument presented in the book and film, but also add some reflections upon the utopian dreams of both right and left, and more importantly consider the Left's continued failure to construct a left vision that captures ordinary people's imagination and enthusiasm.

The dystopia thesis propounds an argument that the structural features of the world political economy are such as to make the problems we collectively face impossible to solve. The dystopia thesis is grounded in present day fact and highly probabilistic trajectories and outcomes as regards the future. The logic and empirical content of the dystopia thesis concludes a near certain hopelessness with respect to avoiding a future of unimaginable horror and suffering. Causally inter-connected, mutually enhancing catastrophes, are around the corner . . . and there is *nothing* we can do to prevent them

Yet at the same time, the dystopia thesis was founded on the contradiction of pessimistic assessment and sincere hope. If one believed absolutely in the hopelessness of any effort to avert catastrophe what would be the point in articulating the argument?

Utopia and dystopia are bound up together in complex ways. Both have their causal effects of interpenetration of imaginaries and realities. For example, both liberal and socialist utopias form a part of contemporary dystopian reality, as ideological barriers to an accurate understanding of both the present and future possibilities. The apocalyptic media visions of life after the bomb . . . or virus or asteroid strike etc. etc., also contribute to a lack of understanding of what is now and what might come to pass in the near future. These imaginaries are part of our dystopian reality because they serve to deceive and mystify us with regard to real problems.

I will begin by summarising the dystopia thesis, giving particular attention to its knowledge, power and ideology component: the theory of structural mystification. I will then reflect upon some of the ways both utopian and dystopian fictions feed into this mystification. Finally, I shall embrace the dystopia thesis's own contradictions (that is to say my own) and discuss how a vision of hope is the only hope we have, how the dystopia thesis ultimately calls for a new Marxist imaginary, a realistically feasible, yet nonetheless inspiring, utopian vision to sustain us in our struggles.

This last component of this piece is perhaps too big to be anything other than a preliminary reflection here. It is a task I have been wrestling with ever since I began my work upon the dystopia thesis. The question of what is to be done was not part of my original project because quite frankly I only had the vaguest of vague ideas about what should be done. I was also, on some levels, persuaded that there was *nothing* to be done. I had only an instinct that sounding the alarm, as it were, might contribute to mitigating the horrors to come. However, as the project progressed it became clear that I simply could not present the dystopian vision and argument without engaging with potential strategies for dealing with the problems

With respect to many of the dystopia thesis's individual components, many people have provided far gloomier assessments than I. I tended to be rather cautious with predictions of catastrophe and apocalypse. But the cumulative emotional effect of seeing put together as a causally inter-linked conclusion, all the worst environmental problems facing humankind, along with all the most extreme suffering of poverty and disease, appeared to be too much for most of the people I consulted with. They told me that *some* strategies for the amelioration of crises had to at least be entertained, along with the analysis of their cause. Some balance of hope *had to be given* along with analysis of calamity

However, my reflections upon the question of what is to be done began with critique. The analysis was of the inadequacies of many of the popular propounded solutions to the problems that were most serious. For example, the technocratic solutions to the world's food or transport problems may have some value but miss the main point: the problems are most significantly political-economic problems rather than technological. For another example, charity may mitigate a small amount of suffering in the immediate present but cannot even begin to address the ocean of pain deriving from the systematically produced extremes of world poverty

Finally, I realized that utopian thinking, the right kind of utopian thinking that is, is actually a necessary counter-point to the dystopia thesis. It is a great irony that left-wing analysis, more specifically Marxist analysis, is everywhere being proven correct and yet is not attended to. Capitalism is in crisis on many fronts. There are rumblings of resistance and revolution in many parts of the world. And yet in the First World, most particularly in the American "heart of the beast", where some of the contradictions of wealth and poverty are most extreme, *the left has never been weaker*. My conclusion with respect to this, is that while intellectual analysis of the problems has never been as acute, there still lacks an inspiring vision of a better world that is realistic enough for masses of people to see beyond the inertia of their present day to day living. Reflection upon this situation shall be the conclusion of the article.

THE DYSTOPIA THESIS

The first argument of the dystopia thesis is that the future of misery and crisis that is dystopia is already here. Perhaps a billion people live lives of such dreadful daily experience as to reduce any concerns about the future to the most immediate. They are starving or close to starving. They are watching their children being sold into the slavery of bonded labour or prostitution. They are dying of malaria or plague or tuberculosis or AIDs or any number of diseases. They live in a mundane poverty-stricken everyday life. Or worse, they are incarcerated and perhaps are being tortured this very second. The list can go on and on through the drama of war and refugees, to the boredom and unpleasantness of under-paid, soul-destroying employment or unemployment. The future is already here for a billion people, if the future is dystopia

The dystopia thesis's predictions of the future are mainly simple probabilistic extensions of present problems being exacerbated. We are just beginning to see the effects of global warming but we can well imagine increased future problems of flooding and hurricanes. And global warming is merely the most dramatic of the wide variety of environmental problems facing us. Many of these link up with issues of resource shortages and energy. So yes, the dystopia thesis is a very simple argument in many respects: things that are bad now and are going to get worse

However, entirely new problems are coming as well. Peak oil will add to existing inequality, suffering, terrorism and warfare. But even more importantly, at some point, it will make our existing socio-political economic system impossible to maintain. There *will* be a post-carbon economy. This is coming whatever we do. But the dystopia thesis predicts an excruciatingly painful transition to this post-carbon future

The dystopia thesis is also a causal analysis. On the one hand, it takes note of the immense complexity of inter-linkages of problems and causality. It observes the positive feedback loops and their snowballing effects. On the other hand, however, it posits a broad context of common structural causality. The world capitalist system possesses structural features that ensures extreme inequality and thus poverty. Poverty is not only an effect that is suffered but is in turn a cause of many, many other problems. In this regard, the dystopia thesis is essentially Marxist. It thus sees inequality, unemployment and poverty as features of the world political economy that are *not* contingent but rather are *fundamental* to the system

Unemployment rates (in any country), for example, may rise or fall; that much is contingent upon a variety of factors; but whether there is to be unemployment or not at all, that is *not* a variable. Some level of unemployment is functionally *necessary* to the system. This is among the reasons why the dystopia thesis rejects reformism as a potential solution to the avoidance of dystopia

The world capitalist system is just that, a *world* system[1]. Globalization is not something new; it is an on-going developing process that emerged simultaneously with the birth of capitalism. The development of the richer countries was dependent upon the lack of development in the poorer. Development and underdevelopment evolved together. The wealth of the rich, whether it be people or nations, is dependent upon the lack thereof by the poor

The particularities of recent global economic change and the neo-liberal economic ideologies and policies that have driven them have had many dire consequences of course. But neo-liberalism *per*

---

1 I am indebted for the World Systems theory here to Immanual Wallerstein and Andre Gunder Frank.

se is not the real problem. *Capitalism* is the real problem. A return to Keynesian economic policies may well save capitalism from some of its contemporary crises . . . but it will not save *us* from dystopia[2]. It will not save the world; inequality will be maintained; the *suffering* of that inequality will be maintained; environmental destruction will continue unabated.

In addition to a structural logic of profit which necessitates inequality, the world capitalist system has a structurally determined time-frame for decision and action. It has a temporal logic, which ensures that potentially beneficial decisions and actions of collective pain avoidance and responsible environmental stewardship will come too late. The peak oil problem can be used to clearly illustrate this.

As we all know, the problem of peak oil is not that we will run out of oil eventually. Rather it is that after the capacity for world production peaks, demand will not slacken but continue its ever increasing pressure. Prices will dramatically rise to a point whereby the present world system of trade and commerce, of energy and transport, of agriculture and consumption, simply will not be able to continue without drastic change. We will move into what people are beginning to call a post-carbon world.

The dystopian point with respect to the peak oil problem is not that a post-carbon world is necessarily a future to be feared. No, the problem, the future to be feared, is the *transition* to it. We could imagine (and people have, which we will discuss in a moment) a post-carbon economy and world as actually a good thing in many ways. What world capitalism will ensure is that the sensible planning in advance that would enable a smooth painless major transition of economy and lifestyle will not occur. Capitalism's political-economic temporal logic forbids it.

There is a further key factor in capitalism which keeps our most serious problems from being effectively engaged with. This is the problem of power and knowledge and ideology.

STRUCTURAL MYSTIFICATION

Structural mystification is the negative side of the dialectical contradiction found in the institutional production of knowledge. Structural mystification exists as a counterpart to the real knowledge production and dissemination practices of the media, the education system and all other institutions fundamentally concerned with the production and dissemination of knowledge

2 See the excellent critique of the return to Keynesian economics by Richard Wolff (2011).

The relationship between power and knowledge has been theorized in innumerable ways. Ideology has also been theorized from many conflicting, and frequently confusing, perspectives. The key points of the theory of structural mystification, however, are clear and relatively simple[3]. Power sometimes corrupts the production and dissemination of knowledge. But it is not as though the production of knowledge could take place *without* the influence of power relations. No, institutional power relations also *facilitate* the production and dissemination of knowledge. This is why the relationship between power and knowledge is dialectical. Knowledge production (and dissemination) most significantly takes place within institutions. The institutions all have within them a dialectical contradiction

For example, the university generally is fundamentally concerned with the production and dissemination of knowledge. This is not a contingent feature but essential to the very nature of what a university is. That that is not all the institution is, does not change this fact. Knowledge production is fundamental in a way that having a football team is not (however important that may be for some universities). But also fundamental to the very nature of a university, is the dialectical opposite to knowledge production and dissemination: the obfuscation of the production of knowledge and the restriction and sometimes outright prevention of the dissemination of knowledge. While all university faculty would be forced to acknowledge that this sometimes occurs, few are aware that it is *not* a contingent feature

The university, amongst other things, is a complex structural hierarchy of power relations. Further, it is connected to the broader hierarchies and complexities of the power relations of the world . . . of the world capitalist system. This is not any simple matter of conspiracy or propaganda or intentional distortion. Rather the production and dissemination of knowledge takes place at the nexus of many different levels of conflict

There is frequently a conflict between the institution and the government in terms of priorities of spending on research and pedagogy, and in terms of academic freedom of speech and critique and dissent. There is an ongoing conflict between the priorities of the board of governors and the university senate. There is a constant scrambling over scarce resources between faculties and departments. There is genuine intellectual debate and politically coerced loyalties and acts of bad faith. There is not only conflict between individuals but conflict *within* individuals.

---

3 For a more complete account see Potter, 2010c.

There is a struggle to "do the right thing" and a struggle to know what that is. It is both a moral and an intellectual struggle . . . and one that takes place very often within a mystifying fog . . . a mystifying fog that they both suffer and frequently help to construct. It is not for nothing that the word "academic" also has a pejorative sense to it. And as Pierre Bourdieu (1988, p. 207) puts it, academics are often "mystified mystifiers" the first ideological victims of the operations of power and classification they perform.

Structural mystification is also structurally embedded within science itself. Yes, even that tremendous tool for acquiring information and potential understanding of so many things is frequently corrupted through its practical and ideological contextualization within the wider political economy. And yet science on another level, is absolutely our only hope of coming to terms with the crises of dystopia.

There is a plethora of examples to choose from to make these points about science here. But I will briefly mention the "hydrogen highway" and hydrogen automobile. The hydrogen car (in a variety of formats) is often propounded by politicians and auto makers as the future solution to the problems of global warming and peak oil. It doesn't use oil and it doesn't pollute (directly). There is not space in this article to go into the practical limitations of this technology in relation to the political economy of it. These have been thoroughly explored elsewhere (see for example Demirbas, 2009, Romm, 2005, and the unattributed article on the Alternative Energies website). No, the major importance of the hydrogen "solution" is mystificatory. Its practical realization is always far enough in the future as to necessitate a continuance of the gasoline vehicle status quo. The utopian promise of the idea is sufficient though, to deflect political action toward any more immediately viable technological solutions

Knowledge production and dissemination, including scientific knowledge production and dissemination, is profoundly affected by politics . . . and politics is profoundly affected by knowledge . . . and the lack of it. The problems of dystopia, whether global poverty or global warming, require *radical* change. Radical change requires significant mass-scale collective political will. Political will requires knowledge. The knowledge gets produced, as does its mystifying ideological counter-arguments and "facts". The knowledge gets distributed . . . on a restricted scale. The knowledge gets produced and receives a restricted dissemination but the ideological counter-points are trumpeted and/or subtly and insidiously whispered in the media, or taught in the schools or even at home

Among the most potent elements of dystopia with respect to knowledge and ideology are the utopian visions that grab the collective imagination. The utopian imaginaries are part and parcel of our dystopian reality.

THE UTOPIAN DREAM OF CAPITALIST REFORM

Slavoj Zizek quotes John Caputo (Caputo and Vattimo, 2009, p. 124-125) to make a point about utopian thinking concerning the possibilities of reforming the capitalist system:

I would be perfectly happy if the far left politicians in the United States were able to reform the system by providing universal health care, effectively redistributing wealth more equitably with a revised IRS code, effectively restricting campaign financing, enfranchising all voters, treating migrant workers humanely, and effecting multilateral foreign policy that would integrate American power within the international community etc., i.e., intervene upon capitalism by means of serious and far-reaching reforms. . . If after doing all that Badiou and Zizek complained that some monster called Capital still stalks us, I would be inclined to greet that Monster with a yawn.

Zizek (2009, p. 79) does not dispute whether such reforms would make for a better world, or even if we might be better able to remain within the system if such far reaching reforms were possible. Instead he argues that:

The problem lies with the "utopian premise" that it is possible to achieve all that within the coordinates of global capitalism. What if the particular malfunctionings of capitalism enumerated by Caputo are not merely accidental disturbances but are rather structurally necessary?

Just to be completely clear, I will answer Zizek's rhetorical question. The "malfunctionings" are not such at all; the ill treatment of migrant workers, for example, is certainly a moral shame, but it is not because of an accidental flaw in the system. No, it and the rest enumerated by Caputo, are *structurally necessary to the system.*

UTOPIAN VISIONS AND DYSTOPIAN REALITIES

Vision. This is what we would like to see in our political leaders. In America, and elsewhere as well of course, but especially in America, vision is in short supply. So we are given utopian fiction. But it is often presented not as a vision of the future but as a pious hope for the present, through the idealized glasses of memory. It was not President Bush or Clinton or Reagan that gave us this poetized vision, a:

... reminder of the time when two powerful nations challenged each other and then boldly raced into outer space. What would be the next thing to challenge us, that makes us go farther and work harder? You know when smallpox was eradicated? It was considered the single greatest humanitarian achievement of the century. Surely we can do it again. As we did in a time when our eyes looked towards the heavens and with outstretched fingers, we touched the face of God.

Yes, poetic indeed, but it was President Bartlett of *The West Wing* (episode 5, 1999), not Obama, that articulated this vision of past and future. Its resonance, of course, is with Kennedy and the beginnings of the "space race". But along with Kennedy's perceived martyrdom (to what exactly?, I often wonder) goes a collective amnesia of the real fear of nuclear holocaust and a total ignorance of what was really going on with the Cuban missile crisis. Forgotten also, is the Bay of Pigs; and most of all it is forgotten that it was with Kennedy that the American involvement in Vietnam began

The eradication of smallpox was undoubtedly a truly wonderful achievement. Bartlett says: "Surely we can do it again". And of course this *should* be true. But this utopian moral imperative, stands alongside the historical reality of the tragic failure to eradicate malaria.

In 1958, the worldwide effort to eradicate malaria began in earnest. It was led by Paul Russell from Harvard's School of Public Health. The United States Congress directly allocated $23 million a year towards the battle. It also provided 90 percent of the World Health Organization's anti-malaria budget and a significant proportion of the budgets of the Pan-American Health Organization and UNICEF (United Nations Children's Education Foundation). This constituted a financial commitment in the order of billions in today's dollars.

It was a serious commitment to eradicate a serious collective human problem. But it also was an effort with a definite time limit to it. Paul Russell in his *International Development Advisory Board Report* emphasized the time line of malaria eradication: four years of DDT spraying and four years of monitoring that there are three consecutive years of no mosquito transmission in an area. He also emphasized the dangers of failing to complete the program of eradication: DDT resistance, renewed disease pandemics and a virtual economic impossibility of having another attempt in the future be successful.

A four-year commitment was made, and four years of funding was what was given. Four years were *nearly* enough. In 1955, Sri Lanka had a million cases of malaria. In 1963, it had only eighteen.

Only another two or three years of concerted effort and financial commitment would have given the world the same success with malaria as it had had with smallpox. But the funding was cut off[4].

The result, of course, was not merely the failure to eradicate something that was eradicable. The result was to make the problem worse, much worse. The insects developed resistance to DDT and other pesticides. The malarial parasites developed resistances to quinine, chloroquine and other drugs. Most importantly, in areas where the mosquitoes and disease would almost certainly make a comeback, many millions of people now lacked all resistance to the disease. By cutting off funding to the eradication efforts, Congress and the other "money people" were condemning millions of people to death in the future. Such is the relationship between the time frame for capitalist political economic planning and future calamity. Such is the relation between eloquent vision and a sad reality.

But if the harsh reality stands in contrast to utopian vision there is something rather pathetic about the vision as well. People often imagine utopia as something very like small town America in the fifties. The dark side of this hope was portrayed nicely in the film *Pleasantville* (Ross, 1998). But as good as this film was, it cannot stand in comparison to the real life utopian monument to this vision of the world. I'm speaking here of the Disney-built small town *Celebration* near *Disney World* in Florida. It looks like Main Street USA in Disney Land but it is a real town that people live and work in. As someone once put it "It just seems to be the perfect little town back in a nicer time. Except it feels creepy".[5]

WHAT IS TO BE DONE?

The answers to the question of what is to be done which I gave in my book and film were all fairly obvious. They could be fundamentally articulated in a number of traditional leftist slogans: "The people (the Left, the workers) united will never be defeated", "Union!", "One Solution, Revolution" "Occupy, Resist, Produce" and so on. I advocated boycotts and protests and taking it to the street. I criticized reformist compromise and charitable band-aids. In short, I advocated what the radical left has advocated for years.

That these activities and slogans are obvious does not diminish their importance nor their power to effect change (witness Tunisia

---

4 I am indebted to Laurie Garret's excellent (1995, p. 48-52) account for all the factual information of this history.

5 Name withheld by request.

or Egypt for recent examples of this). But still, in the face of all the forces of structural mystification, something crucial seems lacking. The masses may have been teeming into the streets of Tunis and Cairo; the poor may have come down from the shanty towns of Caracas to have thwarted the 2002 coup in Venezuela, but. . .while the arrest report of Toronto's 2010 G20 protests was impressive in terms of numbers, the numbers of people who merely peacefully marched in protest was on a relative scale, pitifully small. Most Torontonians, most Canadians, simply went about their ordinary business and watched the violence on TV as a spectacle which had nothing to do with them. My point here again is obvious; Cairo and Toronto are different worlds; the developed and the developing, the core and the periphery, are miles apart in present political potential, as well as in terms of their economies

But the problem is that we are one world; so the "First World" needs a revolution too. But the political consciousness is not there. . .or rather it is not *here*. There are contradictions in this. The majority of the affluent middle classes in countries such as Canada or the US cannot seem to grasp what is obvious to millions of peasants and workers in the developing world. Is it that their affluence blinds them? Some would have us think so. But there is more to it than that

Marxist analysis of capitalism is repeatedly, and everywhere, being proven correct. Right wing ideology is not faring well. We have had, for example, such an intellectual big gun for laissez-faire capitalism as Alan Greenspan admitting he was fundamentally wrong. . . about everything. Yet in North America and Europe, the left has never been weaker. Why?

I don't presume to reduce the answer to this question to a single cause. However, I do want to focus here upon *one* of the causes. The left has thus far failed to articulate a positive vision of the future that truly catches people's imagination!

There is, of course, a good historical and analytical set of reasons for this failure. Early in its history socialist thought divided in terms of hard and soft. Proponents of these softer versions of socialism seemed to spend a lot of time dreaming. For many Marxists the term "utopian socialism" was a pejorative. . .and rightly so. To spell out in great detail a picture of the future without having paid any attention to the process of getting there, without a proper appreciation of the problems of the present, is utopian in this negative sense, simply because the thinking is unrealistic.

It may be the case that there also is a certain, necessarily utopian element, to the dream of overthrowing of Capital. But can one dream and still be realistic? Can we fly and yet be grounded? Good Marxist analysis does not predict too specifically about the future. It rightly concludes that there are simply too many variables for such to be sensibly done. So where does that leave us?

One of the excellent stunts of the Yes Men (2009) has given me an idea in this regard. They printed and distributed a hoax version of *The New York Times*. This satirical version of *The Times* had such headlines as "Iraq War Ends", "Maximum Wage Law Succeeds" "Popular Pressure Ushers Recent Progressive Tilt: Study Cites Movements for Massive Shift in DC" and "Nationalized Oil to Fund Climate Change Efforts". There was a small caption by their Times banner that gave me the idea: "All the News We Hope to Print". We cannot realistically articulate a detailed far-off in the future vision. But we can clearly see what is wrong *now*. This can be our realistically grounded imaginary: the many problems being *immediately solved*

Let us begin articulating things that could be done, things *just beyond* the political realities of the moment, but nonetheless easily imagined. I have had so many conversations with ideology derived ignorant people about socialism. "Well, if all property is going to be shared, does that mean somebody else will be allowed to use my toothbrush?". Or " . . . just how exactly is it going to be organized for people to do their little bit of literary criticism in the afternoon?". The conversation needs to be changed. John Steinbeck articulated the direction of such a change in his classic novel *The Grapes of Wrath*: "What's a Red anyway?" "A Red is somebody who, if you're getting paid 15 cents an hour thinks you should get 25" "Oh . . . I guess I'm a Red then". It is testimony to the power of such simplicity that when Hollywood made their film of this novel they transformed this conversation. In answer to the question of what a Red was the answer was given; "It's hard to say. . . I really don't know". So instead of trying to present some detailed blueprint of the far-off future, let us give a series of questions and strong simple answers to people about the present and the *immediate* future . . . of what could be done.

How can we eliminate hunger in the world? We can take the entire Canadian wheat crop and offer to transport it free to where food is most urgently needed. Could we afford to do this? Yes, it would take an evenly distributed tax increase of only about 2% to afford to have Canada save the world from starvation all by itself! How can we provide basic education and health care to the whole world's population? Well, we could take half of Bill Gates' money, and half of Warren Buffet's money, and this special tax upon the two of them could alone easily finance the effort.

The serious problems of poverty could be realistically costed. These costs could then be presented along with the estimates of individual wealth. Yes, personalizing it would make a great difference. People seem to get lost when one talks about the top one percent of one percent. Four hundred people in the US have a combined wealth greater than the wealth of half of the population of the US (Johnston, 2011). People's heads swim when one talks about the trillions of dollars spent on defense. We need to present to people what could be done for the price of a fleet of battleships or a single stealth fighter. We need to present to people that such and such changes in the national and international laws relevant to generic drugs would save exactly how many lives of people dying of AIDS or TB.

I am not arguing for a single campaign. No, it needs to be bigger than that. The Left, the *world's Left*, needs to continually present a vision of all the things that could be so quickly and easily done to make a better world. "A better world now" could be the new slogan arising from an unflinching look at the horror of dystopia.

REFERENCES

Bichlbaum, Andy and Bonanno, Mike (2009). *The Yes Men fix the World*, Renegade Pictures UK.

Bourdieu, Pierre (1988). *Homo Academicus*, California: Stanford University Press.

Caputo, John and Vattimo, Gianni (2009). *After the Death of God*, pp. 124-125, quoted in Slavoj Zizek *First as Tragedy, Then as Farce*, London: Verso: pp. 78-79.

Demirbhas, Ayhan, (2009). *Biohydrogen: for future engine fuel demands*, Springer Press.

Frank, Andre Gunder (1966). "The Development of Underdevelopment" *Monthly Review*, Volume 18.

_____. (1967). *Capitalism and Underdevelopment in Latin America: Historical Studies of Chile and Brazil*, Monthly Review Press.

Garrett, Laurie (1995). *The Coming Plague: Newly Emerging Diseases in a World out of Balance*, New York: Penguin.

Johnson, Dave (2011). "9 Pictures That Expose This Country's Obscene Division of Wealth" *Alternet.org*. http://bearmarketnews.blogspot.com/2011/02/9-pictures-that-expose-this-countrys.html

Kunstler, James Howard (2005). *The Long Emergency: Surviving the Converging Catastrophes of the Twenty-first Century*, Grove Atlantic.

Paine, Chris (writer/director) (2006). *Who Killed the electric car?* Sony Pictures Classics.

Potter, Garry (2010a). *Dystopia: What is to be done?*, Waterloo: New Revolution Press.

____. (2010b). *Dystopia: What is to be done?* the film version–www. DystopiaFilm.com.

____. (2010c). "Power and Knowledge: A Dialectical Contradiction", *Journal of Critical Realism,* Equinox Publishing.

Romm, Joseph, J. (2005). *The hype about hydrogen: fact and fiction in the race to save the climate,* Island Press.

Ross, Gary (director) (1998). *Pleasantville,* New Line Cinema.

Sorkin, Aaron (writer/director) (1999). "Season One Episode Five" *The West Wing,* NBC.

Turteltaub, Jon (2006) *Jericho,* CBS Paramount Network Television.

Unattributed (2011). "Hydrogen Fuel Vehicles - Looking at the Disadvantages of Hydrogen Fuel Vehicles" http://www.alternative-energy- resources.net/hydrogenfuelvehicles.html

Wallerstein, Immanual (1974). *The Modern World-System I: Capitalist Agriculture and the Origins of the European World-Economy in the Sixteenth Century,* Academic Press Inc.

Wolff, Richard (2011). "The Keynesian Revival: a Marxian Critique", *Alternate Routes,* 22, 103-14

Zizek, Slavoj (2009). *First as Tragedy, Then as Farce,* London: Verso.

Book Review

First As Tragedy Then As Farce

by Slavoj Žižek, London, United Kingdom: Verso Press, 2009. $12.95 U.S paper. ISBN 978-1-84467-2. Pages 1-157

Reviewed by: Aaron Henry[1]

The best way into this review is to start with Slavoj Žižek's opening premise of *First As Tragedy Than As Farce*: Liberalism has died twice in the 21st century. Following 9/11, the retrenchment of democratic rights, the construction of new models of containment and exclusion marked the death of liberalisms promised "liberal-democratic political utopia". The 2008 economic meltdown further revealed that prosperity, contrary to the claims of neoliberal ideologues, could not be delivered through free market mechanisms. As such, using " the ongoing crisis as a starting point" (5) Žižek asks the following: how does ideology function to maintain capitalism as the only option when the inherent irrationality and authoritarian tendencies in the system have been unmasked by liberalisms failures as political and economic ideology? Žižek 's diagnosis is this: the death of liberal ideology leaves us with no other belief, no other imagination of our social bonds other than the non-ideological. This non-ideology maintains or exists in capitalist society through a very cynical functioning, "we only imagine that we do not really believe in our ideology"- which makes it all the more pervasive (3). As such, perception, action and, therein what is politically possible, are now structured by the other of ideology- non-ideology; and, thus, non-ideology is itself the ruling ideology.

The logical question that follows is how does an ideology that is constituted by the fact that we imagine that we do not really believe in it, function and how does it function differently from its twin-form, ideology? The entire first half the book is devoted to this question. At a glance, this non-ideology is in many ways more of less consistent with how 'ideology' functions regularly in Marxist thought (i.e. it normalizes the status quo by positing that existing institutions and relations are directly analogous to human nature or de-historicizes the existence of the

1 Aaron Henry is a Ph.D. candidate at the Department of Sociology and Anthropology, Carleton University (Ottawa, Canada).

established order) The departure, however, is in the specific role non-ideology and the suppression of the possibility of alternatives within a given historical moment. Ideology suppresses the "possibility immanent to the situation": it does this not by fighting actual political opponents but by closing down the "possibility (the utopian revolutionary-emancipatory potential) which is immanent to the situation" (27). Žižek argues that in the 2008 economic crisis this suppression was made through a number of interventions ranging from Pope Benedict's claim "that all is vanity" to Jacques Alain-Miller's assertion that things must be terrible but eventually trust in the monetary system would be restored- by an all 'knowing subject' (28).

It is tempting to level the critique that the suppression of immanent possibilities is not unique to our current moment of capitalist society. After-all, Voltaire's Candide character Professor Pangloss's declaration that "this is the best of all possible worlds" seems to be jib at this very function of ideology. There is a subtle difference though. The idea of the current order being the best of all possible world's and the idea that things are 'bad but are the least bad' do both serve to suppress the possibility of an alternative. However, where the former functions through a utopian optimism- there is nothing better than capitalism- the latter operates through a disavowal of its own cynicism of the existing order (i.e the existing order of relations are broken, miserable and destructive and we no longer believe in this order; and yet things will only be worse without it). Žižek is, arguably, quite convincing here about this shift to cynical suppression of alternatives. After-all was this not the sort of reflex-action behind the financial bail-outs contained within the sentiment, 'the global economy is broken but what can we really do but save it?'

The argument gets somewhat reductive, however, as Žižek traces the function of cynicism of non-ideology into working class and liberal bourgeois forms of consciousness, in the forms of fundamental populism and permissive cynicism, respectively. Žižek argues that the bourgeois liberal (largely in the form of social democrat) clings to the 'symptom' of the repressed truth of the existing order whereas the working class subject fetishizes some other relation in place of the direct truth of its relations. Put concisely, Žižek argues that permissive-cynicism functions insofar as the subject is not aware of the content that belies the form of its initial claim (68). The liberal, for instance, may claim, "I believe everyone has equal opportunity" but they make this claim as something guaranteed by the political sphere; and, thus, the subject here overlooks the unjust social relations that actually underpin the political sphere they articulate their belief of 'equality' through (see Marx's "On the Jewish Question"). In this sense, the political sphere, operates within this form of consciousness as the content (the materiality of the right to equal opportunity) when in fact it is nothing more than the symptom (one could use the word abstraction) of actual existing social relations that are in fact unequal. Populist-fundamentalism, in contrast, operates through a fetishization of something in place of the immediate antagonistic relations one confronts (e.g when Canadians say they worry about immigrants taking all of the jobs, the immigrant is standing in place of capital, de-industrialization and outsourcing etc).

For Žižek, the point of this comparison of the different class relations attached to symptom and fetishism seems to be this: the permissive-cynical subject is the easier of the class positions to mobilize because the form of the subjects ideological belief (i.e equality) can be recognized to be rooted in its content (i.e unequal relations) and as such the subject can simply integrate the content further into the form (i.e we will not be equal politically until we transform our economic relations therefore, let's change economic relations). Conversely, the populist fundamentalist must be told that what they take as the truth of their relations is in itself untrue (e.g. your 'enemy' is not the immigrant but capital). The paradox is that the opposing class position (liberal bourgeois thinkers) is easier to demystify and mobilize than those who 'the left' is actually suppose to support, workers and the down-trodden (68). In this sense, Žižek attempts here, using Lacanian psychoanalysis, an indirect answer to the infamous question that has occupied marxism since the 20th century: why has their not been a working class revolution? I think there are two questions though that arise with Žižek's explanation.

First, and most importantly, I think the idea that fundamental populism can be simply characterized as a movement that puts the fetishized object in place of the real relations it encounters misses the mark on why the 'second death of liberalism', the opening premise of the book, is potentially so dangerous. The death of liberalism has created the opportunity for social forces, previously discredited or marginalized in liberal society, to provide a new narrative on the economy. In particular, take the British National Party (BNP) in the England, this is a perfect example of a fundamentalist-populist force insofar as the BNP pledges to defend working class England from immigrants and 'islamization' and, thus, obscures real exploitative social relations in English society. However, this movement has also critiqued, no doubt with anti-semitic undertones, the bailouts to the big banks and the power of London's financial sector. The point being, Žižek's analysis seems to suggest fundamental-populism simply functions by putting false objects in place of actual relations, the problem though, as Gramsci noted long ago, is that right wing ideology does not simply displace 'true' relations with 'false' relations; rather, it combines them so that one cannot tell one from the other; and, as such, common sense, the mainstay of fascist ideology, always contains some kernel of good sense; thus, common sense contains some form of truth (Gramsci, 2007, 329). In this sense, the problem with fundamental populism is not merely that one displaces the truth of relations with fetishisms but that real relations can be represented (i.e. big bail outs, the privilege of finance capital over labour) and articulated alongside false objects. Arguably, with the death of liberalism is not only that of cynicism but that one now has a situation where a dissatisfaction with the actual relations in liberalism is not only possible to articulate but can be articulated by social forces that liberalism as an ideology previously maligned or discredited; such movements do not displace discontent with real relations with false objects, they merge them.

Second, if we buy Žižek's analysis of fundamental-populism and the cynical permissive subject, we are left with the following question: if the working class is locked in its own modes of populist fetishisms and increasingly we are trapped within the political and economic systems of capitalist society precisely because we imagine we do not believe in them, and thus continually reaffirm them in our actions, how are we to overthrow the system? While Zizek does directly confront the paradox he has constructed around the difficulty of mobilizing the working class his answer is "fidelity to the communist idea" (97).

In particular, for Žižek the communist idea is understood here as eternal idea (one that pivots around the ending the injustice relations between the included and excluded) that needs to be reinvented in each historical period. Žižek argues that in our present day we have four main antagonisms which despite being integral to the reproduction of capital are at the same-time the sites of possible disruption to its functioning: ecological catastrophe, "private property in relation to so-called intellectual property", the science of bio-genetics and "new forms of apartheid, new walls and slums" (91). For Žižek, the relations between excluded and included are fundamentally different from the other antagonisms in that the latter are issues of human survival that can be resolved "through authoritarian measures which will simply intensify existing social hierarchies, divisions and exclusions" (98). As such, the relation of exclusion and inclusion will not just be unresolved by the measures but the relation itself will become the dominant mode of social control. The antagonism of exclusion and inclusion, in contrast, is a relation of justice or rather the injustice of the human condition in its current form; and, as such, because the relation is a question of justice rather than the survival of the species, it is the only antagonism "that justifies the use of the term communism" (96).

As such, Žižek makes the case that we should in fact be wary of 'progressive' political projects that attempt to overcome these antagonisms from a vantage point that does not take the relation of the injustice of exclusion and inclusion as its fundamental starting point. In this regards, Žižek targets the 'progressive' environmental movements that treat the environment as something akin to the Christian tale of the fall from Eden, with simply the industrial revolution sitting in the place of original sin as the event in which we lost our "roots to mother earth", a relationship that must be restored through a deification of nature and the disavowal of modern technology (97). In addition to this he also casts doubt on the Maoist perspective as these approaches have a tendency to "attack the modern subjectivity" as it is understood in Western political thought and society. While these may seem like disparate progressive movements to target, they are united, for Žižek, by the fact that both movements actually destroy the possibility of the communist ideal insofar as the former seeks to abolish the technical productive forces wrought by the industrial revolution, while the latter calls into question the very notions of freedom capable of harnessing the technological forces of capitalism for a project of human emancipation. In this sense, neither project has the capacity to come to terms with the social conditions produced by capitalist society let alone to posit how very possibilities inherent to these conditions could be used to establish an order outside capital. This critique is made quite apparent in Žižek's discussion of the Hegelian mode of subtraction from the situation as the mode of praxis the 'left' must adopt.

In particular, subtraction here is meant to operate simultaneously on three dimensions: withdrawal from a situation in such a way that the relations sustaining the situation itself are exposed so as to see their points of contact (the minimal difference between them) and thus, in exposing these relations, to disintegrate the situation itself (129). Such a process is stillborn without the modern subjectivity insofar as the modern subjectivity posits the critical distance between itself as a reasoning being and the relations of the existing order (Benjamin's notion of the 'stilled present[2]). In other words, to withdraw from the situation, which is in itself to presuppose the possibility of critical distance from the situation itself, is to see the situation as something external to one's own social being. As such, then, subtraction from the situation, a process that requires the critical reflection of the modern subjectivity, reveals the fundamental antagonism of included/excluded, which alone presents the context to reinvent communism in our historical period.

So in the end what are we to make of all this? While Žižek weaves together Starbuck's ads, hotel policy on smoking and export processing zones into an impressive analysis of ideology, one cannot help that the question of the nature of ideology in First As Tragedy Then As Farce is only partially examined. Indeed, while Žižek uses psychoanalysis to try to come to terms with the consciousness of the subject in capitalist society, at times, given that Zizek has introduced his concept of non-ideology in his previous works, it is hard pinpoint what is unique about ideology in capitalist society following the economic death of liberalism. Moreover, the discussion of the working class as a subject that has fallen under the sway of fundamental-populism simply fetishizing false objects is one dimensional and, subsequently, overlooks the complex relations between truth and false objects, the power of the latter arguably needs to be considered in terms of the degree to which ideology allows it to reconcile, rather than displace, itself to the former. In this sense, Žižek delivers an important analysis of ideology in capitalist society, whether this analysis comes to grips with our current situation, however, is another question.

REFERENCES:

Benjamin, Walter. (1968). "Theses on the Philosophy of History." In Hannah Arendt, trans. Harry Zohn. (Ed.), Illuminations. New York: Schocken Books.

Gramsci, Antonio. (2007). "Philosophy, Common Sense, Language and Folklore." In David Forgacs (Ed.), The Antonio Gramsci Reader, selected writings 1916-1935. New York: Lawrance and Wishart.

2 As Benjamin states in *Theses on the Philosophy of History*, "A historical materialist cannot do without the notion of a present which is not a transition, but in which time stands still and has come to a stop" (1968, p. 265).

Book Review

The Ecological Rift: Capitalism's War on the Earth,

by John Bellamy Foster, Brett Clark, and Richard York. New York: Monthly Review Press, 2010. $17.95 U.S.; paper. ISBN: 978-1-58367-218-1. Pages: 544.

Reviewed by: Naomi Alisa Calnitsky[1]

In *Marx's Ecology: Materialism and Nature* (2000), John Bellamy Foster offered a dynamic and in-depth interrogation of the ecological strands of Karl Marx's thought, exploring a number of Marx's critiques of capitalist agriculture and linking his neglected ideas to the modern-day ecological movement. In *Ecology Against Capitalism* (2002), Foster problematized the relationship between contemporary American environmentalism and the needs and preferences of the labour movement, and offered critical insights into the environment's relationship with the economic world, citing critical contemporary examples of the environmental costs associated with the capitalist industrial footprint. His innovative and up-to-date approach placed politicized ecological questions into direct focus, to ask, how might we incorporate the earth into the balance sheet?

Building upon past theoretical approaches and contributions, in *The Ecological Rift: Capitalism's War on the Earth* (2010), Foster, Clark and York offer a radical and comprehensive critique of the planetary environmental crisis as exacerbated by industrial capitalism. Situated within the subfield of environmental sociology, the authors posit arguments which depart from a distinctly Marxist foundation. Their central target is industrial capitalism and its derivative effects, namely, the unsustainable social habits of consumer forces associated with capitalist production, and the unprecedented levels of ecological destruction associated with accumulative capitalism. Foster, Clark and York highlight the alienating tendencies of capitalism, as well as the irreversible changes wrought upon our ecosystem and biosphere from capitalist activities.

---

1 Naomi Alisa Calnitsky is a Ph.D. candidate at the Department of History, Carleton University (Ottawa, Canada), with a focus on the history of Mexican seasonal agricultural workers in Western Canada.

By re-inserting ecological thought into analyses of the human economy, this highly-needed and readable work comprised of scientific arguments and synthetic approaches underscores planetary assaults resulting from the human-industrial footprint and bemoans an apparent lack of concern within social science disciplines towards environmental questions at a time when the planet has approached a red alert status.

Situated within a critical anti-capitalist tradition, the authors point to an abandonment of a critique of capital in existing ecologically-minded social science approaches. They consider the question of "green capitalism," or capitalism's potential or ostensible ability to modernize and adapt along ecologically sustainable lines, in a critical light. Additionally, they question the deceptive phenomenon of "corporate green-washing."

The work emphasizes accelerated transformations in the global environment, where ecosystem degradation and human-induced climate change is linked intimately to the expansion of industrial capitalism. The authors argue that the recovery of the environment may not be ameliorated solely through faith in capitalism's ability to adapt or modernize according to green demands. While this remains a problematic viewpoint, given the fact of capitalism's current position as the dominant economic system governing human economic interrelations across much of the globe, the Marxist critique offered by *The Ecological Rift* nevertheless remains indispensable. One of the book's central strengths is its questioning of the premise of unlimited economic growth from an ecology-centered perspective, in which capital is depicted as an "unstoppable" as well as "crushing" force upon nature.

The Ecological Rift successfully bridges a diversity of academic fields including economics, ecology, and environmental/Marxist sociology, taking its readership into the realm of a yet-to-be established field, that of political ecology. Its authors highlight irreversible ecological transformations such as ocean warming and the degradation of coral reef systems, and place a good deal of emphasis upon scientific proofs for the existence of climate change. Highlights of the work include one imaginative chapter entitled "Capitalism in Wonderland" which illustrates how environmental deterioration has stemmed from human mediations with the natural world and has been propelled by the demands of the capitalist marketplace. Here, our capitalist wonderland is framed by Foster, Clark and York as a thoroughly artificial and alienating human landscape and construct. *The Ecological Rift* has global and international implications, and yet it would likely appeal only to an environmentalist-inclined readership. The work requires attention from ecological and economic schools alike, as its efforts to bridge fields represents a widening of boundaries in the name of ecological urgency.

Significantly, the authors engage with the concept of metabolic rift, defined loosely as the way in which the capitalist system has radically separated natural production from sites consumption, particularly at a global scale and across imperial divides. Capitalism has radically separated humanity from nature, and through "metabolic rift analysis" the authors seek to comprehend environmental catastrophe in terms of the capitalist order of things. Critically entertaining the question of capitalism's ability to modernize and adapt according to the demands of sustainability, *The Ecological Rift* retains skepticism towards the destructive effects of individualist accumulation and prefers socialism as a route towards sustainability. Critically, the work stresses the need for a renewed interrogation into the dynamic relationship between nature and capitalism. It is primarily concerned with an interrogation of capitalism as an anti-ecological force, yet remains wholly devoid of any analysis of capitalism's relationship with gender, avoiding any discussion of capitalism's continued place as male-oriented, rationalized economic regime which exploits and intersects with the natural world in profoundly powerful ways.

Still, the work offers a number of solutions deserving of consideration. Offering a dialogue which incorporates the natural sciences with the social sciences, *The Ecological Rift* is profoundly multi-disciplinary and one of the strengths of the book is its sense of urgency. The authors claim that we are living in an age of unprecedented ecological destruction and only radical ecological approaches may offer sustainable pathways for environmental regeneration. The author's discussion of "Imperialism and Ecological Metabolism" probes the concept of imperialist extraction as it intersected with agricultural production and consumption in metropolitan England, exploring the nineteenth century Peruvian guano trade to Europe from a metabolic standpoint and citing the trade as an example of capitalist exploitation and structural dependency. Marx's humanism, "naturalism" and concept of labour as a metabolic mediation of nature are given due attention. While highly dependent upon Marx's "ecological" mind, without emphasizing contributions from more contemporary ecological thinkers, Foster, Clark and York reinforce their call for social scientists to interrogate capitalism as it intersects with the natural world. Also significantly, the work charts disciplinary transformations and recent theoretical developments in the ecological sciences which have contributed to the genealogy of the sub-discipline of environmental sociology.

Book Review

State Power and Democracy: Before and After The Presidency Of George W. Bush,

by Andrew Kolin. New York, New York: Palgrave Macmillan, 2010. $85.00 U.S., paper. ISBN: 978-0-230-10935-3. 262 Pages.

Reviewed by: Brandon Tozzo[1]

Did America under George W. Bush become a police state? Andrew Kolin's book traces the centralization of control in the presidency at the expense of Congress and American democracy. Kolin argues the extreme security measures taken during the Bush administration are not unique in American history, but part of a longer trend to limit democratic institutions and curtail individual rights and freedoms. According to Kolin, under the Bush presidency America became a police state. The administration used measures to quell opposition through the USA PATRIOT Act, and tortured enemy combatants in military prisons. While Kolin provides a compelling account of the immoral and–under American law–illegal policies before and during the presidency of George W. Bush, the book makes a less persuasive argument that this led to the elimination of domestic American democracy.

The first chapters provide a brief historical account of the consolidation of political power in the executive branch. Starting in the 19th and early 20th century, the American government used the police to investigate political opponents, such as black rights groups, communists, and women's rights advocates. With ascendancy of the United States after World War II, this increased in scope with the formation of the Federal Bureau of Investigations (FBI) and the Central Intelligence Agency (CIA). The external threat of the Cold War and the conflict in Vietnam led to the American executive using the CIA and FBI to infringe on the legal rights of American citizens. Though many facets of the police state started with Nixon in order to repress protest, it has culminated with George W. Bush's response to the terrorist attacks of September 11th, 2001.

The strongest part of the book is the evidence that the American executive is allowed free rein to conduct foreign policy. Other domestic institutions and social forces such as Congress, the media and the public

1 Brandon Tozzo is a Ph. D. Candidate in Political Economy at Queen's University (Kingston, Ontario, Canada).

ignore or are indifferent to the extreme measures taken by American presidents dating back to Richard Nixon. Among the most alarming recent abuses were the use of torture in Guantanamo Bay and the Iraqi Abu Ghraib prison, and the policy of extraordinary rendition to kidnap foreign nationals. All the while, the presidency insulated itself from criminal liability and Congressional oversight. Kolin goes into great detail to outline the lack of accountability for the military and the CIA when it carries out presidential orders, and the need for substantial changes in the way America conducts its foreign policy. Moreover, Kolin outlines how American institutions failed to limit the actions of the Bush administration in fighting the war on terror, a problem that continues under President Obama.

However, Kolin's argument that the Bush administration has instituted a police state in America is less persuasive. A significant issue is that several key concepts are left unclear throughout the book, such as 'police state,' 'democracy' and 'mass democracy'. This is not necessarily problematic–terms and concepts can vary depending on time and location–but there needs more discussion why concepts shift throughout the book. Since the definitions are vague, it often obscures their meaning. For example, there is no discussion of why mass democracy movements such as the Black Panthers and the Socialist Party are favourable to American democracy, while others such as the religious right and Tea Party are not, since they are both mass movements albeit with different agendas. Also, there is little comparative historical analysis of police states. If the United States has developed into a police state under George W. Bush, then some caparison between it and other obvious police states such as Maoist China, Stalinist Russia, and North Korea under Kim Il-sung would have strengthened the book's analysis and provided a more explicit conceptual framework.

More substantively, the Bush administration's elimination of American internal democracy and subversion of the constitution is less convincing when examining contemporary resistance movements in the United States. Kolin argues the Bush administration took radical measures to eliminate formal democracy in reaction to the September 11th terrorist attacks through the USA PATRIOT Act for warrantless wiretaps, and imprisoned and deported over 6000 Muslim non-citizens. However many Muslims detained after 9/11 returned to the United States and sued the Bush administration for compensation. Even some of the more controversial pieces of legislation –such as the warrantless wiretaps -have been struck down by the courts showing that formal democracy may not have been entirely subverted. Such legal recourse does not exist in Guantanamo Bay or in Abu Gharib. Moreover, despite the actions of the Bush presidency to limit dissent, there were mass social movements against the invasion of Iraq and throughout his presidency. The book shows the Bush administration did go too far restricting liberties in the war on terror against enemy combatants, but there was more domestic dissent than presented. Many social groups and formal institutions such as activist groups, the courts, Congress and the media combated the extremism of the Bush presidency. So unlike foreign policy, domestic political forces in the United States had the ability –albeit with varying degrees of success- to contest the extreme policies of the American president.

Kolin's book is an effective warning to readers that the media, Congress and the courts, and social forces must work to prevent the executive from abusing its power and control over America's foreign policy. Without the public forcing American institutions to keep watch, the president can commit illegal or immoral acts in the name of security. This book is recommended for those interested in a comprehensive, and thorough, overview of covert actions taken by the CIA and FBI before and during the Bush presidency, particularly in reaction to the September 11th terrorist attacks.

Book Review

Missing Women, Missing News: Covering Crisis in Vancouver's Downtown Eastside,

by David Hugill. Black Point, NS: Fernwood Publishing, 2010. $17.95 CAD., paper. ISBN: 9781552663776. Pages: 1-111.

Reviewed by Ryan Boyd[1]

In Missing Women, Missing News, David Hugill offers an insightful and critical study of the national newspaper coverage of the crisis of missing women in Vancouver's Downtown Eastside that followed through the proceedings against Robert Pickton, a critique of police responses to the crisis, and an analysis of the roles of the federal, provincial, and municipal governments in creating the socioeconomic conditions of the Downtown Eastside. Hugill charges journalists and police as missing in action after sixty women, most of them sex workers, from this neighbourhood were murdered between 1978 and 2002. On the one hand, he criticizes journalists because mainstream news coverage of the crisis did not appear until 1998. On the other hand, he criticizes police for their contempt and negligence: "At best, they failed to notice. At worst, they failed to care" (p. 10). Hugill argues that the narrative combining down on their luck women, a psychotic serial killer, and bad policing cannot satisfactorily explain why this crisis was ignored for so long. This prudent and topical study reveals the complexity of what was presented as a simple narrative and reassigns the culpability of the crisis to the state.

The crux of Hugill's argument is that news coverage generally offered uncomplicated reasons why these women were neglected and victimized. Media reasoning positioned the local Vancouver police as the negligent party and the women as victims of Pickton alone. Hugill's focus is to reconsider these partial yet dominant explanations by examining additional layers of complexity (p. 22). Hugill explores the historically, politically and culturally pervasive reasons why this crisis was ignored for so long. The state should be implicated as structuring and perpetuating the vulnerability of these women through the lingering impact of

1 Ryan Boyd is a Master's candidate at the Department of Sociology and Anthropology, Carleton University (Ottawa, Canada).

colonialism, prostitution laws and policing patterns, the lack of a federal housing plan, and continued funding cutbacks for social programs directly impacting Vancouver's Downtown Eastside. His consideration of ideology as the primary force of shaping the logic of these narratives is his contribution to several studies already covering the mishandling of the crisis.

Chapter 1 examines the initial limitations of the media coverage and explanations for the crisis, as well as their lasting effects. Hugill's research reveals that newspapers reported that the crisis was largely neglected for two decades because of the negligence of the local Vancouver police department (p. 24). This emerged as the central theme for explaining the crisis in the media. Drawing from Stuart Hall, Hugill suggests that local police negligence became the "primary interpretation" of the crisis, thereby limiting the physical space and parties responsible for the crisis at the local level. This is problematic for Hugill as this interpretation defines both the sources and solutions at the local level, meaning "the narratives of newspapers mask the larger contradictions about the universality of state protection" (p. 24). This primary interpretation sets an ideological limit for the other narratives that would follow. While Hugill commends journalists for implicating local authorities and their role in perpetuating the crisis, he argues that ultimately these groups were the only ones held accountable and that the structural conditions set by the state were neglected.

Chapter 2 is devoted to the role of the state in fostering the conditions that both produced and imperiled marginalized women in British Columbia. Hugill writes that the state is responsible for producing the structural conditions that put these women in danger in three central ways: (1) sweeping retrenchments of state systems of social solidarity beginning in 1983; (2) amendments to the Criminal Code targeted at curbing street prostitution; and (3) the persistent effects of state colonial policy (p. 32). The retrenchment of the state occurred in three distinct periods, beginning in 1983 with provincial budget cuts that "hollowed out social services" (p. 35). The Liberal federal government attacked social services again during the 1990s. Hugill argues that declining federal support both forced and inspired provincial Liberals to further reduce spending beginning in 2001, resulting in the "single deepest cuts to social spending in Canadian history" (p. 37). With this information in hand, Hugill engages with his media analysis and discovers that newspapers report overwhelmingly that women engage in prostitution to support their drug addictions. Despite the reality that many women engage in sex work as a way to supplement reduced or precarious incomes, this reporting has helped produce an ideological conflation with "drug addict" and "prostitute" (p. 39).

Changes to the Canadian Criminal Code under Brian Mulroney in 1985 resulted in pushing already vulnerable women into the unseen margins of the Downtown Eastside and forcing them to work in relative isolation from one another. These changes impeded sex workers from forming cohesive community that could share information about bad dates and pressured them into making quicker, less-informed decisions about their clients. Yet, only six out of 157 articles studied covering the crisis were critical of these sanctions.[2] Hugill's layered work has the potential to inform current debates in prostitution laws, in which the federal government and provincial government of Ontario are appealing an Ontario Superior Court ruling that dismissed laws against keeping a common bawdy house, communicating for the purposes of prostitution and living on the avails of the trade (Jones 2011).

In a critical analysis of the racial component of the state's culpability of endangering sex workers, Hugill's study finds that only thirteen of 157 newspaper articles acknowledged that a significant proportion of missing women were Aboriginal (p. 47). Despite coverage that goes beyond just-the-facts reporting, trying to invoke some deeper meaning to the crisis, journalists overlooked an abundance of research and statistics from well-established authorities that "clearly demonstrates the disproportionate burden of social suffering carried by aboriginal people in this neighbourhood" (p. 47). Hugill questions why this central factor was neglected despite a number of credible sources for answers. His answer is in Canadian commonsense ideology. Our image of Canada as a fair, democratic, and tolerant society creates "race blindness" as a by-product of commonsense. This commonsense reasoning posits that racism cannot possibly exist in this type of society, so it is ignored almost outright. With this layer being ignored, newspaper coverage focused mainly on the exotic nature of violence and drugs, the self-imposed risky lifestyle in society's seedy underbelly, and the presence of a serial killer to add to the well-established coverage of police negligence.

Chapter 3 focuses on reported images of the missing women and sex workers from the Downtown Eastside. Hugill pays special attention to who is speaking on behalf of missing women and prostitutes and their perceived credibility. Hugill suggests that credibility is based on per-

2 While this is mainly a qualitative study, Hugill uses several numerical representations as another way to illustrate the themes in newspaper coverage.

sonal relationships to victims rather than an understanding of the systemic issues facing the Downtown Eastside. His study finds that family and friends of missing women were quoted 109 times, advocates and allies of street women were quoted 25 times, and sex workers themselves were quoted 10 times (p. 62). This is indicative of vastly differentiated access to discourse and shows that sex workers were not in the position to describe themselves, but were rather described by others. One critique is that while it is implied, access to discourse is not something that Hugill writes about in detail. A second critique is that this analysis also would have been more nuanced if details of quotes from police officers and their role in describing the women and the crisis had been included.

When prostitutes were allowed to define themselves it was only to describe their one-dimensional drive for narcotics. Hugill notes that each paper reminds its readers that these murdered women were "real people," but describes them more like caricatures. Conflating prostitution with crime makes it appear self-inflicted or self-selected—especially with drug addiction. Drawing on Hall, Hugill suggests that through conflation with drug use, prostitution is criminalized and therefore depoliticized (p. 75).

Chapter 4 is where Hugill's work in human geography shines through. The aim of this chapter is to detail the ways in which coverage mapped the Downtown Eastside, using a multitude of images on street-level chaos that set the neighbourhood as symbolically distinct and disconnected from the rest of the city. Hugill writes, "[t]hough seemingly disconnected, patterns of divestment in the DTES and patterns of geographically specific tolerance of illicit activity offer potent ways to interrogate the hollowness of the claim that Vancouver's inner city has been "taken over" by a degenerate population" (p. 83). Here Hugill is pointing to the ways in which capital and state interest had slowly disappeared from the area. Furthermore, differentiated police presence and enforcement created a zone of tolerance that ultimately neglected missing women, suggesting that their disappearances were part of the transient nature of the job.

The coverage of the Downtown Eastside is described through text and photographs as if it were ground zero of a zombie apocalypse, where the undead exchange sex for drugs with human beings instead of simply eating them. The neighbourhood is framed as "a horrifying Hobbesian enclosure where the war of all against all is waged with unyielding fury" (p. 92). No one can be trusted and political intervention is seen as futile.

However, Hugill's conclusion suggests that all is not lost. The

Downtown Eastside has shown a great deal of leadership, bottom-up resistance, ground-level support, and ingenuity in a number of groundbreaking programs, such as InSite, Canada's first safe-injection venue (p. 98). He suggests that sex workers must make changes even if they are not officially sanctioned by the state, such as collective work environments, networks that share bad-date lists, or sex worker unions. They must also push for a venue for safer sex work. These suggestions have partially come to fruition in the aforementioned Ontario Superior Court case ruling, which has seen current and former sex workers advocate for safer conditions.

Work like Missing Women, Missing News questions commonsense ideology and urges critical thinking. While Hugill focuses on Vancouver's Downtown Eastside, his work is relevant in current debates surrounding prostitution laws, spatial identities of other urban areas with concentrated poverty[3], and the residual effects of colonialism in an Aboriginal population. The Aboriginal population faces structural issues such as systemic poverty, high rates of incarceration, mental health concerns, and loss of culture, among many others, because of Canada's racist history. This history cannot be ignored because of the contemporary commonsense of tolerance. In the case of vastly disparate birthrates, without developing strategies that problematize and work to resolve the negative impacts of colonialism, institutionally and culturally disenfranchised Aboriginal communities will continue to grow in a culture of contempt and indifference.

REFERENCES:

Aboriginal Peoples in Canada in 2006: Inuit, Métis and First Nations, 2006 Census (2008). Ottawa: Ministry of Industry - Statistics Canada.

Jones, A. (2011, May 4). "Sex-trade workers say Ottawa trivializing their serious claims in appeal". *Maclean's.ca.* Retrieved May 18, 2011 from www.macleans.ca/article.jsp?content=n6755746.

Walks, R. and L. Bourne. (2006). "Ghettos in Canada's cities? Racial segregation, ethnic enclaves and poverty concentration in Canadian urban areas". *Canadian Geographer, 50*(3), 273-297.

3 Walks and Bourne (2006) report a growing trend of racialized concentrated poverty that suggests a 'ghettoization' in major Canadian cities, such Toronto, Saskatoon, and Winnipeg.

Book Review

Economic Democracy: The Working Class Alternative to Capitalism,

by Allan Engler, Halifax: Fernwood Publishing, 2010. $15.95 CAD paper. ISBN 9781552663462. Pages 1-112.

Reviewed by: Chris Hurl[1]

In this world of highly specialized academic discourse, the art of writing a manifesto has all but disappeared. A good manifesto should be short, concise and all-encompassing. Through sharp language it should cut to the core. In this sense, Allan Engler's short book, *Economic Democracy,* should be seen as a contribution to the revival of the manifesto in confronting neoliberalism in Canada and around the world.

As a long-time activist in the labour movement, heading up Local 400 of the International Longshore and Warehouse Union (ILWU) and contributing to a strong left current in the Vancouver and District Labour Council (VDLC), Engler approaches the problems of modern capitalism as an organic intellectual. Building on his earlier work, in which he examines the myth of market individualism, he diagnoses in clear language the many deep-seated problems inherent under capitalism and attempts to prescribe a solution, based on grassroots economic democracy.

Inspired by Marx, Engler situates modern capitalism in the disjuncture between the narrow restriction of property rights and the growing socialization of labour. On the one hand, ownership under capitalism is concentrated into the hands of an "entitled minority". While this is often obfuscated through the apparent freedom of individuals to buy and sell things on the market, Engler argues that market freedom is just another word for "letting the capitalists decide" (18). Engler traces the implications of minority entitlement over the past three hundred years, which has entailed the destabilization of the world market, the destruction of the environment, the rise of colonial wars and the exploitation of peripheral regions by the core countries.

On the other hand, people are increasingly interdependent, tied together in a complex division of labour. Less and less capable of existing

1 Chris Hurl is a Ph.D. candidate at the Department of Sociology and Anthropology, Carleton University (Ottawa, Canada).

outside of market relations, they become dependent on social cooperation in order to survive. With the growing socialization of labour, the myth of competitive individualism becomes open to contestation as, increasingly, working people come to recognize that productivity cannot be simply attributed to the entrepreneurial spirit of individual capitalists, but is the outcome of complex relationships advanced between workers, communities, and nature.

While Engler goes some distance in diagnosing the problems of modern capitalism, he does not quite meet his mark. The key to writing a good manifesto is not only exposing the dark and dismal reality, but also evoking the collective protagonist that promises a way out, cobbling together a shared sensibility that transcends the relationship between author and reader. A good manifesto stands between voluntarism and determinism, such that the transformation envisioned is neither the result of the inevitable march of progress, nor is it simply a matter of waking people up out of false consciousness.

On the one hand, the book falls short to the extent that it falls back on deterministic arguments. Just like the transition from feudalism to capitalism, Engler argues, the movement to a post-capitalist world will be a gradual one. It will not be produced through a revolutionary dictatorship or armed uprising. No single event will bring it about. In fact, the change will be incremental through the advancement of workplace organization, community mobilization and democratic political action. Through slowly extending the power of social ownership, the powers of the "entitled minority" will be necessarily weakened. Eventually, a "tipping point" will be reached and the system will be transformed as a whole.

But how will the power of "social ownership" be advanced? At times this reads as an inevitable process. From the emergence of the early industrial unions through to the development of social security and the advancement of the rights of women and people of colour, Engler's account of twentieth century history appears as a ceaseless movement forward fuelled by the growing socialization of labour. However, barring a few comments on the deregulation of capital flows, he fails to sufficiently explain the significant shift in ruling relations over the last forty years. The rise of neoliberalism is simply attributed to the failure of trade union leaders and single-issue social activists to challenge the system as a whole. It is attributed to the lack of faith by the working class that a viable alternative to capitalism exists.

Missing from Engler's analysis is an in-depth discussion of "socialized labour," which he defines as "people who depend on income from their labour" (45). The rise of socialized labour is in part attributed to a process of primitive accumulation, by which people are dispossessed of their land and are compelled to sell their labour for a wage. It is fuelled by a process of technological innovation, through which people are integrated into an increasingly complex social machine. However, the notion of socialized labour is limited. To the extent that it includes *everyone*, this category lacks analytical power. It does not provide an adequate means of understanding the divisions in progressive social movements or the problem of building solidarity in the broader community.

On the other hand, Engler poses the solution as a matter of proper consciousness. It is simply a matter of showing people that a world of human equality, democracy and cooperation is practical and attainable. "Once the scaffoldings of capitalist property relations have been removed, people will understand that well-being everywhere depends on human equality" (62). Unfortunately, Engler does not convincingly show how such a world is possible. Instead, he falls back on the evocation of the hypothetical situation, that moment when revolution has been achieved, minority entitlement has been abolished and the community finally sits down to make its own decisions.

The problem is that Engler does not explain who or what this "community" is. This can, in part, be attributed to his latent populism. He tends to target forces *external* to the community that are responsible for its downfall. The "working class alternative" is purely negative, in the sense that it is simply contingent on denying minority entitlement. However, there is no sense of how this is a positive program. Aside from a few hints of union organizing and social activism, there is no discussion of existing movements that are taking concrete steps towards a better world. In the absence of such a discussion, the advancement of alternatives is inevitably abstract and schematic. At times, Engler appears as a makeshift fortune-teller, promising an end to war, environmental degradation and social inequality, viewing this more as a natural outcome than as a process that must be actively pursued through the adoption of specific strategies and tactics over the course of struggle.

"Socialized labour" and "community" are the two black-boxes that Engler leaves unexplained. However, the book does take us in the direction of rethinking these terms and their relationship in practice. Certainly, the rise of neoliberalism over the past forty years reflects the advancement of a fractured landscape upon which citizenship and wage labour have been unevenly inscribed. In this context, how can we effectively struggle to reconstitute the relationship between "work" and "citizenship" in a manner that undermines the market individualism that has been so prevalent over the past forty years? For instance, how does this play out on the ground through the struggles of public sector workers to retain their collective bargaining freedoms? Or in the struggles of illegal immigrants to obtain the right to residence, gaining access to public schools and hospitals? In appraising the prefigurative possibilities of such struggles, it is not enough to simply invoke the universal protagonist that promises a way out. Rather, it is important to recognize how these struggles come to develop concrete relationships with a broader community in practice.

Book Review

The Politics of Genocide

by Edward S. Herman and David Peterson. New York: Monthly Review Press, 2010. $12.95; paper. ISBN: 978-1-58367-212-9. Pages: 159.

Reviewed by: Matthew Nelson[1]

While genocide commonly refers to the killing or attempted killing of an entire ethnic group or people, its definition is highly controversial and the subject of extensive debate. The term is often used to describe diverse forms of direct or indirect killing, which has resulted in its "frequency of use and recklessness of application" over the past several decades (103). In *The Politics of Genocide*, Herman and Peterson argue that while members of the Western establishment and news media have rushed to denounce bloodbaths in Bosnia-Herzegovina, Rwanda, Kosovo, and Darfur, they have largely remained silent over war crimes and mass atrocities committed by allied regimes in Southeast Asia, Central America, the Middle East, and Sub-Saharan Africa. As Noam Chomsky suggests in the foreword to the book, since the end of the Cold War, we have witnessed the emergence of an era of virtual "Holocaust denial" or "genocide denial with a vengeance" (7-9).

In substantiating their argument, Herman and Peterson draw on years of meticulous research, careful documentation and in-depth, empirical analysis of atrocities and bloodbaths around the world. The authors have done an excellent job at exposing the double standards of the US news media and its hypocritical system of propaganda. In this sense, *The Politics of Genocide* offers a needed corrective to those who manipulate and abuse the genocide label for the purposes of promoting the expansion of imperial power interests around the globe. Similar to Herman's past work, however, the book offers less in the way of a theoretical addition to debates surrounding the nature of genocide and imperialism, instead providing a series of well-documented case studies. Like the five 'filters' in Herman and Chomsky's *Manufacturing Consent*, the phenomenon of genocide is simply classified through four categories—in this case, of bloodbaths. Moreover, while Herman and

1 Matthew Nelson is a Ph.D. candidate at the Department of Political Science, Carleton University (Ottawa, Canada).

Peterson, like Chomsky, do perceive imperialism fundamentally in race and class terms, their use of terms such as 'elite' and Western 'establishment' rather than class or ruling class tends to obscure the real material links between genocide, capitalism and Western imperialism.

For Herman and Peterson, "a remarkable degree of continuity stretches across the many decades of bribes and threats, economic sanctions, subversion, terrorism, aggression, and occupation ordered-up by the policy-making elite of the United States" (13). After the US emerged from the Second World War in a dominant economic, political and military position, it had to confront numerous nationalist upheavals in former colonial areas by peoples seeking "independence, self-determination and better lives" (14). To counter these increasingly popular demands for improvement in living standards, the US supported a series of dictatorships in countries like Indonesia, South Vietnam and Chile. Although these "national security" states were "torture-prone" and "deeply undemocratic," they helped improve the overall climate of capitalist investment by keeping their majorities fearful and atomized (14). When local dictators failed, direct US military intervention often followed, as illustrated in the cases of Vietnam, and more recently, in Iraq and Afghanistan.

The authors draw on the framework for analyzing mass killings provided by Chomsky, and Herman himself in their *Counter-Revolutionary Violence: Bloodbaths in Fact and Propaganda* (CRV), first published in 1973. In this work, Herman and Chomsky conclude that it is obvious and demonstrable that US officials, with the help of the established media, would engage in "atrocities management," by producing incessant propaganda to deflect attention away from US-approved violence, and onto its enemies. In its framework of analysis, CRV provided four categories of bloodbaths: "Constructive," "Benign," "Nefarious," and "Mythical" (a sub-category under Nefarious). As Herman and Peterson explain, "[t]hose bloodbaths carried out by the United States itself or that serve immediate and major US interests are Constructive; those carried out by allies or clients are Benign; and those carried out by US target states are Nefarious and (sometimes) Mythical" (16). In essence, instances of mass violence are evaluated differently by the US political establishment and media depending on who is responsible for carrying them out. The authors apply this analytical framework in their current work by subsuming more recent bloodbaths under the four categories, which they argue are "eerily applicable to the present", and "apply now with the same political bias and rigor" (17-19). Using empirical measures such as the coverage of key events in the media, what the authors offer the reader is more or less a classificatory schema or conceptual model for understanding bloodbaths rather than a specific interjection into theoretical debates surrounding critical accounts of genocide, imperialism and international law.

Today's leading 'experts' on genocide and mass atrocities, including many journalists, academics, legal scholars and policymakers, are often careful to exclude from consideration the Vietnam War, the 1965-1966 Indonesian massacres, and the invasion and occupation of East Timor by Indonesia in 1975, the latter of which resulted in the deaths of somewhere between 100,000 and 200,000 civilians (although this is a hugely debatable claim) (18). The Vietnam War, and the massive "sanctions of mass destruction" directed at Iraq during the 1990s, are examples of *Constructive* atrocities, where the victims of war crimes are deemed *unworthy* of our attention. However, when the perpetrators of genocide are considered enemies of the West, the atrocities are *Nefarious* and their victims are seen to be *worthy* of our focus and sympathy. Examples of *Nefarious* atrocities include: Cambodia under the Khmer Rouge, Iraq under Saddam Hussein, Halabja, Bosnia, Rwanda, Kosovo and Darfur. When systematic violence is carried out by US clients—such as Indonesia in East Timor from 1975-1999, Israel in the Gaza Strip and West Bank from 1967 to the present, or Rwanda and Uganda in Congo—they are viewed by the US political establishment as *Benign* and not worthy of condemnation. The final category, *Mythical*, results from the inflation of numbers or invention of incidents by the US government, media sources and NGOs to implement pre-planned interventions such as sanctions, embargoes and the funding of various 'color revolutions.'

The Politics of Genocide has done much to emphasize the biases and contradictions of US foreign policy, but it should be read in conjunction with other theoretical contributions to themes related to genocide, imperialism and international law. First, while Herman and Peterson recognize that the history of ethnic cleansing and crimes against humanity demonstrates "the centrality of racism to the imperial project" (22), there is little discussion of why advanced capitalist powers and oppressed nations are, in the first place, not equal partners in shaping the world. Due in part to their use of terms such as 'elite' and Western 'establishment' rather than class, their analysis should be complimented by recent work that is more explicit in highlighting the centrality of racism to issues of class, capitalism and imperialism in the international system.

While not directly touching on the topic of genocide, Marxist theorists writing on current modes of imperialism such as Leo Panitch and

Sam Gindin (*Global Capitalism and American Empire,* 2004) and David Harvey (*The New Imperialism,* 2003) emphasize the extent to which current modes of imperialism continue to exacerbate racial as well as global class inequalities. Identifying the class basis of the new imperialism would help identify some of the underlying reasons for why media coverage of genocides in the West is often silent with respect to crimes committed by the various client regimes of advanced capitalist states. Second, Herman and Peterson are highly critical of the "selective investigation" and "selective impunity" of the International Criminal Court (ICC) in prosecuting alleged perpetrators of genocide, especially, in the contemporary age of 'responsibility to protect,' the exclusion from its jurisdiction of the international crime of aggression, judged at Nuremburg to be the "*supreme international crime*" (21).

However, on this theme, the authors seem to imply that the responsibility to protect doctrine and the very notion of human rights are to be located outside of contemporary imperialism. In this sense, they are often ambiguous on whether they seek to defend a position of legal neutrality, holding out hope for the reformed international law and institutions, which Marxist theorist of international law China Miéville has recently argued in *Between Equal Rights* (2006), are completely incapable of adequately resisting imperialism. Not only does legal equality, in this sense, mask actually existing inequality, the appeal to international law tends to undermine the most effective avenue for advancing necessary political resistance against the new imperialism—building solidarity as widely as possible through social movements centered not only on anti-racism, but also on class struggle.

Alternate Routes: A Journal of Critical Social Research

Edited by Carlo Fanelli (Carleton University)
& Bryan Evans (Ryerson University)

The Global Economic Crisis and Canada: Perception Versus Reality

2013 Conference & Journal Call For Papers

It is now broadly recognized that the global economic crisis that struck in late 2007 is by far the most significant and wide-ranging since the Depression years of the 1930s. While there have been signs of tepid recovery over the last five years, the International Monetary Fund has recently warned that "[t]he global economy is in a dangerous new phase. Global activity has weakened and become more uneven, confidence has fallen sharply recently, and downside risks are growing... Thus, the structural problems facing recession-hit economies have proven more intractable than expected, and the process of devising and implementing reforms more complicated. Given fears of an ongoing recession, particularly as a result of Europe's sovereign debt crisis and a record level U.S. budget deficit, the global recession that struck in 2007 is by no means over.

In Canada, however, the economic downturn has been shorter and milder than many of its G7 counterparts. In fact, according to Statistics Canada, while the Canadian economy began contracting in the fourth quarter of 2008 by the third quarter of 2009 the recession had already passed. Indeed, the Great Recession was no greater than previous slumps such as those in the early 1980s and 1990s as measured by job losses, home sales, bankruptcies, credit availability and consumer spending. But numbers rarely, if ever, tell the whole story. *Alternate Routes* is seeking contributions that go beyond the rhetoric of recession versus recovery as measured by narrowly economistic factors. We are seeking papers that chart the full affects of the global economic crisis and its implications for Canada. In what ways has international instability affected Canada? To what extent are such features structurally-induced, the product of contemporary circumstances, the result of specific policies of particular administrations, or some combination of other factors? What new challenges and opportunities have been created? How should progressives respond? We are seeking papers that address, but are not limited to the following:

- How have public services (e.g. health care, education, pensions) been affected?
- Has economic volatility led to political instability, or new political alignments?
- To what extend has the downturn varied across age, ability, ethnicity, race, gender, etc?
- In what ways has the nature and quality of work and labour changed?
- How has the Canadian recession differed across regional and industrial lines?
- How have public/private sector unions and civil society groups been affected and responded?
- Has poverty and inequality increased?

If interested in presenting your research at *Alternate Routes'* conference to be held at Ryerson University (Toronto, Canada) on Friday March 16th 2012, please send an abstract of no more than 300 words and brief biography to editor@alternateroutes.ca by January 15th 2012. Accepted submissions may be solicited for publication in our 2013 issue.

If you would like to have your article considered for publication in our 2013 issue, please see www.alternateroutes.ca for submission guidelines. Articles must be submitted by April 31st, 2012 to editor@alternateroutes.ca.

For all other inquires, please see www.alternateroutes.ca, or send an email to: editor@alternateroutes.ca

www.ingramcontent.com/pod-product-compliance
Lightning Source LLC
LaVergne TN
LVHW091027080826
845145LV00002B/388

9781926958156